War in the Bible
and Terrorism in the Twenty-First Century

Bulletin for Biblical Research Supplements

War in the Bible
and
Terrorism in the Twenty-First Century

Edited by

RICHARD S. HESS and ELMER A. MARTENS

Winona Lake, Indiana
EISENBRAUNS
2008

Library of Congress Cataloging-in-Publication Data

War in the Bible and terrorism in the twenty-first century / edited by
Richard S. Hess and Elmer A. Martens
    p. cm. — (Bulletin for biblical research supplements ; 2)
    Includes bibliographical references and indexes.
    ISBN 978-1-57506-803-9 (hardback : alk. paper)
    1. War—Biblical teaching.   2. Terrorism—Religious aspects—
Christianity. I. Hess, Richard S. II. Martens, E. A.
    BS680.W2W37   2008
    261.8′73—dc22

                                  2008004670

Contents

Rev. Ian Durie

Dedication

This volume is dedicated to the memory of Rev. Ian Durie, Major General (Retired), Executive Chairman of ACCTS MMI, and Commander of the British Artillery Group in the First Gulf War. Ian's dedication to his faith and to the service of humanity, as well as his own experience in war, render him a model of a Christian who sought to address the most difficult of ethical questions in our age. He participated in the conference at Denver Seminary, and his paper is published in this volume. Ian died in a traffic accident on April 21, 2005, while on a mission to teach the ethics of leadership in Romania.

Preface

In February 2004, Denver Seminary's annual Biblical Studies conference addressed the question of the teachings of biblical ethics regarding modern war. The conference was envisioned as a collaborative effort between Cal Dunlap, the director of the Association for Christian Conferences, Teaching, and Service, and the Biblical Studies division of Denver Seminary. A year earlier, the invasion of Iraq had taken place. The questions created by this event prompted an urgency in the consideration of the topic. ACCTS, which sponsors international symposia in military ethics with officers from armed forces across the globe, provided ethicists and practitioners from within the military of both the U.S. and Great Britain. We also solicited papers from leading theologians and advocates of pacifist and just-war views. In the end, we sought a relatively small group of representative Christians from all perspectives who would come together to debate and discuss from the standpoint of their individual heritages and biblical roots the questions of war with regard to ethical dilemmas.

The result was a remarkable two days of presentations and interactions that remain a testimony to the earnest search for biblical and ethical approaches to the greater questions of war and the Bible. Many of the papers from that conference are collected here, and they provide a representative sampling of the issues and possible movement toward solutions to the wars and violence of our age. They are a unique survey of a variety of positions and views. They also display profound respect for other perspectives. The reader will not necessarily find an answer for the question of what position to take on the issue of warfare, but he or she will appreciate the depth and rationale of the positions represented here.

Miroslav Volf's essay lays a foundation for the basic question regarding war and the Bible: Does the Bible, and especially Christianity's interpretation of it, advocate warfare? Arguing that it does not, Volf provides the necessary basis for any discussion of the Bible as a source of moral direction. Following my essay, which summarizes perspectives on warfare, Elmer A. Martens and M. Daniel Carroll R. examine specific questions regarding the Bible's teaching on warfare from an exegetically informed perspective of pacifism. Martens traces the message of the divine warrior in the Old Testament through to the cross of the crucified Christ in the New Testament. The result is a portrait of a Christian whose life of self-sacrifice surrenders the fighting to God. Carroll's examination of the historical and theological contexts of Isaiah develops themes that reject politics as usual and seek salvation elsewhere.

The following section directly addresses current ethical questions facing the Bible reader. Daniel R. Heimbach leads in a direction that is different from the previous essays, but it is necessary because it addresses the moral and ethical implications of Christian involvement in states that go to war. He considers what constitutes a just cause for a just war. In doing so, he directly addresses the 2003 invasion of Iraq and the war that proceeded from this invasion. Tony Pfaff addresses an issue that in hindsight seems prescient in its importance: the definition of noncombatants in the context of a war with terrorists and the responsibility in just-war tradition to avoid harming noncombatants. The late Ian Durie, a retired British Major General, addresses the definition of terrorism and, in the context of the just-war tradition, the significance of this definition in terms of an ethical response to terrorist attacks. For those unfamiliar with the just war tradition, Durie discusses the criteria on pp. 123–25.

A concluding essay by Glen H. Stassen returns to the biblical ideals of peace and introduces the theme of just peacemaking as a counterpoint to just war. The result is a positive direction for understanding and working together toward the achievement of peace in the present age, all the while realizing that the fullness of peace lies beyond this world.

I must express gratitude for several of the many people who made this volume possible. Foremost is Cal Dunlap, director of ACCTS, who assisted the Biblical Studies division of Denver Seminary in engaging the speakers who came. Without his efforts, the conference and this subsequent volume would not have been possible. The faculty of the Biblical Studies division, Craig L. Blomberg, M. Daniel Carroll R., William W. Klein, and I also collaborated to bring about the conference. It is a delight to thank both ACCTS and Denver Seminary, who cosponsored the event. Denver Seminary in particular provided the facilities and the publicity for the conference. Luanna Traubert's dedication to the many details of that Friday and Saturday enabled everyone to participate and learn in a comfortable context.

I should also like to thank Eisenbrauns for their agreement to publish this volume and for their customary attention to detail in the final stages of its production, printing, and distribution. The Institute of Biblical Research deserves credit for allowing this work to appear as one of the first volumes in their new series, the Bulletin for Biblical Research Supplement Series. Finally, as coeditor I would like to express my special gratitude to Elmer A. Martens, who, along with his wife, Phyllis, worked diligently to complete the editing of all the contributions that appear in this volume. Without their labors, it would not have been published.

Richard S. Hess
Englewood, Colorado
May 19, 2007

Contributors

M. Daniel Carroll R. (Rodas) is Distinguished Professor of Old Testament at Denver Seminary, Denver, Colorado; adjunct professor at El Seminario Teológico Centroamericano, Guatemala City, Guatemala.

Ian G. C. Durie†, a Major General (Retired) in the British Army, was Executive Chairman of ACCTS Military Ministry International, UK.

Daniel R. Heimbach is Professor of Christian Ethics at Southeastern Baptist Theological Seminary, Wake Forest, North Carolina.

Richard S. Hess is Earl S. Kalland Professor of Old Testament and Semitic Languages at Denver Seminary, Denver, Colorado.

Elmer A. Martens is President Emeritus and Professor Emeritus of Old Testament at the Mennonite Brethren Biblical Seminary, Fresno, California.

Tony Pfaff is a Lieutenant Colonel and a Middle East Foreign Area Officer in the United States Army and a former professor of Philosophy at West Point.

Glen H. Stassen is the Lewis B. Smedes Professor of Christian Ethics at Fuller Theological Seminary, Pasadena, California.

Miroslav Volf is the Henry B. Wright Professor of Systematic Theology at Yale University Divinity School, where he is also the Director of the Yale Center for Faith and Culture.

Abbreviations

General

ACCTS	Association for Christian Conferences, Teaching, and Service
A.D.	Anno Domini
B.C.	Before Christ
LXX	Septuagint
MMI	Military Ministries International
MT	Masoretic Text
NIV	New International Version
NRSV	New Revised Standard Version
NT	New Testament
OT	Old Testament
SBC	Southern Baptist Convention
UN	United Nations

Reference Works

AB	Anchor Bible
ABRL	Anchor Bible Reference Library
BibInt	*Biblical Interpretation*
BZ	*Biblische Zeitschrift*
CBQ	*Catholic Biblical Quarterly*
COS	Hallo, W. W., editor. *The Context of Scripture*. 3 vols. Leiden: Brill, 1997–2002
ESHM	European Seminar for Historical Methodology
HBT	*Horizons in Biblical Theology*
Int	*Interpretation*
JAOS	*Journal of the American Oriental Society*
JBL	*Journal of Biblical Literature*
JCS	*Journal of Cuneiform Studies*
JSOT	*Journal for the Study of the Old Testament*
JSOTSup	Journal for the Study of Old Testament: Supplement Series
LHBOTS	Library of Hebrew Bible / Old Testament Studies
NCBC	New Century Bible Commentary
NICOT	New International Commentary on the Old Testament
NIDOTTE	Van Gemeren, W. A., editor. *New International Dictionary of Old Testament Theology and Exegesis*. 5 vols. Grand Rapids: Zondervan, 1997
OBT	Overtures to Biblical Theology
OTL	Old Testament Library
OTS	Old Testament Studies
R&T	*Religion and Theology*

REMHI/CIIR   Proyecto Interdiocesano Recuperación de la Memoria Histórica /
             Catholic Institute for International Relations
RLT   *Revista Latinoamericana de Teología*
SBLSymS   Society of Biblical Literature Symposium Series
SHCANE   Studies in the History of the Ancient Near East
THAT   Jenni, E., and Westermann, C., editors. *Theologisches Handwörterbuch zum
             Alten Testament.* 2 vols. Munich: Kaiser / Zurich: Theologischer Verlag,
             1971–76
TynBul   *Tyndale Bulletin*

CHAPTER 1

Christianity and Violence

MIROSLAV VOLF

The Current Resurgence of Religion

In the aftermath of the terrorist attack on the World Trade Center on September 11, 2001, it was not unusual to hear that the attack "changed everything." "Everything" is certainly an exaggeration, but 9/11, as the terrorist attack is sometimes called, did change a good many things, including our relation to religion. The attack, in which more than 3,000 lives were lost and the economic life of the nation was disrupted in a major way, was partially motivated by religion. Religion, we were led to conclude, is alive and well today and is a force not only in the private but also in the public lives of people around the globe.

This is not what the mainstream sociologists of the 20th century, who followed in the footsteps of Karl Marx, Max Weber, and Emil Durkheim, were predicting. Instead of slowly withering away or lodging itself quietly in the privacy of worshipers' hearts, religion has emerged as an important force on the national and international scenes. It is too early to tell how permanent this resurgence of religion will be. The processes of secularization may well continue, though likely not in the older sense of an overall decline of religious observance but, rather, in the newer sense of the diminishing influence of religion in contemporary social structures. Nevertheless, religion is presently alive and well on the public scene, so much so that a collection of essays entitled *Religion, the Missing Dimension of Statecraft* (which, when originally published in 1994, was seen as pushing the boundaries of its discipline) has become obligatory reading for diplomats in many countries, Western and non-Western.[1]

In many people's minds, the reassertion of religion as a political factor has not been for the good. It seems that the gods are mainly concerned with terror, as suggested by the title of Mark Juergensmeyer's book on the global rise

---

1. Douglas Johnston and Cynthia Sampson, *Religion, the Missing Dimension of Statecraft* (New York: Oxford University Press, 1994).

of religious violence, published before 9/11.[2] Among the intellectual elite in the Western cultural milieu, the contemporary coupling of religion and violence feeds most decisively on the memories of the wars that plagued Europe from the 1560s to the 1650s, in which religion was "the burning motivation, the one that inspired fanatical devotion and the most vicious hatred."[3] These wars contributed a great deal to the emergence of secularizing modernity.

A secularizing impact of the wars of religion was felt even as far afield from everyday concerns as theories of knowledge are sometimes deemed to be. As Stephen Toulmin has argued in *Cosmopolis*, modernity did not emerge, as is often claimed, simply as a result of its protagonists' endeavor to dispel the darkness of tradition and superstition with the light of philosophical and scientific reason. It was not accidental that Descartes "discovered" the one correct method to acquire knowledge in a time when "over much of the continent . . . people had a fair chance of having their throats cut and their houses burned down by strangers who merely disliked their religion."[4] A new way of establishing truth "that was independent of, and neutral between, particular religious loyalties" seemed an attractive alternative to war fueled by dogmatic claims.[5]

Like key Enlightenment figures, many contemporaries see religion as a pernicious social ill that needs aggressive treatment rather than a medicine from which a cure is expected. Did not the perpetrators of the 9/11 terrorist attack appeal to religion as the primary motivating force for their act? In the recent war in the Balkans, did not the Serbs fight for the land on which the holy sites of their religion stood? Is not the difference between Catholicism and Protestantism at the heart of the civil war in Northern Ireland? Is not religion a major factor in clashes in India? The contemporary resurgence of religion seems to go hand in hand with the resurgence of religiously legitimized violence — at least in the public perception. Hence, the argument goes, it is necessary to weaken, neutralize, or eliminate religion outright as a factor in public life.

Contesting the Claim That Christianity Fosters Violence

In this essay, I will contest the claim that the Christian faith, as one of the major world religions, predominantly fosters violence and will argue that it should be seen as a contributor to more-peaceful social environments. This

---

2. Mark Juergensmeyer, *Terror in the Mind of God: The Global Rise of Religious Violence* (Berkeley: University of California Press, 2000).

3. R. Scott Appleby, *The Ambivalence of the Sacred: Religion, Violence, and Reconciliation* (Lanham, MD: Rowman and Littlefield, 1999) 2. See Ronal Asch, *The Thirty Years War: The Holy Roman Empire and Europe, 1618–48* (New York: St. Martin's, 1997).

4. Steven Toulmin, *Cosmopolis: The Hidden Agenda of Modernity* (New York: Free Press, 1990) 17.

5. Ibid., 70.

may seem a bold claim. Lest I be misunderstood from the start, let me clarify my thesis. I will not argue that the Christian faith was not and does not continue to be employed to foster violence. Obviously, an argument of this sort cannot be plausibly made. Not only have Christians committed atrocities and engaged in less egregious forms of violence during the course of their long history but they have also drawn on religious convictions to justify them.[6] Moreover, there are elements in the Christian faith that, when viewed in isolation or when excessively foregrounded, can plausibly be used to legitimize violence. In addition, I will not argue that Christianity has been historically less associated with violence than other major religions. I am not sure whether this is or is not the case, and I am not sure how one would go about deciding the issue. I will leave these important but difficult questions unaddressed.

What I will argue is that, at least when it comes to Christianity, the cure for religiously induced and legitimized violence is almost exactly the opposite of what an important intellectual current in the West since the Enlightenment has been suggesting. The cure is not less religion but, in a carefully qualified sense, *more* religion. I do not mean, of course, that the cure for violence lies in increased religious zeal; blind religious zeal is at the heart of the problem. Instead, it lies in a stronger and more intelligent commitment to the faith as faith. In terms of how Christian faith is conceived, my thesis is this: The more we reduce Christian faith to a vague religiosity that serves primarily to energize, heal, and give meaning to a life the content of which is shaped by factors other than faith (such as national or economic interests), the worse off we will be. Conversely, the more the Christian faith matters to its adherents and the more they practice it as an ongoing tradition with strong ties to its origins and with clear cognitive and moral content, the better off we will be. *"Thin" but zealous practice of the Christian faith is likely to foster violence; "thick" and committed practice will help generate and sustain a culture of peace.*[7] This thesis

---

6. For a survey, see Gottfried Maron, "Frieden und Krieg: Ein Blick in die Theologie- und Kirchengeschichte," in *Glaubenskriege in Vergangenheit und Gegenwart* (ed. Peter Herrmann (Göttingen: Vandenhoeck & Ruprecht, 1996) 17–35. See also Karlheinz Deschner, *Kriminalgeschichte des Christentums* (6 vols.; Reinbeck bei Hamburg: Rohwolt, 1986ff.) and a response to his work in *Kriminalizierung des Christentums? Karlheinz Deschners Kirchengeschichte auf dem Prüfstand* (ed. H. R. Seeliger; Freiburg im Breisgau: Herder, 1993).

7. The best way to explain my use of the words *thick* and *thin* is to compare it with the usage of others. Clifford Geertz has popularized the use of the contrasting pair "thick" and "thin" (*Interpretation of Cultures* [New York: Basic Books, 1974] 3–30). He in turn has borrowed it from Gilbert Ryle. Both use the terms in the syntagm of a "thick" or "thin" description of the same phenomenon. A typical case of a "thin" description is "rapidly contracting his right eyelids," and a "thick" description is "practicing burlesque of a friend faking a wink to deceive an innocent into thinking a conspiracy is in motion." Michael Walzer has introduced an altered sense of "thick" and "thin," applying the terms to moral argument. He writes, "[I]t is not my claim to offer a thick description of moral argument, rather to point to a kind of argument that is itself 'thick'—richly

amounts to the claim that approaching the issue of religion and violence by considering the *quantity* of religious commitment—more religion, more violence, less religion, less violence—is unsophisticated and mistaken. The most relevant factor is, rather, the *quality* of religious commitment within a given religious tradition.

This thesis will be supported by countering several influential arguments about the violent character of Christianity. This is only half—the negative half—of what is needed to make my thesis plausible. The other, positive half is to show that at Christianity's heart, and not just at its margins, lie important resources for creating and sustaining a culture of peace.[8] In the past, scholars have argued in a variety of ways that the Christian faith fosters violence. I will engage four arguments that, in my estimation, go to the heart of the matter.[9]

---

referential, culturally resonant, locked into a locally established symbolic system or network of meaning. 'Thin' is simply a contrasting term" (*Thick and Thin: Moral Argument at Home and Abroad* [Notre Dame, IN: University of Notre Dame Press, 1994] xi n. 1). For a different, more recent use of "thick" and "thin" in which these designations refer to "the two types of human relations," and in which "thick relations are in general our relations to the near and dear" and "thin relations are in general our relations to the stranger and the remote," see Avishai Margalit, *The Ethics of Memory* (Cambridge: Harvard University Press, 2002) 7, 37ff. My use is similar to Walzer's, in that, just as Walzer claims that in relation to morality one arrives at the "thin" understanding and practice of the faith by abstraction from the "thick" understanding and practice. I define "thick," for instance, as a worshiper expressing a conviction that God is triune and understanding this conviction to be governed by the story of Jesus Christ and to imply an obligation to act in certain ways; "thin" is Serbian soldiers' flashing three fingers in what looks like a victory sign but is in fact a sign of a Trinitarian faith reduced by this very act to nothing more than an empty marker of cultural difference. Or consider an example from the United States: "thin" is the draining of specific religious content from the words *under God* in the Pledge of Allegiance so that they become a cultural tradition rather than a theological assertion; "thick" is when "God" in the Pledge refers to the God of Jesus Christ or to Allah or to Yahweh, which would render the phrase unconstitutional under the "no establishment" clause. See the editorial, "Taking on the Pledge," *The Christian Century* (July 17–30, 2002) 5. Walzer's and my concerns, however, are different. I am concerned to show how the "thinning" of religious practice opens religious convictions to be misused to legitimize violence because it strips away precisely what in "thick" religious faith guards against misuse of this sort, whereas Walzer is concerned to show that morality is "thick" from the beginning and that the "thin" morality, which is universal, always resides within the "thick" morality, which is particular (Walzer, *Thick and Thin,* 4).

8. See my *Exclusion and Embrace* (Nashville: Abingdon, 1996).

9. There are other arguments for the same thesis, some of which I will address indirectly. One is based on the combination of the claims about God's omnipotence, omniscience, and implacable justice, for instance. A belief in an all-powerful God who sees everything and wills punishment for every transgression is central to the Christian faith, the proponents of the argument claim, and is bound to lead to violence. Another argument for the violent character of the Christian faith is based on the authoritarian character of every revealed religion. Adherents of a religion that is based on the irrational authority of revelation tend to adjudicate disputes, not through rational means and compromise but through assertion of irrational authority. Space restrictions do not allow me to address these and other arguments. But my comments below address them indirectly.

The Argument That Religion by Its Nature Is Violent

The first argument for the violent character of Christianity is that religions are violent by nature and that the Christian faith, being a religion, is therefore violent by nature. Mark Juergensmeyer's *Terror in the Mind of God* rests on this reading of religion. A central reason that violence has accompanied religion's renewed political presence, he argues, is "the nature of religious imagination, which always has had the propensity to absolutize and to project images of cosmic war."[10] Cosmic war is waged not for its own sake but for the sake of peace, of course. Precisely because cosmic war lies at its core, religion has been "order restoring and life affirming."[11] But in order for religion to avoid leaving a trail of blood and tears in its pursuit of peace, it cannot be left to its own devices. It needs "the temper of rationality and fair play that Enlightenment values give to civil society."[12] Religion qua religion is violent. To have a socially positive role, religion must be redeemed by Enlightenment values.

The argument that a religion that counts Augustine, Thomas Aquinas, and Luther among its great teachers must learn to be "rational" from Enlightenment thinkers betrays a rather narrow understanding of "rationality." But at least this account of rationality is plausible. Implausible, however, is the claim that a religion that counts St. Francis of Assisi among its greatest saints does not have resources of its own to learn about fair play but must borrow them from Enlightenment thinkers. The pressure to make implausible claims of this sort comes from "thinning" Christian convictions to general religious beliefs and then placing images of cosmic war at the heart of these general beliefs. In the process, everything specific to the Christian faith has been lost.

Whereas Juergensmeyer asserts that religion is inherently violent by appealing to the images of the cosmic war that allegedly lie at its heart, Maurice Bloch argues for the same assertion by offering a general theory of religion. In his book *Prey into Hunter*, he argues that the "irreducible core of the ritual process" involves "a marked element of violence or . . . of [a] conquest . . . of the here and now by the transcendental."[13] He explains,

> In the first part of the ritual the here and now is simply left behind by the move towards the transcendental. This initial movement represents the transcendental as supremely desirable and the here and now as of no value. The return is different. In the return the transcendental is not left behind but continues to be attached to those who made the initial move in its direction; its value is not

---

10. Juergensmeyer, *Terror in the Mind of God*, 242.

11. Ibid., 159.

12. Ibid., 243.

13. Maurice Bloch, *Prey into Hunter: The Politics of Religious Experience* (Cambridge: Cambridge University Press, 1992) 4–5.

negated. Secondly, the return to the here and now is really a conquest of the here and now by the transcendental.[14]

This return from the transcendental sphere motivated by the goal of conquest, Bloch continues, explains "the often-noted fact that religion so easily furnishes an idiom of expansionist violence to people in a whole range of societies, an idiom which, under certain circumstances, becomes a legitimation for actual violence."[15]

Let us assume that Bloch has analyzed the core of the ritual process correctly. The question remains whether one should examine the core of the ritual process, stripped of the texture as well as the larger context that a concrete religion gives it, in order to understand the relation of religions to violence. Consider this thought experiment: Imagine that the first part of the ritual—the leaving of the here and now by moving toward the transcendental—is understood by a religion as death to her own self-centered desires and as her entry into a transcendental space of harmonious peace. And suppose that the religion stipulates that the second part of the ritual—the conquest of the here and now by the transcendental—must be achieved in a peaceful way, consistent with the content of the transcendental. If the formal structure of ritual expressed this content, would this religion serve as "a legitimation of actual violence"? Would not the "conquest," if successful, be precisely the victory of the "transcendental" peace over the violence of the here and now?

As readers are certainly aware, this sort of religion need not be imagined as hypothetical. What I have asked the reader to imagine is precisely how the Christian faith, at least in some of its important strands, understands itself and its initiation ritual, baptism. Bloch engages the Christian faith directly and envisages a possibility that might allow it to avoid underwriting violence. But in his account, this possibility is predicated on Christianity's "refusal of the second phase of rebounding violence, that is, a refusal of the conquest of external vitality which is therefore ultimately a refusal to continue with earthly life."[16] The Apostle Paul's Christianity, he believes, is an example of this sort of refusal—or rather, an example of a half-hearted refusal because Paul also undertook "prudent organization of a well-organized church firmly embedded in the continuing practical and political world."[17]

A more careful study of the apostle's writings will show that he advocated neither a full-fledged nor a half-hearted refusal of the "conquest." Explaining the significance of baptism for earthly life, the apostle writes, "Therefore we have been buried with him by baptism into death, so that, just as Christ was

14. Ibid., 5.
15. Ibid., 6.
16. Ibid., 90–91.
17. Ibid., 94.

raised from the dead by the glory of the Father, so we might walk in the new-ness of life" (Rom 6:4). Paul understands walking in "newness of life" as *imita-tio Christi* and therefore as "repetition" of the transcendental sphere in the here and now. So he seeks "conquest." But as significant as the conquest itself is the character of the conquest, for conquering in the right way is the only way to conquer. Because Christ died in self-giving love for the godless, Paul must affirm a nonviolent conquest of the here and now. I paraphrase Paul's famous summary of the Christian life in the world: to seek to conquer evil with evil is to be conquered by evil; evil can be overcome only with good (Rom 12:21).

Will Christianity, understood as a peaceful conquest of a violent world by the God of peace, foster violence? One could argue that any victory of the "transcendental" over the here and now amounts to violence. But if non-coercive victory of peace over violence is itself implicated in violence, then one may legitimately wonder whether the notion of violence has been hope-lessly muddled. Put differently, one would need to show why "violence" un-derstood thus is not desirable rather than objectionable.

As applied to Christianity, the victory of the transcendental over the here and now is violent only if the notion of the transcendental is stripped of its particular content and infused with the values of the here and now around which the conflicts rage. This often happens when the Christian faith is em-ployed to legitimize violence. We declare God to be on our side and we see ourselves as soldiers of God, so that the earthly goals acquire a "transcendent" aura and the struggle for them becomes a religious duty. One may describe this as inverse projection—not the projection of what humans deem su-premely valuable onto a heavenly screen, a practice that 19th-century critics of religion deplored, but the projection of heavenly values onto earthly goods. The second projection is more dangerous because the first generates reli-giously sanctioned passivity in the context of oppression and suffering, whereas the second generates religiously sanctioned violence in the context of struggle for scarce goods. This sort of projection of transcendent values onto earthly goods can only succeed, however, if Christian faith is illegiti-mately stripped of its "thick" content in order to support an engagement in a struggle that was already under way and carried out for other-than-religious reasons and by means not sanctioned by the religion.

The Argument That Monotheism Entails Violence

Some scholars, such as Regina Schwartz in her book *The Curse of Cain: The Violent Legacy of Monotheism*, attempt to argue for the Christian faith's com-plicity in violence by pointing not to the general features of the Christian faith as religion but to one of its characteristic components. Along with Juda-ism and Islam, Christianity is a *monotheistic* religion and, therefore, Schwartz argues, an *exclusive* and *violent* religion. "Whether as singleness (this God against the others) or totality (this is all the God there is), monotheism abhors, reviles, rejects, and ejects whatever it defines as outside its compass."[18] Given that the belief in one God "forges identity antithetically," monotheism creates a mistaken notion of identity ("we are 'us' because we are not 'them'") and contributes to violent practice ("we can remain 'us' only if we obliterate 'them'").

In addition, monotheism imports the category of universal "truth" into the religious sphere. Jakov Jukic, a Croatian sociologist of religion, has noted that this fact lies at the heart of monotheism's exclusivity. To believe that there is only one God entails belief in the only *true* God. Moreover, because this claim to the truth of the one God must be universal, it is inescapably public. Universal public claims cause strife when they encounter opposing claims, of either a particular or a universal sort. For this reason also, monotheism is bound to have a violent legacy, the argument goes.[19] "We," the faithful, have on our side the one true God and stand in opposition to "them," the infidels and renegades.

This argument should be taken seriously. And yet it is not clear that an affirmation of divine oneness *in itself* leads to violence. Does not a monotheistic claim to universal truth also work against the tendency to divide people into "us" and "them"? If one accepts the belief in one God, in an important sense everyone is "in," and everyone is "in" on precisely the same terms. True, "being in on the same terms" may feel like violence if one does not want to be "in," or one wants to be "in" on different terms. But if one removes monotheism, the division and violence between "us" and "them" hardly disappears, and if "we" or "they" are religious, each will appeal to his/her respective god to wage war. In fact, this happens whether religion is monotheistic or tribal. In a polytheistic context, violence may reassert itself with even more force because it will necessarily be justified by locally legitimized or arbitrary preferences, against which, in the absence of a divinity who overarches the parties, there can be no higher court of appeal. Even if monotheism is taken vaguely and abstractly as belief in one God without further qualification, it is not clear that it is likely to generate more violence than polytheism or atheism.

None of the monotheistic religions espouses this vague and abstract monotheism. Specifically, Christian monotheism contains a further important pressure against violence, especially violence caused by self-enclosed and exclusive identities of the type criticized by Schwartz; for Christian monotheism is

---

18. Regina Schwartz, *The Curse of Cain: The Violent Legacy of Monotheism* (Chicago: University of Chicago Press, 1997) 63.

19. Jakov Jukic, *Lica i Maske Svetoga: Ogledi iz drustvene religiologije* (Faces and Masks of the Holy) (Zagreb: Krscanska sadasnjost, 1997) 242–43.

Trinitarian.[20] What difference does Trinitarianism make?[21] One of the most important social aspects of the doctrine of the Trinity is its notion of identity. To believe that the one God is the Father, the Son, and the Holy Spirit is to believe that the identity of the Father, for instance, cannot be understood apart from the Son and the Holy Spirit. The Father's identity is from the start defined by the Son and the Spirit, and therefore it is not undifferentiated or self-enclosed. One cannot say without qualification that the Father is not the Son or the Spirit because to be the Father means to have the Son and the Spirit present in one. The same is true, of course, of the Son and the Spirit in relation to the Father and one another.

Moreover, the divine persons as non-self-enclosed identities are understood by the Christian tradition to form a perfect communion of love. The persons give themselves to each other and receive themselves from each other in love. None need wrest anything from the others, none need impose anything on the others, and none need secure himself from the incursions of the others. Far from being a life of violence, the life of the divine being is characterized by mutually uncoerced and welcomed generosity.

It would be difficult to argue that monotheism of this sort fosters violence. Instead, in Maurice Bloch's terminology, it grounds peace here and now in the transcendental realm, in the love and peacefulness of the divine being. The argument for inherent violence in Christianity's monotheism works only if one illegitimately reduces the "thick" religious description of God to naked oneness and then postulates this abstract oneness to be of decisive social significance. I do not dispute that this reduction actually happens within the Christian community. I do contend, however, that this fact does not attest to the inherent violence of Christianity but is a sign that the Christian faith has not been taken seriously enough. Instead, nonreligious values have taken precedence.

The Argument That Creation Is an Act of Violence

So far, I have argued that Christian faith may generate violence in its "thin" but not in its "thick" form—when a "thick" character of the divine being's differentiated and complex identity is reduced to an undifferentiated "one" and when divine engagement with the world to make it a world of harmonious peace is rendered as generalized "conquest." But what about the argument that

---

20. For a critique of Schwartz along these lines, see my "Jehovah on Trial," *Christianity Today* (April 27, 1998) 32–35.

21. For the following, see my "'The Trinity Is Our Social Program': The Doctrine of the Trinity and the Shape of Social Engagement," *Modern Theology* 14 (1998) 403–23.

some very "thick" and "concrete" Christian convictions generate violence? Central here are the convictions about the world's creation and redemption.

It is a basic Christian claim that God *created* the world. In her influential book *Sexism and God-Talk*, Rosemary Radford Ruether starts with the observation that in the Hebrew Bible the creator is like an artisan working on material outside his own nature. God does so, she argues, by "a combination of male seminal and cultural power (word-act) that shapes it 'from above.'"[22] In this sort of account, creation is a result of an imposition of form on formless matter from outside by an alien force. Hence, creation is an act of violence.

What is wrong with this account of creation? Everything—almost. Even if one assumes that creation is best described as "forming" preexisting material, one must admit that this material is "something" and that it is a specific kind of "something" that deserves respect. But it is not clear at all that chaos, which according to this account of creation God formed, is a "something." And if the chaos were a "something," why would it not be something analogous to a boulder from which an artisan can fashion a sculpture? Despite all the sparks flying from his chisel, Michelangelo working on *David* can hardly be described as perpetrating violence. In order to classify the activity of "forming" as an act of violence, the entity that is formed must possess an integrity of its own that demands respect. If someone were to smash Michelangelo's *David* into pieces of granite, this would be an act of violence.

On the whole, however, the Christian tradition has not understood creation as "forming." Instead, it has underscored that God the creator is not a demiurge working on preexisting matter; God created *ex nihilo* 'out of nothing'. The consequences of this understanding of creation for its putative violent character are significant. As Rowan Williams explains in *On Christian Theology*, when we say that God creates, we do not mean that God "imposes a definition" but that God "creates an identity." He continues, "Prior to God's word there is nothing to impose on."[23] From this, it follows that creation is not the exercise of an alien power—indeed, that it is not the exercise of power at all, understood in the usual sense. Williams writes,

> Power is exercised by x over y; but creation is not power, because it is not exercised on anything. We might, of course, want to say that creation presupposes a divine potentiality, or resourcefulness, or abundance of active life; and 'power' can sometimes be used in those senses. But what creation emphatically isn't is any kind of imposition or manipulation: it is not God imposing on us divinely willed roles rather than the ones we 'naturally' might have, or defining us out of

---

22. Rosemary Radford Ruether, *Sexism and God-Talk: Toward a Feminist Theology* (Boston: Beacon, 1983) 77.

23. Rowan Williams, *On Christian Theology* (Oxford: Blackwell, 2000) 68.

our own system into God's. . . . And this implies that the Promethean myth of humanity struggling against God for its welfare and interests makes no sense: to be a creature cannot be to be a victim of an alien force.[24]

Creation, then, is not a violent act. Indeed, one may even argue that, in the absence of a doctrine of creation, relationships between entities in the world, especially human beings, will necessarily be violent.[25] If identities are not created, then boundaries between identities must emerge out of interchanges between these entities. And these interchanges themselves must be described as violent, because boundaries, precisely because they are always contested, are arbitrary from a vantage point that transcends either of the contesting entities. Given scarce resources, boundaries will always be the product of power struggles, even if these power struggles take the form of negotiations. Moreover, no appeal for arbitration between the contending parties can be made to something that ultimately stands outside the power struggle.

The Argument That the Intervention of a New Creation Generates Violence

If creation is not a violent act, Christian convictions about creation do not generate violence—provided, of course, that they are not stripped of their specific texture and reduced to the formula "*x* forms *y*, which possesses integrity of its own," so that they can be employed in ways contrary to their inner logic. But what about the eschatological *new creation*? What about God's activity to redeem creation from consequences of sin? Clearly, the new creation is not *creatio ex nihilo* 'out of nothing', but *creatio ex vetere* 'out of old creation'. This "old" and "sinful" creation does possess an integrity of its own (even if it is an integrity in tension with its true character), and it can and does assert its will over and against God. In redeeming the world, God intervenes into the existing sinful world in order to transform it into a world of perfect love. Is this intervention not violent and does it not therefore generate violence on the part of human beings?

The most radical critique of redemptive divine engagement as violent and violence-inducing comes from poststructuralist thinkers. They believe that any determinacy of the goal to be achieved by divine transformation of this world and any specificity about the agent of transformation already breeds violence. By their account, in order for what must *come* (in contrast to what *is*), to be nonviolent, it must always remain completely other and cannot be

---

24. Ibid., 68–69.

25. See John Milbank, *Theology and Social Theory: Beyond Secular Reason* (Oxford: Blackwell, 1990).

expressed as an "onto-theological or teleo-eschatological program or design."[26] As John Caputo, speaking in the voice of his teacher, Jacques Derrida, states, "[I]f the Messiah ever actually showed up . . . that would ruin everything."[27] Any and every Messiah is problematic because he would necessarily exclude something or someone. Hence, the only acceptable goal of desirable change is "absolute hospitality," a posture of welcoming the stranger without any preconditions, just as the only acceptable engagement to achieve change is "radical and interminable, infinite . . . critique."[28]

"Absolute hospitality" seems generous and peaceful, until one remembers that unrepentant perpetrators and their unhealed victims would then have to sit around the same table and share a common home without adequate attention to the violation that has taken place. The idea ends up too close for comfort to the Nietzschean affirmation of life, in which a sacred "yes" is pronounced to all that is and "but thus I willed it" is said of all that was, including all the small and large horrors of history.[29] Absolute hospitality would in no way amount to absence of violence. To the contrary, it would enthrone violence precisely under the guise of nonviolence because it would leave the violators unchanged and the consequences of violence unremedied. Hospitality can be absolute only once the world has been transformed into a world of love in which each person is hospitable to all. In the world of injustice, deception, and violence, hospitality can only be conditional—even if the will to hospitality and the offer of hospitality remain unconditional.

Transformation of the world of violence into a world of love cannot take place by means of absolute hospitality. It would require radical change and not simply an act of indiscriminate acceptance for the world to be transformed into a world of love. The Christian tradition has tied this change to the coming of the Messiah, the crucified and the resurrected One, whose appearance in glory is still awaited. Is this messianic intervention violent? Does it sanction human violence? The answer is simple regarding the Messiah's first coming. Jesus Christ did not come into the world in order to conquer evildoers through an act of violence but to die for them in self-giving love and thereby reconcile them to God. The outstretched arms of the suffering body on the cross define the whole of Christ's mission. He condemned the sin of humanity by taking it upon himself; and by bearing it, he freed human beings from its power and restored their communion with God. Though suffering on the

26. Jacques Derrida, *Spectres of Marx: The State of the Debt, the Work of Mourning, and the New International* (trans. Peggy Kamuf; New York: Routledge, 1994) 75.

27. John Caputo, *The Prayers and Tears of Jacques Derrida* (Bloomington: Indiana University Press, 1997) 74.

28. Derrida, *Spectres of Marx*, 90.

29. See Friedrich Nietzsche, *Thus Spoke Zarathustra*, in *The Portable Nietzsche* (trans. Walter Kaufmann; New York: Penguin, 1954) 139, 253.

cross is not all Christ did, the cross represents the decisive criterion for our understanding of all his work.

Does the belief in the Crucified generate violence? Beginning at least with Constantine's conversion, the followers of the Crucified have perpetrated gruesome acts of violence under the sign of the cross. Over the centuries, the seasons of Lent and Holy Week were, for the Jews, times of fear and trepidation; Christians have perpetrated some of the worst pogroms as they remembered the crucifixion of Christ, for which they blamed the Jews. Muslims also associate the cross with violence; crusaders' rampages were undertaken under the sign of the cross.

However, an unbiased reading of the story of Jesus Christ gives no warrant for this perpetration of violence. The account of his death in 1 Peter summarizes well the witness of the whole New Testament:

> For to this you have been called, because Christ also suffered for you, leaving you an example, so that you should follow in his steps. He committed no sin, and no deceit was found in his mouth. When he was abused, he did not return abuse; when he suffered, he did not threaten; but he entrusted himself to the one who judges justly. He himself bore our sins in his body on the cross, so that, free from sins, we might live for righteousness. (1 Pet 2:21–24)

If there is a danger in the story of the cross in relation to violence, it is the danger that it might teach simple acquiescence to being mistreated by others; the danger is not that it might incite someone to mistreat others. Whenever violence was perpetrated in the name of the cross, the cross was depleted of its "thick" meaning within the larger story of Jesus Christ and "thinned" down to a symbol of religious belonging and power—and the blood of those who did not belong flowed as Christians transmuted themselves from would-be followers of the Crucified to imitators of the people who crucified him.

Finally, what about the Messiah who is still to come in glory? He will come with grace for his followers. But does not the book of Revelation portray him as a Rider on a white horse whose "eyes are like a flame of fire," whose robe is "dipped in blood," from whose "mouth comes a sharp sword with which to strike down nations," and who is coming to "tread in the wine press of the fury of the wrath of God the Almighty" (19:11–16)? Some New Testament scholars have attempted to reinterpret the Rider to make him fit the generally non-violent stance of the New Testament. What is right about these efforts is that in Revelation the *martyrs* are the true victors so that, paradoxically, the "Beast's" victory over them is their victory over the "Beast." In this, they mirror Jesus Christ, the slaughtered Lamb, who conquered his enemies precisely by his sacrificial death.[30]

---

30. See Richard Bauckham, *The Theology of the Book of Revelation* (Cambridge: Cambridge University Press, 1993) 74, 90.

However, the Rider is not simply the Lamb; he is the Lamb in his function as the final judge. But why is the final judgment necessary? Without it, we would have to presume that all human beings, no matter how deeply steeped in evil they are, will either eventually succumb to the lure of God's love or, if they fail to do so, will willingly embrace not only the evil they do but the destructive impact of evil upon their own lives. This belief is little more than a modern superstition, borne of the inability to look without flinching into the "heart of darkness." It is true that evil is self-contradictory and, if unchecked, is bound to self-destruct. But evildoers are so much "better" as evildoers, as they improve their ability continually to make themselves thrive while wreaking havoc on others. There is no doubt that goodness can and does overcome evil. But the power of evil rests in great measure on the fact that, the more one does evil, the thicker the shield becomes that protects the evil from being overcome by good. The book of Revelation rightly refuses to operate with the belief that all evil will either be overcome by good or self-destruct. It therefore considers the possibility of divine violence against the persistent and unrepentant evildoer. There is redemption from violence so that we can practice love by means of love. However, those who refuse such redemption will of necessity be excluded from the world of love.

How should we understand this possible divine violence? In the context of the whole Christian faith, it is best described as a symbolic portrayal of the final exclusion of everything that refuses to be redeemed by God's suffering love. Will God finally exclude some human beings? Not necessarily. I called the divine "violence" "possible," for it is predicated on a human being's refusal to be made into a loving person and therefore to be admitted into the world of love. Will some people refuse? I hope not—and the Bible along with the best of the Christian tradition has never affirmed with certainty that some will refuse and therefore be excluded.[31]

It is possible (though not necessary) that the coming about of the new creation will require the divine violence of excluding what is contrary to the world of perfect love. The crucial question for our purposes is whether this possible divine violence at the end of history sanctions actual human violence in the middle of history. The response that resounds throughout the New Testament, including the book of Revelation, is a loud and persistent "No!" Though imitating God is the height of human holiness, there are things that only God may do. One of them is to deploy violence. Christians are manifestly not to gather under the banner of the Rider on the white horse but to take up their crosses and follow the Crucified. If they were to do otherwise, once again, they would be involved in "thinning" out a "thick" element of faith and

---

31. On the important distinction between hope for and belief in universal salvation, see Hans Urs von Balthasar, *Dare We Hope That All Men Will Be Saved?* (trans. David Kipp and Lothar Krauth; San Francisco: Ignatius, 1988).

making a mischievous use of it. They would be arrogating for themselves what God has reserved only for himself, to transpose the divine action from the end-time to a time in which God explicitly refrains from deploying violence in order to make repentance possible, and, finally, to transmute a possibility of violence into an actuality. "Thick" reading of Christian eschatological convictions will not sanction human violence; on the contrary, it will resist it.

Misusing the Christian Faith to Underwrite Violence

I will underscore one more time that my point in this essay is not to deny that the Christian faith has been used to legitimize violence or to claim that there are no elements in the Christian faith on which these uses plausibly build. Rather, my point is that neither the character of the Christian faith (its being a religion of a monotheist type) nor its most fundamental convictions (such as that God created the world and is engaged in redeeming it) are violence inducing. The Christian faith is *misused* when it is employed to underwrite violence.

How does this misuse happen and how should we prevent it? If we strip Christian convictions of their original and historic cognitive and moral content and reduce faith to a cultural resource endowed with a diffuse aura of the sacred, we are likely to get religiously legitimized and inspired violence in situations of conflict. If we nurture people in historic Christian convictions that are rooted in its sacred texts, we will likely get militants for peace, if anything. This, I think, is the result not only of a careful examination of the inner logic of Christian convictions but also of a careful look at actual Christian practice. R. Scott Appleby has argued in his book *The Ambivalence of the Sacred*, on the basis of case studies, that contrary to a widespread misconception, religious people play a positive role in the world of human conflicts and contribute to peace not when they "moderate their religion or marginalize their deeply held, vividly symbolized, and often highly particular beliefs" but, rather, "when they remain religious actors."[32]

In conclusion, I will briefly address the question why misconceptions about the violent character of Christian faith abound. I have already given part of the answer: Christians have used and continue to use their faith to legitimize violence that they deem necessary. Misconceptions of the Christian faith reflect the widespread misbehavior of Christians; and the misbehavior of Christians results from misconstruals of their own faith, from "thinning" its "thick" and original elements.[33] But there is more. One can easily show

---

32. Appleby, *Ambivalence of the Sacred*, 16.

33. Michael Sells's account of religion's relation to genocide in Bosnia is founded on an extremely "thin" account of the Christian faith; it functions more as a cultural resource with little connection to its origins than as a living faith committed to the sacred Scriptures and the best of

that the majority of Christians (and the majority of religious folks in general) are nonviolent citizens, peace lovers, peacemakers, sometimes even peace activists; and they are these things precisely for religious reasons. The purveyors of violence who seek religious legitimation are statistically a minority among Christians.

So why is the contrary opinion widespread? The reasons are many. What Avishai Margalit writes about ethnic belonging applies equally to religion: "It takes one cockroach found in your food to turn the most otherwise delicious meal into a bad experience. . . . It takes 30 to 40 ethnic groups who are fighting one another to make the 1,500 or more significant ethnic groups in the world who live more or less peacefully look bad."[34] One may describe this as *inflation of the negative*, the tendency of the evil to loom larger than the, comparatively, much-larger good.

This general tendency is strengthened in the modern world in which information flows are so pervasively dominated by mass media. Consider the following contrast. The Serbian paramilitary who rapes Muslim women with a cross around his neck has made it into the headlines and is immortalized in books on religious violence. Katarina Kruhonja, a medical doctor from Osijek, Croatia, and a recipient of the alternative Nobel prize for her peace initiatives, remains relatively unknown, as does the motivation for her work, which is thoroughly religious. She writes that she became a peace activist when, during the Serbian shelling of Osijek, the recentering of her own self on the crucified Christ "freed [her] will," and she "was able to resist the power of exclusion and the logic of war."[35] People such as Ms. Kruhonja remain obscure partly because the success of their work demands low visibility. But our unawareness of them is significantly based on the character of mass-media communication in a market-driven world. Violence sells, so viewers are shown violence without qualms about the disproportion between represented and actual violence.

The mass media create reality, but they do so by building on the proclivities of viewers. Why does the Serbian paramilitary rapist seem more "interesting" than Ms. Kruhonja? And why are we prone to conclude based on the cross he is wearing around his neck that his religious faith is implicated in the acts, whereas it would never occur to us to conclude based on the ring on his finger that the institution of marriage is to blame? Religion is more associated with violence than with peace in the public imagination partly because the public is fascinated with violence. We, the peace-loving citizens of nations

---

the tradition (*The Bridge Betrayed: Religion and Genocide in Bosnia* [Berkeley: University of California Press, 1996]). The "thinning" was, of course, not undertaken by him but by people he studied.

34. Margalit, *The Ethics of Memory*, 100.

35. Katarina Kruhonja, personal communication.

whose tranquility is secured by effective policing, are insatiable observers of violence. And as voyeurs, we show ourselves to be vicarious participants in the very violence we outwardly abhor. We are particularly drawn to religious violence because we have, understandably, a strong interest in exposing hypocrisy, especially of a religious sort. When these two factors are considered together—the inner deployment of violence and our delight in its exposure—we are revealed as fascinated with religious people's engagement in violence partly because we ourselves are violent but expect them to act otherwise.

If we were more self-critical about our own hidden violent proclivities and more suspicious about the presentation of violence in media, we might observe on the religious landscape not only eruptions of violence but also a widespread and steady flow of work that religious people do to make our world into a more peaceful place. Our imagination would then not be captured, for instance, by religion as a motivating force for the dozen or so not-particularly-religious zealous terrorists who destroyed the Twin Towers. Instead, we would be impressed by the degree to which religion served as a source of solace and orientation for the majority of Americans in a time of crisis and by the motivation it gave to many of them to help the victims, to protect Muslim coreligionists from stereotyping, and to build bridges between religious cultures estranged on account of violence triggered largely by nonreligious motives. These anonymous people acted out of the true spirit of Christian faith.

CHAPTER 2

War in the Hebrew Bible:
An Overview

RICHARD S. HESS

From the perspective of the Western world, the understanding of war and
its ethical issues must begin with a consideration of the Hebrew Bible or the
Old Testament. This is not merely because this source has been used throughout history as a primary means of justifying all stances on the moral questions
raised by war but also because the Hebrew Bible preserves a tradition that
continues in an unbroken connection from a time removed from the present
day by millennia. Beginning with the Hebrew Bible serves two purposes.
First, it allows the student to consider the issue of war in an ancient and different culture and time and thereby to evaluate the validity of modern arguments with the additional evidence of another age. This exercise minimizes
the prejudice that we all have, limited as we are by our own culture and experience. The second purpose, however, is equally important. A fresh examination of the teaching regarding war in the Hebrew Bible allows the Westerner
to consider how much has changed in views of war since ancient times.

This topic is vast in scope. Virtually every one of the 39 books of the Hebrew Bible mentions the subject of war, and some deal with it in great detail.[1]
Furthermore, there is no unanimity among biblical authors regarding war.
Views vary from book to book and, at times, from page to page. Indeed, in the
Hebrew Bible war is assumed from the outset as a necessary part of the world
in which the ancients found themselves. Neither the speeches of God nor the
actions of people who are considered saints ever envisioned the absence of
war in the world. It is true that passages such as Isa 2:2–4 and Mic 4:1–4 look
forward to a time of universal peace and the complete cessation of hostilities.
This vision is not unlike the harmonious relationship ascribed to the first
human couple in the opening two chapters of Genesis. However, neither of

---

1. Ruth and the Song of Songs are exceptions, according to Cyril S. Rodd (*Glimpses of a
Strange Land: Studies in Old Testament Ethics* [Edinburgh: T. & T. Clark, 2001] 185). See, however,
Song 3:7–8, where both military equipment and warriors appear.

these ideals was a historical reality in the periods in which the writers of the books of the Bible lived. Every generation knew war.

In light of the complexity of this subject and the issues involved, the purpose of this essay is to survey recent studies on the subject of war in the Old Testament and to evaluate their contributions. The essay will limit itself to several contributions related to the ethics of war as it is described in the Hebrew Bible. This delimitation of scope requires a focus on studies related to the moral view of warfare in the ancient world, excluding, for example, studies that consider the materials and strategies used in ancient warfare and in biblical battles. Even given this limitation, the questions related to war in the Bible remain complex and multilayered. While the issue of whether war in principle is "right" or "wrong" is never addressed in the Old Testament, it is not correct to assume that the Bible presents all wars from a single perspective. Nor is it correct to assume that war was either good or bad based on the extent to which it served the purposes of God or some other key character.

Instead, there are at least three levels on which warfare must be examined. First is the question of the nature of God as a warrior who leads his people in battle. This depiction of God is foundational for most of the understanding of war in the Hebrew Bible. Examination of this concept is necessary, for the people who worshiped the God of Israel were surely influenced and guided by the character of the God whom they honored. Second is the analysis of the different types of war described in the Bible and the explicit reflections on war that are suggested by the text. While this inquiry is complex and multifaceted, it provides the most important layer of understanding for appreciating the role of Israelites at war and the ethics that may have governed their prosecution of battle. Third, there remains the critical evaluation of the purpose behind the text's presentation of battles. This raises questions of ideology and propaganda. To what extent is the biblical presentation of warfare a distortion of the historical events, designed to serve the political purposes of the power elite of Jerusalem?

What is war in the Bible? The verb 'to make war' (*nilḥam*) occurs in its customary Niphal-stem formation some 164 times in the Bible. The noun form *milḥāmâ* 'war' appears about 320 times.[2] This relatively high frequency reflects the importance of the subject in the Bible. As others have noted, the practice and ideology of war was shared by the Israelites and other peoples of antiquity.[3] Most references to war concern Israel's battles in the wilderness, at the entrance into Canaan, and against various enemies of the nation (for example: Philistines, Amalekites, Arameans, and later powers). The role of

---

2. H. D. Preuss, "*milḥāmâ*," *TDOT* 8:334, 343.
3. Ibid., 336.

Israel's God Yahweh as warrior also significantly influences biblical usage of the term, and I will now examine this usage.

Yahweh as Warrior

Beginning with Exod 15:1–18 and forward, Yahweh is portrayed as a warrior who leads his people in battle and fights for them. Significantly, this is the manner in which Yahweh first reveals himself to Israel in conjunction with Israel's liberation from Egypt. The role of Yahweh as a warrior is the model against which all other fighters and their warfare are measured. This is the first model that Longman and Reid propose in their discussion of God as a warrior.[4] It is also the earliest model in the Bible used as an image for war.

The writer of Exodus celebrates God's defeat of the Egyptian army in the waters of the Re(e)d Sea in the following song:

> [1]Then Moses and the Israelites sang this song to the LORD: "I will sing to the LORD, for he is highly exalted. The horse and its rider he has hurled into the sea. [2]The LORD is my strength and my song; he has become my salvation. He is my God, and I will praise him, my father's God, and I will exalt him. [3]The LORD is a warrior; the LORD is his name. [4]Pharaoh's chariots and his army he has hurled into the sea. The best of Pharaoh's officers are drowned in the Red Sea. [5]The deep waters have covered them; they sank to the depths like a stone. [6]Your right hand, O LORD, was majestic in power. Your right hand, O LORD, shattered the enemy. [7]In the greatness of your majesty you threw down those who opposed you. You unleashed your burning anger; it consumed them like stubble. [8]By the blast of your nostrils the waters piled up. The surging waters stood firm like a wall; the deep waters congealed in the heart of the sea. [9]The enemy boasted, 'I will pursue, I will overtake them. I will divide the spoils; I will gorge myself on them. I will draw my sword and my hand will destroy them.' [10]But you blew with your breath, and the sea covered them. They sank like lead in the mighty waters. [11]Who among the gods is like you, O LORD? Who is like you—majestic in holiness, awesome in glory, working wonders? [12]You stretched out your right hand and the earth swallowed them. [13]In your unfailing love you will lead the people you have redeemed. In your strength you will guide them to your holy dwelling. [14]The nations will hear and tremble; anguish will grip the people of Philistia. [15]The chiefs of Edom will be terrified, the leaders of Moab will be seized with trembling, the people of Canaan will melt away; [16]terror and dread will fall upon them. By the power of your arm they will be as still as a stone—until your people pass by, O LORD, until the people you bought pass by. [17]You will bring them in and plant them on the mountain of your inheritance—the place, O LORD, you made for your dwelling, the sanctuary, O LORD, your hands established. [18]The LORD will reign for ever and ever. (Exod 15:1–18, NIV)

---

4. Tremper Longman III and Daniel G. Reid, *God Is a Warrior* (Studies in Old Testament Biblical Theology; Carlisle: Paternoster, 1995) 31–47.

Consider this text in light of what it says regarding warfare. The focus is on Yahweh as the leader of the army and the prosecutor of the war. Twice at the beginning and once in the middle, the poem emphasizes the destruction of the Egyptian army (vv. 1, 4–5, and 7). Again, in vv. 10 and 12, there is reference to the waters and then the earth covering the enemy. In this text, Yahweh's activity in battle is a response to the boast of the enemies in v. 9, who claim superiority to Israel and, by implication, to its God. The central text of this construction is v. 7, in which the expressions do not primarily describe the specific event of the drowning of the Egyptians but use general and universal terms to outline God's victory over all opposition. By this means, the psalm becomes more than an account from early Israel. It is a picture of Israel's God who, from the beginning, affirms his superiority over all rivals, whoever they are.

Of particular interest is the dominant theme of the first twelve verses of the passage. They do not focus on the battle itself but constitute a hymn of praise to God. The greatness of Yahweh is described in terms of his role as Savior of his people, and he is portrayed as greater than any of the surrounding deities and as possessor of might and power (vv. 1a, 2–3, 6, 8, 11, and 12a). His might and power are affirmed through the image of his right hand (vv. 6 and 12), as well as his mighty breath (vv. 8 and 10). The image of the right hand, found also in the Psalms, is used in Egyptian literature earlier than this passage to describe the military security that pharaoh provides. Exodus 15, therefore, is an intentional polemic against pharaoh; Yahweh is portrayed as superior to the gods of Egypt by his defeat of the Egyptian army and his subsequent appropriation of Egyptian honorifics and expressions of superiority.

The second half of the hymn of praise emphasizes that the purpose of the victory is not the destruction of the enemy but the salvation of Yahweh's people (vv. 13–18). He leads Israel through the midst of their enemies and settles them on the secure mountain of his choosing. The ultimate theme of this psalm is not war but peace. God leads Israel and ultimately settles them in peace.

The purpose of the warfare in this text is to overcome obstacles that prevent God from achieving the purpose that he has for his people. Furthermore, the battle is portrayed as defensive. It is initiated by the Egyptians, who boast of their ability to attack and destroy Israel. Clearly, the view of the psalm is that this battle is not a slaughter of innocents but the containment of violence that otherwise would be directed at God's people.

The image of Yahweh as a warrior forms the basis for God's presence with his people as he leads them to success in their battles. In the wilderness, Israel repeatedly fought because they were attacked in a manner that far outweighed any provocation on their part. Thus, the Amalekites initiated attacks against Israel (Exod 17:8–16). Other examples are found in Numbers 21, in which the king of Arad (v. 1), the king of Heshbon (v. 23), and the king of Bashan (v. 33) all initiate battles with Israel. The nation's going to war is portrayed as a defensive response to the aggression of the enemies.

This perspective culminates in the dynastic oracle given to King David in 2 Samuel 7. Yahweh identifies with the line of David in such a way that the wars of Israel become the wars of God. While the oracle identifies Israel's wars as Yahweh's wars, and this identification is reflected in many psalms that celebrate the line of David (for example, Psalms 2, 78, 110), the narrative accounts of battles in the successive generations do not often exemplify this approach.

Longman and Reid also discuss the image of Yahweh as warrior in which he fights not against Israel's enemies but against his own people. This aspect of war frequently appears in the prophetic books of the Old Testament. It also appears in the historical books of Kings in their account of the destruction of the Northern and Southern Kingdoms. One biblical writer describes the fall of the Northern Kingdom in moral terms that suggest a direct relationship between Israel's sin and God's allowing the kingdom to fall into the hands of its enemies:

> [21]When he tore Israel away from the house of David, they made Jeroboam son of Nebat their king. Jeroboam enticed Israel away from following the LORD and caused them to commit a great sin. [22]The Israelites persisted in all the sins of Jeroboam and did not turn away from them [23]until the LORD removed them from his presence, as he had warned through all his servants the prophets. So the people of Israel were taken from their homeland into exile in Assyria, and they are still there. (2 Kgs 17:21–23, NIV)

Notice that it is not weakness on the part of Yahweh that permits this destruction and deportation. Instead, the deportation is part of his response to the rebellion of his people. More than a generation before these events, the prophet Amos had proclaimed that Israel held no privileged place in God's evaluation: "'Are not you Israelites the same to me as the Cushites?' declares the LORD. 'Did I not bring Israel up from Egypt, the Philistines from Caphtor and the Arameans from Kir?'" (Amos 9:7, NIV).

This prophet and others like him pronounce Yahweh's words of judgment against the enemies of Israel and in the same breath turn to the people of God and launch the fiercest and most sustained attack on them. The fact that Yahweh, as a warrior, could turn against his people was not a late development, however. It was already in place at the beginning of the nation's history (Exodus 32—34). At Mt. Sinai, when Israel turned away from God to pursue other deities, God was prepared to destroy the nation until Moses and other faithful Israelites interceded for the people.

The two pictures of Yahweh as warrior, fighting both for Israel and against Israel, are consistent only if one recognizes that Yahweh's warfare forms part of his commitment to preserve his holiness. When his people join in his holiness through faithfulness to him, they experience his battle on their behalf. However, when they turn away from him and no longer observe his covenant agreement with them, they face Yahweh's wrath and the threat of the loss of their land and national identity (Deut 28:49–68). The prophets capture this theme in their depictions of the Day of the Lord, on which God will visit judgment on all peoples, both Israel and the other nations, inflicting terror and destruction on those who have turned their backs on him and giving hope and salvation to the faithful.[5]

In this manner, the picture of Yahweh as warrior developed from traditions regarding divine acts of salvation on behalf of God's people, to a God who acts against his own people, and finally to a God who is the embodiment of rightous judgment. This development sidetracks the issue of the ethics of warfare among historical nations. However, the theme that resonated in the reality of war for Israel was that their success depended on their relationship to the divine warrior. Additionally, Craigie comments that, despite the sinfulness of war as a human activity, the role of God as warrior provides hope.[6] He notes that, for the Israelite and for the faithful individual who understands the nature of God as warrior, "even in his human dilemma, with the concomitant human sin, he may seek God and find him." God's presence in war, for example, will not justify it or make it holy, but it does provide hope in a situation of hopelessness.[7] Thus, the ethics of war were already relativized in the Judeo-Christian tradition by the presence of God.

Israel at War

Most discussions of the ethics of warfare as described in the Hebrew Bible consider it important to distinguish the different types of warfare in which Israel participated. Among these, the best known is the "holy war," initially described by the theologian Gerhard von Rad.[8] The basic elements of holy war may be summarized as a summons by God to battle, consecration of the warriors, sacrifices, receiving an oracle, Yahweh's movements in front of the army, loss of courage by the enemy, enactment of the *ḥērem* 'ban' (Deut 20:10–18 and

---

5. See the book of Joel. Also see Longman and Reid on other important texts (*God Is a Warrior*, 61–82).

6. Peter C. Craigie, *The Problem of War in the Old Testament* (Grand Rapids: Eerdmans, 1978) 41.

7. Ibid., 43.

8. See Gerhard von Rad, *Holy War in Ancient Israel* (ed. and trans. Marva J. Dawn and John H. Yoder; Grand Rapids: Eerdmans, 1991).

elsewhere), and a dismissal of the warriors of Israel.[9] Although this form may be present in texts such as Joshua's attack on Jericho (Joshua 5–6) and accounts of later Israelite wars described in Chronicles (especially 2 Chronicles 20), there is no consistent usage of this form of war.

Despite the tendency of some to refine or expand the idea of holy war,[10] Craigie, for example, finds no basis to consider any war to be particularly holy.[11] In fact, no ancient war was entirely secular. Despite the horror of battle, the ancient world understood all its wars to be sacred, if not holy. That is, war involved the powers of heaven as well as earth. Therefore, every war that was prosecuted by an ancient people, whether great or small, was dependent on the favor of the gods for its success. The case was no different in Israel. Thus, while the demand for a precise form and particular terminology as proposed in von Rad's theory of holy war may be criticized as inaccurate, he was certainly correct to connect the prosecution of war with the larger picture of Israel's God as a warrior.

The above-mentioned *ḥērem* 'ban' appears in Deut 20:10–18 as a guideline for Israel's engagement with enemies on the territory that God had given to the nation. This "ban" required the total destruction of all warriors in the battle and (in some way) the consecration to Yahweh of everything that was captured. Niditch goes to some length to portray this activity as initially related to a sacrifice to God, part of a larger picture of human sacrifice.[12] However, she writes that this changed: "The dominant voice in the Hebrew Bible treats the ban not as sacrifice in exchange for victory but as just and deserved punishment for idolaters, sinners, and those who lead Israel astray or commit direct injustice against Israel."[13]

A 9th-century stele of King Mesha of Moab describes his destruction of an Israelite town and its sacrificial devotion to his god Chemosh as a *ḥērem* 'ban'. However, this language does not prove that the same theology dominated in Israel. And, indeed, there is no explicit evidence for human sacrifice to Yahweh in the early texts. The fact that God commanded Abraham to sacrifice Isaac in Genesis 22 must be balanced against the denial that any sacrifice of this sort was ever performed. God explicitly stopped it and provided an animal substitute. Therefore, this story is not a strong case for the adoption of human sacrifice as an approved form of Yahweh worship.

---

9. Lori L. Rowlett, *Joshua and the Rhetoric of Violence: A New Historicist Analysis* (JSOTSup 226; Sheffield: Sheffield Academic Press, 1996) 51; Rodd, *Glimpses of a Strange Land*, 187–88.

10. John A. Wood, *Perspectives on War in the Bible* (Macon, GA: Mercer University Press, 1998).

11. Craigie, *The Problem of War*, 49.

12. Susan Niditch, *War in the Hebrew Bible: A Study in the Ethics of Violence* (New York: Oxford University Press, 1993) 28–55.

13. Ibid., 45.

Nevertheless, the ban as an enactment of God's justice appears in these texts as well as in 1 Samuel 15, in which the prophet criticizes Saul for allowing Agag, the king of the Amalekites, to live, when he had commanded that all must be destroyed. This is the first type of warfare that Niditch discusses. It is portrayed as having an "us-versus-them" quality, in which "a group that fears loss of its identity attempts to define itself" by eliminating "foreigners," both outside and within the group, who are perceived as a threat.[14] An example of a threatening foreigner within the group is Achan in Joshua 7, who, although an Israelite, must be put to death for not observing the absolute demands of the *ḥērem*. A related example appears in Numbers 31, where Moses allows the virgin daughters of the defeated to live,[15] even though, according to the *ḥērem*, they should have been killed (also see Judges 21). Although these texts tend to reduce women to the level of chattel for trading, they also recognize the uncleanness that must be associated with the brutality of war.

A second type of war is the bardic tradition.[16] This is found in the story of David and Goliath and in other stories of the life of David before he became king. Expected rules of warfare were assumed and followed. Wars of this tradition were most conducive to recitation. Niditch identifies their origin in "a courtly bardic tradition produced in glorification of a young nation state, its king, its 'mighty men,' and the heroes of previous generations."[17]

"Tricksterism" often appears in the bardic tradition and in battles in which the Israelites or their representatives are at a military disadvantage and must use some sort of clever ruse to overcome their weakness. Niditch notes many stories involving women in this category, including the rape of Dinah (Genesis 34), the victory by Jael over Sisera (Judges 4–5), and the story of Esther.[18]

A third category of war is the ideology of expediency, in which whatever force is necessary should be used to eradicate the enemy and thus render it unable ever to fight again. Niditch cites many examples of this type of warfare from the life of David after he became king, but she also includes the story the Danite's annihilation of the inhabitants of the town of Laish in order to take it for themselves (Judges 18). Accounts of the ideology of expediency include the manner in which David captures the Ammonites (2 Sam 12:30–31) and makes them laborers, while placing the crown of their deity on his own head. The pragmatic and blood-drenched intrigues and wars of

---

14. Ibid., 74.
15. Ibid. Niditch calls this the priestly ideology of warfare and identifies it as a separate type.
16. Ibid., 90–105.
17. Ibid., 105.
18. Ibid., 106–22.

David have received much discussion; the various views have been summarized by Baruch Halpern.[19]

Niditch concludes her perspectives on war in the Hebrew Bible with what she calls an ideology of nonparticipation.[20] This study includes the critique by the prophet Hosea of Jehu's bloody purge of Ahab's dynastic house, despite the sin of the dynasty (Hos 1:4). The study also discusses the criticism of the expedient approach that is implicit in the tale of Abimelech (Judges 9). Other critiques include Jacob's negative evaluation of the rape of Dinah (Gen 49:5–7) and Amos's criticism of the injustices perpetrated by various nations in their martial activities (Amos 1–2). Although there are exceptions, the accounts in Chronicles tend to omit many of the cruelties of David and other blood-filled war traditions that are preserved in Samuel and Kings. God's protection of the weak and the future anticipation of a millennial age without war also belong to this ideal perspective of nonparticipation.

Accounts of War as Propaganda

A further issue that must be considered is the purpose of the accounts of warfare in the Hebrew Bible. Why did the authors record their battle stories? Niditch has already alluded to an answer in her analysis of the bardic tradition, discussing the role of entertainment and, by implication, the passing on of values. However, she also describes the universal need in human society to justify the killing of other people. War accounts provide a justification for killing when they establish the legitimacy and even the necessity of the taking of human life. The Bible, as noted above, also contains implicit criticism of warfare (as in some of the prophets). This critique of war has led some to believe that the role of Yahweh as warrior provides a substitute for human involvement in war and thereby to assert a pacifist stance.[21] While accounts such as Israel's victory over the Egyptians (Exodus 14–15) and some later wars of Israel (for example, 2 Chronicles 20) support the noncombatant status of Israel as it merely bears witness to Yahweh's victory over its enemies, both the legal prescriptions for war in Deuteronomy 20 and the actual wars fought by Israel under divine direction clearly presume the involvement of the nation in the taking of human life. Thus, the Bible prescribes for Israel neither a total ban on war nor permission for the nation to fight however it wishes.

---

19. See Baruch Halpern, *David's Secret Demons: Messiah, Murderer, Traitor, King* (The Bible in Its World; Grand Rapids: Eerdmans, 2001).

20. Niditch, *War in the Hebrew Bible,* 134–49.

21. Millard C. Lind, *Yahweh Is a Warrior: The Theology of Warfare in Ancient Israel* (Scottdale, PA: Herald, 1980).

Nelson and Rowlett represent scholars who perceive a fundamentally propagandistic purpose in the war accounts of the book of Joshua.[22] Denying or
ignoring any significant historical basis for these texts, these scholars argue
that the texts support the later reforms of King Josiah by describing the ideal
warrior, Joshua, and the military successes that he and the nation of Israel en-
joyed as they conquered the land. This literary fantasy then forms the basis
for Josiah's call for religious reform, coupled with his commitment to restore
the borders of ancient Israel in a series of campaigns in the final decades of
the 7th century B.C. Rowlett advances this thesis by arguing that the word pictures and rhetoric of battles in Joshua 1–12 were created in Josiah's court by
scribes who drew upon Neo-Assyrian models of recording war campaigns.
These annals of the 8th and 7th centuries B.C. preserve verbal images (just as
Neo-Assyrian reliefs preserve pictorial images) of violence and torture of defeated opponents. Horrific pictures of this sort were designed to reinforce
obedience among the vassals of the Neo-Assyrians and to win respect for their
empire. Josiah borrowed them in order to serve similar purposes for his developing empire.

This theory fails to convince anyone who has studied the ancient Near
Eastern evidence. First, the descriptions in the Neo-Assyrian annals are designed to evoke terror in the defeated population in a manner not found in the
book of Joshua. Rowlett notes the example of the treatment of the five kings
of the southern coalition whom Joshua captured and killed. The text describes his invitation to the army generals of Israel to place their feet on the
necks of each king, how he killed the kings, and how he hung their bodies on
trees until evening, at which point he buried them in a cave, marked by a pile
of rocks (Josh 10:25–28). Whatever effect this story may have had on the nation of Israel, no enemy of Israel is described as a witness to this event. This is
contrary to the Neo-Assyrian method. Their brutality toward all prisoners of
war and not only kings exceeded the brutality of other nations. They flayed
some of their victims alive and impaled others on poles and heaped up the
bodies of the rest of the population that they intended to kill. These horrid
sights were not temporarily visible only to the army of Assyria; their purpose
was to make a public spectacle to all onlookers. Assyrian writers and artists recorded the horrors in detail in both visible reliefs and in their annals. Few can
read the accounts of the 10th-century Assyrian king Asshurnasirpal without
shuddering at the delight that he took in describing these atrocities. This is

---

22. Richard D. Nelson, "Josiah in the Book of Joshua," *JBL* 100 (1981) 531–40; idem, *Joshua: A
Commentary* (OTL; Louisville: Westminster John Knox, 1997); Rowlett, *Joshua and the Rhetoric of
Violence.* See the broader survey by Robert B. Coote and Mary B. Coote, *Power, Politics and the
Making of the Bible: An Introduction* (Philadelphia: Fortress, 1990).

propaganda on a level that far exceeds the four brief verses in Joshua, which only mention the five leading kings and not dozens or hundreds of hapless prisoners of war. The same is true of the remainder of the book of Joshua. Furthermore, neither the account of Josiah's reign in Kings nor the parallel account in Chronicles describes anything resembling the atrocities that the Neo-Assyrian kings committed. Thus, it is too much of a leap to ascribe similar propagandistic motives to the biblical writers of wars such as the campaigns of the book of Joshua.

Nonetheless, it is not inappropriate to find in the description of Joshua a model of leadership that later kings such as Josiah emulated. However, in comparing the accounts of warfare in the Bible with extrabiblical accounts, especially of the Neo-Assyrian and Neo-Babylonian empires, one suspects that there is far less record of brutality in Israel's practice of war. This is true despite the formal similarities between war accounts in Joshua and other ancient Near Eastern literature.[23] The biblical text simply does not linger over the gruesome details. There is little suggestion that war is an act of human sacrifice to a god who demands it. Finally, although the Israelites do receive permission to drive out the inhabitants of Canaan, as recorded in Joshua, they never have divine authority to expand their territories beyond what is initially given to them. In this sense, all wars subsequent to the taking of the land in the book of Joshua are wars of defense. This, of course, stands in stark contrast to the nature of the battles of all the major empires surrounding them. Whether the battle was with the Hittites or Egyptians in the second millennium or involved the Arameans, Assyrians, Babylonians, Persians, or Greeks in the first millennium, Israel's military contact with these groups in Canaan was always a defense against an aggressor entering Israel's homeland.

To what extent are the conquests described in Joshua genocidal wars of extermination that have no place in any reasonable ethic of warfare? In my view, a description of this sort would be inaccurate and distorted. References to the destruction of noncombatants in these wars, that is, to "men and women," are scarce, referring only to Jericho and Ai (Josh 6:21 and 8:25). However, there is reason to suspect that these references in Joshua are stereotypical phrases that emphasize the complete destruction of everyone. On the other hand, Jericho and Ai, the initial two sites of conquest, instead of being towns or cities, may have been military forts guarding the routes from the Jordan Valley up to population centers in the hill country such as Bethel and Jerusalem. Evidence for this conclusion includes (1) the complete absence of references to specific noncombatants such as women and children with the exception of Rahab and

---

23. K. Lawson Younger Jr., *Ancient Conquest Accounts: A Study in Ancient Near Eastern and Biblical History Writing* (JSOTSup 98; Sheffield: JSOT Press, 1990).

her family, who are not killed; (2) the lack of evidence for settlement at Jericho and Ai during the time of Israel's emergence in Canaan, suggesting that these were not cities but military forts; (3) the use of the term *melek* 'king' to mean a military leader in Canaan at this time; (4) the lack of indication in the biblical text that these were large cities (unlike Gibeon and Hazor, which are thus described); and (5) the meaning of the name Ai 'ruin', which suggests the reuse of earlier fortifications to serve as a temporary fort instead of a more permanent site of habitation.[24]

The other two major battles, which were against the northern and southern coalitions, are represented in the biblical text as defensive wars (Joshua 10–11). In both cases, they begin as the coalitions assemble against Israel or its ally and therefore force the people of God into battle (Josh 10:3–5, 11:1–5). Note, furthermore, that the eight or more references to complete destruction of the cities represented by these coalitions (in which nothing was left alive) could plausibly be stereotypical descriptions for the purpose of demonstrating obedience to the command to drive out the Canaanites (Josh 10:28, 30, 32, 35, 37, 39; 11:11, 14).[25] It is possible that, after the defeat of the army, the populations fled rather than remaining in a relatively defenseless city. Furthermore, we know that many of these "cities" were used primarily for government buildings, and the common people lived in the surrounding countryside.[26] Therefore, it is not certain that there was a population remaining in these cities to be destroyed. There is no indication in the text of any specific noncombatants who were put to death. In any case, there is clear evidence that there were Canaanites remaining in the areas where Israel settled (Judg 2:10–13).

For the purposes of this essay, it is not relevant to ask whether these battles were truly defensive or whether they were even historical. It is enough to observe that this is how the writers of the Bible presented them. They were, in every case, justified wars against combatants. Does this mean that biblical Israel never killed anyone unjustly? Certainly not. The wars recorded in Judges become increasingly brutal, until the final chapters depict a civil war with killing that resembles a massacre. However, as in other descriptions of battles in the Bible, there is no suggestion in Judges that these wars and atrocities reflected the ideal that Israel was expected to follow in obedience to its God, the true warrior. The same can be said of later battles, including the campaigns of David (especially after he became king); they are not held up as an ideal to emulate.

I must emphasize that we must always preserve the distinction between a record of what happened, or at least a story about it, and a moral evaluation of

---

24. See my *Joshua: An Introduction and Commentary* (Downers Grove, IL: InterVarsity, 1996).
25. See Younger, *Ancient Conquest Accounts.*
26. See my *Joshua*, 137–38.

the account.[27] To highlight this distinction, the biblical writer may stress, for example, the peaceful and defenseless nature of the city of Laish that the tribe of Dan attacks (Judg 18:7–10, 27–29). However, it is wrong to argue that the writer of the account "sees this as divine providence," as Rodd maintains.[28] The writer nowhere makes this claim. Instead, it is reported that the tribe of Dan determines that God has given the city into their hands. Whether this is true or not and whether they have any right to murder the innocents in the city are points not discussed. This is characteristic of the writers of Judges who, especially in the final chapters, record events and dialogue but leave moral and theological evaluations to the readers. Indeed, Rodd seems intent on offensive interpretations of the biblical texts about war when none are warranted. In a similar vein, he notes regarding David's slaughter of Moabites and Edomites that "there is no hint of any criticism of David's military zeal."[29] Like the writers of Judges, the composers of the books of Samuel often reserved judgment and merely described the events. Plenty of criticism of David's ethics is placed in the mouths of Nathan the prophet and others, but it is part of the narrative and not a task of the narrator.

Rodd represents the postmodernist view of the biblical tradition, stressing the differences between various texts and arguing that there are "many different strands within the Old Testament, often contradictory and impossible to harmonize."[30] Rodd concludes that Deuteronomy's attempts to regulate war are idealistic, that peace in the Bible often implies total subjugation of enemies rather than positive actions, and that the Old Testament glories in war in a manner that is ethically unacceptable, though a few prophecies provide a bit of hope of future peace. For this reason, all the recent treatments of the ethics of war in the Old Testament fail to address seriously the major moral issues involved. The view of T. R. Hobbs, that warfare was necessary for the survival of ancient Israel, is inadequate because it does not address what the Old Testament has to say regarding war in the modern age.[31] Nevertheless, Rodd's own conclusions seem to follow Hobbs in arguing the inadequacy of the Old Testament to speak to issues of war (and other ethical issues) in the modern age. While he is severely critical of all who have attempted to address this issue, he does not explain why Old Testament ethics are inadequate. It remains to be proved that the Hebrew Bible glories in war. The evidence of Exodus 15 may be multiplied throughout the Bible; whenever war is associated with God's

---

27. John J. Collins, "The Zeal of Phinehas: The Bible and the Legitimation of Violence," *JBL* 122 (2003) 20.

28. Rodd, *Glimpses of a Strange Land*, 187.

29. Ibid.

30. Ibid., 193.

31. T. Raymond Hobbs, *A Time for War: A Study of Warfare in the Old Testament* (Wilmington, DE: Michael Glazier, 1989).

activities, the majesty of God receives far more attention and praise than the war that he prosecutes. What is true of the divine warrior is also true of his human counterparts.

In the end, neither Rodd nor other writers have succeeded in overturning the observation of Craigie that war is an evil necessary to the fallen human condition. In this regard, Rodd's comment is relevant: "We may grant that the ancient Israelites felt the anguish of pain, grieved over their dead, and longed for security, yet this does not mean that they even glimpsed the reaction to war which two world wars and countless conflicts since then have evoked in many today."[32]

However, the events of September 11, 2001, have thrown this conclusion into stark relief. For many, the relativism of the late 20th century, embodied in postmodernism, is no longer the final answer to the difficult questions surrounding war and peace. Nor is it acceptable to take a text such as the Bible, which has influenced the entirety of Western tradition, and merely to parade a collection of contradictions from its many and diverse pages. When each text is examined in its context, different results often appear. In the end, the Bible reflects a variety of reasons for war, but it does so with a moral tenor that ultimately recognizes battle as a necessary evil in the context of a greater, cosmic struggle between good and evil.

---

32. Rodd, *Glimpses of a Strange Land,* 203.

CHAPTER 3

Toward Shalom:
Absorbing the Violence

ELMER A. MARTENS

The cross is a distinctive Christian symbol known worldwide. For some, the cross is a huge scandal: violence against an innocent person. Others hold that God was being implicated in violence. For some, because God presumably had the power to forestall the violence at the cross and did not, he is like an abusive father, a "blood-thirsty God."[1] Indeed, some claim that God is characterized by violence. Based on this assumption, Regina Schwartz subtitles her book *The Violent Legacy of Monotheism*.[2]

"On the contrary!" cry believers. The cross does not depict a God of violence but of love. The cross may be foolishness, even a stumbling block, to the unbeliever, but for all people the cross is potentially the power of God unto salvation. The cross is the symbol par excellence of sacrificial love (John 3:16). Schwartz's book title is misleading and downright wrong. The legacy of biblical monotheism is shalom, not violence.

The intent of this essay is to sort out these two contradictory interpretations. I argue here that the cross along with the resurrection is the centerpiece of the Christian gospel, that its message is fundamentally reconciliation and peace, and that the method for achieving reconciliation and peace is absorbing the violence. Christians, followers of God's way, share this message of reconciliation and peace and both advocate and practice nonviolence. Shalom is ultimately possible because of God's intervention. An alternate title for this essay might be: "The Legacy of Biblical Monotheism: Shalom."

Author's note: I extend my gratitude to Willard Swartley, Tom Yoder Neufeld, and Allen Guenther for their critique and help. I benefited from feedback from a joint faculty colloquium of Mennonite Brethren Centenary Bible College, Shamshabad, India; and Andhra Christian Theological College, Hyderabad, India, where an earlier version of this essay was presented.

1. Joanne C. Brown, "Divine Child Abuse," *Daughters of Sarah* 18 (1992) 24–28. See also J. C. Brown and Rebecca Parker, "For God So Loved the World?" in *Christianity, Patriarchy and Abuse: A Feminist Critique* (ed. J. C. Brown and C. R. Bohn; New York: Pilgrim, 1989) 1–30.

2. Regina M. Schwartz, *The Curse of Cain: The Violent Legacy of Monotheism* (Chicago: University of Chicago Press, 1997).

My primary interpretive method is biblical theology, a method that emphasizes integrating the diversity of the Bible, not philosophically as does systematic theology, but by employing the biblical narrative and using biblical categories. Biblical theology penetrates to the heart of the Bible's message and organizes various themes around it. My claim is that God's heartbeat is about shalom. I will document this claim, address the countervailing arguments, and hint at the implications of this claim for ethics.

God's Heartbeat: Shalom

The claim that God's heartbeat for humanity and the cosmos is peace and reconciliation is firmly based biblically.[3] God's grace-oriented project is to eliminate the enmity that exists between humanity and himself; the clearest demonstration of this project is the cross. The cross both incorporates the message of peace and exhibits the method by which peace is made. Two theologians, Paul and Isaiah, make this point.

The Cross of Christ: The Message and Method of Shalom

Paul writes to the Ephesians about breaking down walls of partition. "For he is our peace; in his flesh he has made both groups into one and has broken down the dividing wall, that is, the hostility between us" (Eph 2:14). He is speaking of Jews and Gentiles, the enmity defined laterally. Earlier, he addressed the vertical enmity. "But now in Christ Jesus you who once were far off [from God] have been brought near by the blood of Christ" (Eph 2:13). God is intent on establishing one new humanity, "thus making peace, [reconciling] both groups to God in one body through the cross, thus putting to death that hostility [should we read 'violence?'] through it" (Eph 2:15b–16, NRSV). The result: shalom, an all-embracing well-being.[4] The means: the cross, where the incarnate Christ absorbed violence.

A text that corroborates this conclusion is Isaiah's description of the suffering servant. "He was wounded for our transgressions . . . upon him was the

---

3. By one count, the term *shalom* occurs 240 times in the Old Testament. For monographs on the subject, see Walter Brueggemann, *Living toward a Vision: Biblical Reflections of Shalom* (Philadelphia: United Church Press, 1978; repr., *Peace* (Understanding Biblical Themes; St. Louis: Chalice, 2001); Richard McSorley, *New Testament Basis of Peacemaking* (3rd ed.; Scottdale, PA: Herald, 1985); Perry Yoder, *Shalom: The Bible's Word for Salvation, Justice and Peace* (Newton, KS: Faith and Life, 1987); and Perry Yoder and Willard M. Swartley, eds., *The Meaning of Peace: Biblical Studies* (Louisville: Westminster John Knox, 1992; repr. with a revised, extensive bibliography, Elkhart, IN: Institute of Mennonite Studies, 2001).

4. For an extended elaboration of the meaning of *shalom* offered by ten European scholars, see Yoder and Swartley, *The Meaning of Peace*. In this volume, Claus Westermann notes based on 2 Kgs 4:23 that the English word *okay* corresponds well with the nuance found in the Hebrew *shalom* ("Peace [Shalom] in the Old Testament," 21).

correction (*mûsār*) that ensured our shalom" (Isa 53:5). The message arising from the servant's work is shalom. In the same servant song, the method by which shalom is secured is specified: "He was oppressed, and he was afflicted, yet he did not open his mouth; like a lamb that is led to the slaughter, and like a sheep that before its shearers is silent, so he did not open his mouth" (Isa 53:7). Isaiah's servant is a shalom-bringer, not working through coercion or the exercise of brute power but through self-giving, absorbing the blows of the wicked (us).

Old Testament theologians may not have summarized the message of the Old Testament by using the word *shalom* specifically, but they have suggested this in different words. Walther Eichrodt and more recently Bernhard Anderson, with an emphasis on covenant, readily incorporate in their writings the notion of shalom. They claim that the purpose of covenant is to bring rapprochement and even bonding to parties that are distant from each other.[5] Walter C. Kaiser Jr., stressing the promise-blessing theme, echoes what I have said about shalom.[6] My own synthesis of the Old Testament, which focuses on the themes of deliverance, covenant, relationship, and blessing, is essentially shot through (excuse the military language) with the shalom motif.[7]

New Testament scholar Richard Hays observes that "the cross and resurrection define the hermeneutical lens through which Scripture as a whole is to be read." Basing his discussion on Luke 24:25–27, he adds, "As this text suggests, the cross and resurrection require, and enable, a transformative rereading of the story of Jesus and the stories of Israel."[8] George Ladd, a New Testament theologian, posits that the kingdom of God is a centralizing rubric,[9] a kingdom appropriately described as a peaceable kingdom. Given the reality of the cross, the variety of biblical themes that connect with shalom and, more importantly, the explicit statements in both testaments that God wills shalom, it is credible to claim that God's heart beats for shalom.[10]

---

5. Walther Eichrodt, *Theology of the Old Testament* (trans. John A. Baker; 2 vols.; Philadelphia: Westminster, 1961–67); Bernhard Anderson, *Contours of Old Testament Theology* (Minneapolis: Fortress, 1999).

6. Walter C. Kaiser Jr., *Toward an Old Testament Theology* (Grand Rapids: Zondervan, 1978).

7. See my *God's Design: A Focus on Old Testament Theology* (3rd ed.; Richland Hills, TX: Bibal, 1998). See Bernard Ott, *God's Shalom Project* (trans. T. Geddert; Intercourse, PA: Good Books, 2004).

8. Richard Hays, "The Future of New Testament Theology" (Inaugural Lecture to the George Washington Ivey New Testament Chair, Duke Divinity School, Durham, NC, January 28, 2003) 9.

9. George Ladd, *A Theology of the New Testament* (2nd ed.; Grand Rapids: Eerdmans, 1993).

10. J. Lawrence Burkholder asserts: "Central to the vision of the rule of God is peace [*shalom*]." "How Do We Do Peace Theology?" in *Essays on Peace Theology and Witness* (ed. Willard Swartley; Occasional Papers 12; Elkhart, IN: Institute of Mennonite Studies, 1988) 14.

Shalom: Basic in Jesus' Teaching and Practice

To substantiate the claim that the point of departure for a biblical theology is shalom (not only as message but as method), I appeal to the canonical divisions, beginning with the New Testament. In enlisting portions of Scripture, I will not use proof-texts, but I will instead highlight material that confirms the theme of shalom. If Christ's message was peace (see John 14:27), so also was his method, for he pronounced, "Blessed are the peacemakers" (Matt 5:9). The apostles seized on Christ's peacemaking modus operandi by urging that Christians not resort to force, in *imatatio Christi*. Peter explains how Christians should deal with enmity and opposition; Christ left an example to follow, says Peter: "When he [Christ] was abused, he did not return abuse; when he suffered, he did not threaten, but he entrusted himself to the one who judges justly" (1 Pet 2:21, 23). This method of peacemaking, absorbing violence and trusting the God who judges justly, becomes, in anticipation of my conclusion, foundational for a Christian ethic. The message that is peace is calibrated with the method for peace-bringing.

Shalom Urged in Wisdom

Books within the Writings, the third division of the Old Testament canon, such as Psalms and Proverbs, support the New Testament ideal of a peaceable society and encourage peaceful means to achieve this society. The sages in Proverbs advocate a peaceable lifestyle and offer advice on responding to provocations. "Her [Wisdom's] ways are ways of pleasantness, and all her paths are peace" (Prov 3:17, 15:1). This foundational statement for a godly lifestyle is beautifully illustrated in Abigail's conciliatory response to David by which she mitigates his anger and forestalls revenge (1 Sam 25:2–42). The wisdom dimension of this story surfaces, among other ways, in the words 'understanding' (*śekel*) and 'foolishness' (*nābāl*).[11] The peace process extends even to enemies, as the wise man counsels, "If your enemies are hungry, give them bread to eat; and if they are thirsty, give them water to drink" (Prov 25:21; cf. 12:20). In establishing shalom within the society, God is clearly involved: "When the ways of people please the Lord, he causes even their enemies to be at peace with them" (Prov 16:7).

The Psalms urge us to "seek peace, and pursue it" (34:14), an exhortation written by one who is teaching his family the fear of the Lord. The Psalms promise that "there is posterity for the peaceable" (37:37, NRSV; "there is a future for the man of peace," NIV). Someone may retort that the imprecatory

---

11. See my "Way of Wisdom: Conflict Resolution in Biblical Narrative," in *The Way of Wisdom: Essays in Honor of Bruce K. Waltke* (ed. J. I. Packer and Sven K. Soderlund; Grand Rapids: Zondervan, 2000) 75–90.

psalms strike a different note; the point is conceded: human emotions run high when people are provoked. But, strikingly, the imprecatory psalms call on God to take punitive action in accord with his promise/principle, "Vengeance is mine; I will repay"—a major plank in the shalom position (Deut 32:35). The Writings segment of the canon advocates a strategy of desisting from personal vengeance when provoked.

Shalom Highlighted in the Prophets' Vision

Christianity is a religion of hope in a God who transforms individuals and circumstances and ultimately the evil-permeated cosmos itself. So while the prophets often portray judgment as violent, they leave no doubt about God's ultimate design for the world. Some texts are centerpieces for larger peace sections. One powerful, classic depiction is of an eschatological time when the lion lies down with the lamb (Isa 11:6).

Another peace text in Isaiah reads:

> In days to come . . . all the nations shall stream to it [the highest of the mountains] . . . that he [God] may teach us his ways and that we may walk in his paths. For out of Zion shall go forth instruction. . . . He shall judge between the nations . . . they shall beat their swords into plowshares, and their spears into pruning hooks; nation shall not lift up sword against nation, neither shall they learn war any more. (Isa 2:2–4, NRSV)[12]

The vision is of a world without the violence of war. Reading the phrase *wehāyâ be'aḥărît hayyāmîm* as 'in the last days', scholars customarily assert that only in the eschaton when the Messiah rules will this vision be fully realized. This reading shortchanges the exegesis. The expression *wehāyâ be'aḥărît hayyāmîm* is translated in the NRSV as 'in days to come' and should be understood as 'whenever'. Hence, whenever and wherever (including here and now) the word of Yahweh's instruction is embraced, the outcome will be eliminating weapons of destruction and instead forging implements of agricultural production. The oracle offers hope for the future, but it also addresses the immediate circumstance. Proof of this conclusion is that the virtually duplicate passage in Micah continues: "For all the peoples walk, each in the name of its god, but we will walk in the name of the Lord our God forever and ever" (Mic 4:5). There can be no doubt: to follow God is to walk in the way of peace, not only at a future time but now.[13]

---

12. See other Isaiah passages on peace, for example, Isa 9:6–7, 11:6–9, 32:17, 55:12.

13. For the same conclusion, forcefully argued, see the essay by Hans Walter Wolff, "Swords into Plowshares: Misuse of a Word of Prophecy?" in *The Meaning of Peace* (ed. Yoder and Swartley; Louisville: Westminster John Knox, 1992) 110–26. He sees the text as misread when "the watchword 'Swords into plowshares' is banned from the historical present . . . and is relegated to an indefinite, far-off future for the nations (or else applied to spiritual inwardness)" (p. 123).

God's intent is peace. This means that God's people should not only pursue the way of nonviolence but, more accurately, that they should be peacemakers or, in the words of another writer, take a position of constructive nonviolence.[14] Certainly, if peace will be established in the eschaton, then it is incumbent on God's people to work in the present toward this goal. "The eschatological vision of a new world of peace remains decisive for the evaluation of war in history."[15] The verdict on human warfare is "No!" Shalom must be established by methods other than war.

Exhortation toward peace rather than violence comes from other prophets as well. In one telling incident, the prophet Elisha directed that the enemy Arameans, miraculously struck with blindness, were to be brought into the city of Samaria and fed, even given a feast (2 Kgs 6:15–23). Jeremiah counseled his compatriots not to fight the Babylonians but to surrender to them (Jer 29:11–12). How were they to live in a militaristic nation such as Babylon? Jeremiah answered, "Seek the welfare of the city [Babylon], and pray to the Lord on its behalf, for in its welfare (*šālôm*) you will find your welfare" (Jer 29:7). This shalom is to be established by methods other than warfare (compare Paul's encouragement to pray for governments, 1 Tim 2:1–2). Jeremiah's counsel to pray for enemies antedates by centuries the words of Jesus, "Love your enemies" (Matt 5:44). Both Jeremiah and Jesus advocate constructive nonviolence, the initial act of which is prayer. The prophetic vision of future peace begins practically in the here and now. Pray! Love the enemy!

Shalom: Overtures in the Torah

The Torah, the first section of the canon (some consider it to be more foundational and significant than either the Prophets or the Writings) communicates the message of shalom as well but more as an overture than a sustained theme. The creation account presents an idyllic picture of shalom. Phinehas is awarded a "covenant of peace" (Num 25:12). Later, the rules of military engagement for Israel include offering terms of peace to the town that is about to be besieged (Deut 20:10). God motivates Israel to keep his commandments with the promise: "I will grant peace (*šālôm*) in the land" (Lev 26:6). Most arresting is the well-known benediction, "The Lord bless you and keep you. . . . The Lord lift up his countenance upon you, and give you peace (*šālôm*)" (Num 6:24–25). Shalom is a subtheme within the Pentateuch.

---

14. The phrase is from James Juhnke, "How Should We Then Teach American History? A Perspective of Constructive Nonviolence," in *Must Christianity Be Violent? Reflections on History, Practice, and Theology* (ed. Kenneth Chase and Alan Jacobs; Grand Rapids: Brazos, 2003) 107–18.

15. R. P. Knierim, "Justice in Old Testament Theology," in *The Task of Old Testament Theology* (Grand Rapids: Eerdmans, 1995) 105. See also his "On the Subject of War in Old Testament and Biblical Theology," *HBT* 16 (1994) 1–19.

Laws (for example, cities of refuge, Num 35:6–39) and narratives also illustrate the method by which shalom is established. For example, the story of Isaac's contest with the Philistines over the ownership of wells for water in Gerar country involves provocation and demonstrates a nonviolent resolution to conflict (Gen 26:12–33). When the Philistines had filled Abraham's wells with refuse, Isaac's men redug the wells and subsequently dug new wells, including an artesian well; however, the Philistines repeatedly claimed ownership. In each instance, Isaac absorbed the loss without retaliation and moved on to dig yet another well. There are scholars who conclude that Isaac lacked backbone.[16] In my opinion, however, based on God's confirming theophany to Isaac and the amiable ending of the story with a nonaggression pact with the Philistines, this story of a peaceful resolution to a potential conflict must be assessed positively. Isaac was not a wimp; he was a hero who dared to trust God in conflict situations. As Abraham did when challenged for grazing land by Lot and his servants (Gen 13:1–12), so Isaac yielded and absorbed the loss instead of fighting.

Both patriarchs, Abraham and Isaac, exemplify the way to peaceful coexistence: a nondefensive posture and conciliatory action. Oswald Chambers is astute when he applies this principle to Christians: "The only right a Christian has is the right to give up his rights."[17] It is through peacemaking actions of this sort that God's promise that Abraham will be a blessing to all nations is fulfilled (Gen 12:1–3). In contrast, the "resolution" to the confrontation between Jacob's sons and the sons of Hamor at Shechem over Jacob's daughter Dinah, with its attendant deceit and ugly killings, does not represent the conveyance of blessing in the least (Gen 34:1–31).

This brief sketch highlights the prominence of shalom throughout the Bible's canon: the Old Testament with its Torah, Prophets, and Writings, as well as the New Testament, in both the Gospels and the Epistles. Equally important, these Scriptures demonstrate that the path to shalom is nonviolent. This observation is critical, because the point of departure for a discussion of violence is crucial. If the subject were the environment, should one not begin with the creation story, in which God pronounced all things good? If the topic were salvation, should one not hear clearly the words of our Lord to the woman at the well about living water (John 4:10)? My subject is neither creation nor salvation but violence. Following the trajectory from the Old Testament to the New Testament (the better clarified because we began with the New Testament), the increasingly dominant word is shalom, and the path to it is nonviolent.

---

16. See discussion in my "Way of Wisdom," 76–81.

17. Oswald Chambers, *Our Portrait in Genesis* (London: Marshall, Morgan & Scott, 1957) 29.

Wrestling with the Countervailing Evidence of Violence

I readily admit that the emphasis I have placed on shalom is one-sided, for the Bible depicts humans as agents of violence; it even reports that God commands acts of violence. A cursory explanation is that violence can be compared to the minor chords in a musical composition that sometimes immediately precede the final major chord of resolution. Readers of the Bible must be attentive to the dominant chord (shalom) even while recognizing the discordant note of violence.

However, I cannot avoid addressing the violence in the biblical record. By violence, I mean the infliction of harm, mostly physical harm by force, even to the extent of destroying life. Violence is anti-shalom. Violence is the vandalizing of shalom.[18] The frequency of human-to-human violence mentioned in the Bible, some 600 times, demands that one directly address what is a countervailing reality to shalom language. One can best approach the contravening literature of violence by classifying it, according to agent, in three categories: violence in society generally; violence by Israel at God's command; violence of which God is more directly the agent.[19]

Violence in Society Generally

One can easily cite biblical incidents of violence and war precipitated by human initiative, mostly from the Old Testament but also from the New Testament. Cain murders his brother Abel (Genesis 4). Abraham engages with four kings to recapture Lot (Genesis 14). Jacob's sons take revenge on the people at Shechem, killing the males of the family (Genesis 34). Moses kills an Egyptian (Exod 2:11–12). War breaks out between the house of Saul and the house of David (2 Sam 3:1). Joab avenges Abner's murder of Asahel by stabbing Abner to death (2 Sam 3:26–30). Ishbaal is murdered (2 Sam 4:5–8). Amnon, who raped Tamar, is treacherously killed (2 Sam 13:23–29). War between Aram and Israel continues for three years (1 Kgs 22:1). Jehu ruthlessly kills 42 of the relatives of King Ahaziah (2 Kgs 10:12–14), and under pretenses kills the prophets of Baal and the Baal worshipers (2 Kgs 10:18–27). To these I must add

---

18. This vocabulary is borrowed from Cornelius Plantinga Jr., *Not the Way It's Supposed to Be: A Breviary of Sin* (Grand Rapids: Eerdmans, 1995) 7–27. Some writers enlarge the definition. Violence "is intended to hurt, harm, damage, destroy, to otherwise disempower a person. It is an intrusion on the dignity of another" (Vern Neufeld Redekop, *From Violence to Blessing* [Toronto: Novalis, 2002] 21). See his chart (p. 163) for ways of inflicting violence.

19. Raymund Schwager, whose work I examined after deciding on this classification, proceeds similarly (*Must There Be Scapegoats? Violence and Redemption in the Bible* [San Francisco: Harper & Row, 1987] 43–135). For the statistic of 600 occurrences, see p. 47. Two Anabaptist-Mennonite periodicals have each devoted an issue to the subject: *Direction* 32 (*Responding to Violence*; Spring 2003); and *The Conrad Grebel Review* 21 (*Is God Nonviolent? A Mennonite Symposium*; Winter 2003).

the "texts of terror," stories of violence against women, two of whom are the unnamed Levite's concubine (Judg 19:1–30) and Jepthath's daughter (Judg 11:29–40).[20] In the New Testament, King Herod puts to death babies who are under two years of age (Matt 2:16). Herod also committed violence against believers and had James the brother of John killed with the sword (Acts 12:1–2).

Recounting the violence is part of biblical realism. Accounting for it in order to procure a remedy is the concern of secularists as well as theologians. A theological answer is given by two analysts of violence, Rene Girard and Regina Schwartz. The Cain and Abel story remains in the immediate background for both.

Regina Schwartz, a teacher of literature and Director of the Chicago Institute of Religion, Ethics, and Violence, proposes a theory to explain why the world is violent. Cain acted violently because God disapproved of his offering. Why, asks Schwartz, was God so stingy, even picky, with his affirmations? In her answer she cites the scarcity motif: one God, one land, one people. She argues that a myth of scarcity, which is grounded in monotheism, results in violence. The paradigm of scarcity is illustrated in the first commandment: no other gods are permitted as objects of worship. "Monotheism . . . is a doctrine of possession, of a people by God, of a land by a people, of women by men."[21] Alongside the scarcity theme as an explanation for violence, she posits the issue of identity formation, which is purchased at the expense of the Other. She argues that "imagining identity as an act of distinguishing and separating from others, of boundary making and line drawing, is the most frequent and fundamental act of violence we commit."[22] God's covenant with Israel forges a collective identity, but it means that others are excluded, thus setting the stage for conflict and violence. Behind human violence is an ultra-narrow-minded God.

Given this analysis of the reason for violence, Schwartz's proposed methods to reduce violence include altering or extending boundaries by means such as the retelling (reshaping) of stories to produce more elastic boundaries and a reconceiving of Truth to make it plural, based on plenitude, not scarcity. "To open the biblical canon is my concluding call. . . . My re-vision would produce an alternative Bible that subverts the dominant vision of violence and scarcity with an ideal of plenitude and its corollary ethical imperative of generosity. It would be a Bible embracing multiplicity instead of monotheism."[23]

---

20. Phyllis Trible, *Texts of Terror: Literary-Feminist Readings of Biblical Narratives* (Philadelphia: Fortress, 1984).

21. Schwartz, *The Curse of Cain*, 71; cf. 119.

22. Ibid., 5, 19.

23. Ibid., 175–76. "Perhaps instead of rewriting the *historical* narrative with versions that may allow us to feel better about it, we should reopen and rewrite the *biblical* narrative" (ibid., 158; emphasis in original).

She speaks forthrightly about rewriting the biblical narrative. In a sense, some Christians have already done this; sections from the Psalms that, because of expressions of violence, are an "embarrassment" have been eliminated from certain liturgical readings.[24] Schwartz's "solution" is radical and problematic.

Rene Girard ponders the same issue: what accounts for violence among humans? Girard, like Schwartz, is a teacher of literature—specifically, French literature at Stanford. His point of departure into an investigation of violence is to examine the great literary pieces, such as Greek tragedies, Shakespeare's works, and the novels of Dostoevsky.[25] He posits that humans are given to imitation (mimesis). First, they desire what their models desire. Before long, the desire for "whatever" becomes a rivalry with the model that possesses this "whatever." Within the larger society, these forces produce a conflict that readily becomes violence. On a national scale, the conflict erupts into war.[26] Girard proposes that humans do not have a natural bent toward peace; their immediate bents are aggressive aggrandizement and, connected with this desire, the intent to kill.

Girard observes that a solution of sorts to violence is the implementation of a scapegoat mechanism. Not infrequently, an innocent person becomes the focus for the hostility of all. The innocent is killed, an event that has an awe-inducing effect and strangely causes the conflicted parties to achieve equilibrium, a kind of shalom.

Though working as a theorist and not as theologian or exegete, Girard has put forth a hypothesis about the origin of violence that readily aligns with the biblical evidence.[27] Cain desires what Abel has, namely, the assurance of God's favor. Denied this favor, he turns his hostility on the model whom he is imitating. The two struggle. Cain kills Abel. A Christian theologian, interpreting this same material, can agree to some extent with Girard on the reason for the violence but concludes that the human predicament is the sins of selfishness and rebellion, one of the consequences of which is violence. The conclusion is inevitable: where sin reigns, violence is inevitable.

---

24. Erich Zenger, *God of Vengeance? Understanding the Psalms of Divine Wrath* (Louisville: Westminster John Knox, 1996), for example, 30.

25. Rene Girard's hypothesis is set out in several of his writings. See *Violence and the Sacred* (Baltimore: Johns Hopkins University Press, 1977); *Things Hidden since the Foundation of the World* (Stanford, CA: Stanford University Press, 1987); and *The Girard Reader* (New York: Crossroad, 1996). A crisp summary of Girard's position can be found in Schwager, *Must There Be Scapegoats?* 1–42, esp. 46–47. See Robert G. Hamerton-Kelly, *Sacred Violence: Paul's Hermeneutic of the Cross* (Minneapolis: Fortress, 1992) 13–39.

26. Journalist Chris Hedges, who has been embedded in war situations, writes that war "exposes the capacity for evil that lurks not far below the surface within all of us" (*War Is a Force That Gives Us Meaning* [New York: Public Affairs, 2003] 3).

27. See Willard Swartley, ed., *Violence Renounced: Rene Girard, Biblical Studies and Peacemaking* (Telford, PA: Pandora, 2000).

What may be said, from the biblical view, about restraining or even eradicating violence? The answer is that God does not remain aloof but takes a decisive role in human events. God is depicted as entering the human fray intent on preventing violence. God gives Cain a word of warning: "Sin is lurking at the door; its desire is for you, but you must master it" (Gen 4:7). God is in the business of preventing violence from the outset; to negate incipient violence, it is necessary that Cain undergo a change of will and a change of heart. The rest of Scripture is the story of how God accomplishes this transformation, to the extent that the heart of stone, intent on violent behavior, can become the heart of flesh, whose new desires for compassion and peace determine actions (Ezek 36:26). From a transformed heart will issue not an intent to kill nor an attempt to defy God but an urge to obey God, to forswear violence, and to love one's neighbor, even the enemy neighbor, with a divine kind of love.

God's project, to restore shalom, involves God's ultimate offering of himself as the scapegoat, the ultimate absorber of human violence. Intermediately, in his administrative justice, he hears the blood of Abel, the victim, crying from the ground and removes Cain. However, even in the midst of punishment, the God of grace places a protective mark on Cain's forehead. God can be trusted to intervene in and undo human violence. For Girard, the violence is indeed curbed by means of the scapegoat mechanism—but only temporarily. Another set of desires and thus another conflict could erupt at any time, leading to another round of violence. As Schwager explains, the effect of embracing the scapegoat solution is temporarily redemptive, in the sense of liberating the individual from sinful desire for vengeance.[28] In a more permanent solution, God has "rolled" sin, with its impulse to commit violence, onto Christ Jesus, who became sin for us (2 Cor 5:21). Based on this is the promise that violence-prone sinners can become new creations.[29] Paul, who was fond of the indicative-imperative schema, enjoins: You are children of light [new creation]; walk as children of light [no violence].

In sum, sin-caused violence is intercepted by Jesus Christ. Shalom is the result, but its purchase price is the total self-giving of the deity, the absorption of violence.

Violence in Human Affairs Commanded by God

A second category of violence—violence perpetrated at God's command—is more difficult to explain. Texts in which God instructs Israel to annihilate her enemies, ruthlessly it seems, represent a conundrum.

---

28. Schwager, *Must There Be Scapegoats?* 174–80.

29. Two books that stress the transformation of heart are: John Dear, *Disarming the Heart: Toward a Vow of Nonviolence* (Scottdale, PA: Herald, 1993); and Stanley Hauerwas, *The Peaceable Kingdom: A Primer in Christian Ethics* (Notre Dame, IN: University of Notre Dame Press, 1983).

But as for the towns of these peoples that the Lord your God is giving you as an inheritance, you must not let anything that breathes remain alive. You shall anni-hilate them—the Hittites and the Amorites, the Canaanites and the Perizzites, the Hivites and the Jebusites—just as the Lord your God has commanded. (Deut 20:16)

Joshua, representative of God, commands, "The city [Jericho] and all that is in it shall be devoted to the Lord for destruction" (Josh 6:17).[30] These texts grate on modern sensibilities. How should these texts be heard within the larger message that God is a God of love?

Proposed Solutions

Some responses are hardly satisfactory, such as the sociologically oriented explanations. Proponents of these explanations assert that the Israelites justi-fied their dispossession of the Canaanites on the contrived notion that they were God's elect and that their deity had promised the land to them; invoking God was war propaganda. Another version of this rationalistic approach is that Israel misunderstood God.[31] The idea that God would order Israel to be so ruthless with their enemies, it is claimed, betrays the human element in the Bible's origin. Yet another variation of the anthropological approach to the is-sue is to argue that these stories belong to the genre of mythology and should be understood within a symbolic world and/or as mythology. Interpreters who are more sympathetic to the biblical account as reliable history skirt the ques-tion by asserting that this sort of language about God as a warrior is meta-phorical. Or, as Bernard Anderson argues, the conquest stories of violence must be read in light of the symbolic world of the literature.[32]

These responses to the issue of violence, though they have some value, are basically limp, because they do not face head-on the biblical claim that God is a warrior and that as Yahweh Sebaoth—"Lord of Hosts," commander-in-chief of the universe—he directed his people to wage war. Various proposals

---

30. The root 'devoted' (Heb. *ḥrm*) appears in both verbal and noun forms. The noun *ḥērem* is "reserved for things and cattle in Deut 7:26; 13:17[18]; Josh 6:17; 7:1, 11, 12, 15; 22:20; 1 Sam 15:21; 1 Chron 2:7)." Jackie A. Naudé notes, "Rarely in these contexts does the nom. refer to human be-ings (*THAT* 1:635–39)"; see "Ḥ R M," *NIDOTTE* 2:277. This observation softens the harshness in some instances. See Mark Fretz, "*Ḥērem* in the Old Testament: A Critical Reading," in *Essays on War and Peace: Bible and Early Church* (ed. Willard M. Swartley; Occasional Papers 9; Elkhart, IN: Institute of Mennonite Studies, 1986) 7–44.

31. C. S. Cowles et al., *Show Them No Mercy: Four Views on God and Canaanite Genocide* (Coun-terpoints; Grand Rapids: Zondervan, 2003) 38–41. Other views involve the difference in dispen-sations and the case for spiritual continuity.

32. B. W. Anderson, in a chapter entitled "God and War," offers this theory (*Contours of Old Testament Theology*, 171–80).

attempt to sanitize the issue by calling into question the veracity of Scripture. Thus, the argument, at least for evangelicals, shifts to the larger question of the veracity of the record and pivots on inspiration. However, I cannot follow up on the issue of inspiration in this essay.

Some scholars, unsure of how to treat the troubling war passages in the Old Testament, have relied heavily on progressive revelation: God accommodated himself to the culture of the time; but, based on the New Testament, the "corrected" message is peace, not war.[33] This answer is also less than satisfactory because it denigrates the status of the Old Testament and is too similar to the Marcionite heresy, rejected by the church, in which the primitive God of anger in the Old Testament is differentiated from the loving God of the New Testament.

A more sophisticated, theological reply to the problem of God's ordering violence is given by R. Schwager. His argument, largely following Klaus Koch, is that God is involved remotely, if at all, in these requirements for brutality. Schwager emphasizes the view that actions already possess within themselves the consequences of good or evil. Evil actions necessarily produce evil consequences. The built-in order of the universe runs its course. In this order, the evil actions already carry within themselves the seeds of evil reprisals. God is depicted as a God who commands wars and, even worse, calls for brutal annihilation of all human life. But this must be understood in a highly indirect, even abstract way, on the order of God's "giving them up" (Rom 1:24, 26, 28).[34] Although this emphasis on the link between acts and consequences is important, God is not off the proverbial hook by use of this casuistry. The Bible represents God as commanding war and actually stipulating the 'ban' (*ḥērem*), devoting everything to destruction. Liberals, evangelicals, and Catholics make the valiant and even helpful efforts cited here to evade the discomfort that these commands cause, but in the end their arguments are limited and less than compelling.

A Theological Point of Entry: Holiness, Righteousness, and Justice

A more helpful approach that is indebted to the method of biblical theology is to observe the priority of topics such as holiness, righteousness, and justice in Scripture. A fundamental assertion in the Bible is that God is holy (Exod 15:11; Lev 19:2; Hos 11:9b). Holiness is commonly but inadequately defined as separateness. A better definition of holiness, as John Gammie has

---

33. For example, Myron Augsburger, "Christian Pacifism" in *War: Four Christian Views* (ed. Robert G. Clouse; 2nd ed.; Downers Grove, IL: InterVarsity, 1991) 81–97.

34. Schwager, *Must There Be Scapegoats*, 63–75, 214–20.

explained, is "cleanness, purity."[35] The tabernacle structure and, more particularly, the priestly ritual, along with the food laws, illustrate that holiness involves freedom from contamination or blemish. John Hartley correctly states: "[S]eparation does not get at the essential meaning of holiness—neither in reference to God, the Holy One, nor in reference to the variety of items described as holy—for it fails to provide any content to the concept of being holy. . . . 'Holy' is a word descriptive of God, his 'quintessential character.'"[36] As human beings, we are strangers to this impeccable, immaculate, fully transparent state of being. However, humans can glimpse part of what is entailed in holiness, expressed as righteousness and justice, which are more readily delineated. Though righteousness and justice often appear in combination (for example, Amos 5:24), one may regard righteousness as the inner disposition to be and do what is divinely prescribed as right and justice as "honorable actions," the overt, observable behavior that is in accord with God's directives. Every discussion of holiness, righteousness, or justice must account for the asymmetry that exists between God and humans, so that each of the three words has a rarity, a purity, and an intensity of meaning when applied to God that it cannot have when applied to humans.

The concept of justice, cradled within God's holiness, is a helpful point of entry into the issue of God-commanded violence. There should be no doubt of the theological importance of "justice." Isaiah announces, "I the Lord love justice" (Isa 61:8). The psalmist declares that the foundation of God's rule is righteousness and justice (Ps 89:14).[37] Regarding the highly complicated question of the meaning of *mišpāṭ* 'justice', I can only sketch some major contours, one of which is the dispassionate exercise of reward and punishment (Gen 18:25; Ps 82:1–4). It is this notion of fairness that is foremost in the English word *justice*. But fairness represents only a small part of what is meant by Hebrew *mišpāṭ* 'justice'; we may call it the "hard edge" of justice. However, the Hebrew understanding of justice entails what may be called a "soft edge." The God of the Bible, in the interest of justice, has regard for the poor, for the victims of oppression, and for honorable relations generally. Thus, in Psalm 82, the deities in the divine council are cast earthward because of their failure to

---

35. John Gammie, *Holiness in Israel* (Minneapolis: Fortress, 1989).

36. John Hartley, "Holy and Holiness, Clean and Unclean," *Dictionary of the Old Testament: Pentateuch* (ed. T. Desmond Alexander and David W. Baker; Downers Grove, IL: InterVarsity, 2003) 420. See B. W. Anderson, who labels Part I of his Old Testament theology, "Yahweh, the Holy One of Israel," noting that "it [holiness] is the Wholly Other, which exceeds everything worldly: all human conceptuality, all moral categories, all metaphors. It is the power that belongs to 'the very essence of deity'" (*Contours of Old Testament Theology*, 46).

37. Brueggemann observes that the main force in the Mosaic revolution, "a theological *novum*," was "to establish justice as the core focus of Yahweh's life in the world and Israel's life with Yahweh" (*Old Testament Theology* [Minneapolis: Fortress, 1997] 735).

implement justice, a failure defined in terms of callous indifference to the poor.[38] Indeed, honorable relations, if conceptualized in alignment with biblical demands, encompass the essentials of *mišpāṭ* 'justice'.[39]

Violence and the Hard Edge of Justice. To conceive of justice as honorable relations implies that God discloses, even in a limited way, the reasons for his action. God does not owe us an explanation for his action. Nevertheless, as a God of justice—that is, honorable relationships—he discloses clues to the reasons for his commands and announcements (for example, the prophetic judgment speeches in which the accusations present the rationale for the announcements).

One reason for the destruction of the Canaanites/Amorites was that they had corrupted themselves by sinning and were ripe for judgment. Their cup of iniquity was full (Gen 15:16; compare Deut 9:4). The archaeological work at Ugarit, for example, has provided literature written by peoples of this region, some of which is morally gross in the extreme, a reminder of Paul's description of human perversity that grew to the extent that, in retribution, God gave people up to their evils (Rom 1:24, 26, 28). In Israel as well, sin engendered God's hostility (Lev 26:23–25). God exercises patience with the evildoer, but his patience is not infinite (Exod 34:6–7).

A second rationale for the drastic act of mass extermination is given in Deuteronomy. The population in Palestine—Hittites, Amorites, Canaanites, Perrizites, Hivites, and Jebusites—is to be annihilated "so that they may not teach you to do all the abhorrent things that they do for their gods, and you thus sin against the Lord your God" (Deut 20:18). This is God's case for the preemptive strike. An evil act is allowed in order to prevent a worse evil. From a human point of view, the argument is certainly understandable, though the follow-through is painful. In the arena of health, this principle is illustrated by the drastic action taken, whether in the United Kingdom, Canada, or the Unted States, because of the discovery of animals infected with mad cow disease. In several instances, thousands of cattle—surely not all of them infected—have been slaughtered. The action was taken in order to arrest the spread of the evil and to safeguard the population. Similar drastic action was taken in Asia in connection with the bird flu. God understands the proportions to which evil can grow and takes drastic action to halt the downward spiral. The story of the

---

38. A king's mandate to do justice will involve punishing the evildoer, but it should also pay attention to the victim. "O house of David! Thus says the Lord: Execute justice in the morning, and deliver from the hand of the oppressor anyone who has been robbed" (Jer 21:12).

39. Rolf Knierim champions justice as a major biblical motif ("Justice in Old Testament Theology," in *The Task of Old Testament Theology* [Grand Rapids: Eerdmans, 1995] 86–122). On "justice," see H. G. Reventlow and Y. Hoffman, eds., *Justice and Righteousness: Biblical Themes and Their Influence: Festschrift for S. B. Uffenheimer* (JSOTSup 137; Sheffield: JSOT Press, 1992).

Flood can be interpreted as an unfeeling outburst of rage on the part of the Almighty or, in the words of Genesis, which specifically mentions the term *violence* in association with the event, as a means of grace, lest humankind become altogether unsalvageable (Gen 6:5–13).

The fact that God remains just even when resisting evil is evident in God's even-handed treatment of peoples. God commands war against corrupt populations. But he also sets himself as an adversary against a corrupt Israel. Isa 63:10 is telling: "But they [Israel] rebelled and grieved his holy spirit; therefore he became their enemy; he himself fought against them" (cf. Isa 8:1–15, 29:3–10; Jer 5:10–17, 21:3–9, 29:16–19). Israel is not immune to the severe actions of God, as though its chosenness exempts it from God's disciplinary action. So the command to destroy is circumstantial. The punitive dimension of God's justice cannot be ignored; as nations become his agents and/or targets of destruction, violence will ensue.

Even within the framework of hard-edged justice, it must be noted that war and violence are not necessarily automatic solutions in dealing with the "enemy." If the command to exterminate is problematic (and it is), we must at a minimum acknowledge situations in which God said "no" to war (for example, Numbers 14; 1 Chr 22:6; Isa 30:1–2). When the Israelites faced a potential clash with the Moabites en route to the promised land, God's directive was to negotiate with them and not to resort to war (Deut 2:9). Moreover, the prophets did not advocate war when Israel was in difficulty. Jeremiah's counsel for Judah was to surrender to Babylon, the invader. Prophets did not seize on the traditions of conquest wars, for example, in order to legitimize war.

Violence and the Soft Edge of Justice. Justice involves honorable relationships. There comes a point at which a holy God, in the interest of justice, takes harsh action, such as commanding war. But the same holy God, in the interest of justice with a compassionate edge, eschews violence if it can be avoided. God instructs that, when his people encounter an opposing force, their first gesture should be peaceable. "When you draw near to a town to fight against it, offer it terms of peace" (Deut 20:10). Another approach to the enemy is illustrated in the story of Jonah and Nineveh: instead of destroying the Assyrian enemies, God commands Jonah to evangelize them—to invite Nineveh, the enemy, to repent and thus reap life and not death. The hard-edge commands of God for Israel to exterminate the population groups of Palestine must not be read without hearing also the (apparently) contradictory but equally passionate words of Yahweh through Ezekiel: "Have I any pleasure in the death of the wicked, says the Lord God, and not rather that they should turn from their ways and live?" (Ezek 18:23, NRSV). God is not capricious, inflicting violent destruction on the earth with reckless abandon. His basic stance is salvific. In other words, the grand narrative that culminates in Jesus is proof that God's purposes are bent toward salvation.

It is in light of the soft edge of justice that one should discuss what God reveals through warfare. In the context of war, God reveals his power and sovereignty but also his condescension. Yahweh engages the historical process. Walter Brueggemann addresses the violent aspects of the conquest: "The theological outcome of Josh 11 concerns the will and capacity of Yahweh to overturn the present historical arrangements of society which are judged to be inequitable and against the purposes of Yahweh. Yahweh is here revealed as the true governor of the historical-political process."[40] God enters the fray of sin-caused violence. God's entry into the war scenes of ancient Israel as chief warrior is something of an overture to the larger theme to be played out in the incarnation of our Lord Jesus Christ. In Jesus Christ, God bodily entered the human fray, exemplifying what is entailed in meeting the enemy: faith in God rather than in brute force. The good news is that God's entry into violence is a harbinger of the incarnation. "And the word became flesh and lived among us" (John 1:14).[41]

Through war, Yahweh educates his people in the meaning of trust, faith, and his sovereignty. Already at the Red Sea, with the Egyptians in pursuit, the message of the Yahweh wars becomes explicit. Israel's role in engaging the enemy is to trust God. "The Lord will fight for you, and you have only to keep still" (Exod 14:14). Absent is the participation of Israelite troops.[42] The battle belongs to God: "Do not be afraid, stand firm, and see the deliverance that the Lord will accomplish for you today; for the Egyptians whom you see today you shall never see again" (Exod 14:13). This principle—letting God do the fighting—obtains at the conquest of Jericho and the defeat of the Canaanite commander, Sisera (Judg 5:19–23).

The meaning of faith is forcefully explicated in the story of Gideon and the Midianites (Judg 7:1–25). What likelihood of success do 300 Israelites armed with weapons of less-than-mass destruction such as pitchers, torches, and trumpets have as they oppose oncoming soldiers armed with swords and

---

40. Brueggemann, *Revelation and Violence: A Study in Contextualization* (Milwaukee: Marquette University Press, 1986) 54–55.

41. Exposition along these lines can be found in P. C. Craigie, *The Problem of War in the Old Testament* (Grand Rapids: Eerdmans, 1978) 99–100.

42. Millard Lind has traced the Yahweh wars to underscore the importance of letting Yahweh do the fighting (*Yahweh Is a Warrior* [Scottdale, PA: Herald, 1980]). See Wolff's assertion: "One cannot miss hearing in the Old Testament a decisive 'No' to every trust in any kind of weapons" ("Swords into Plowshares," 115). True, Israelite armies would fight, defeat, and destroy enemies (2 Chr 14:13–15). As John Howard Yoder notes, "Yet what was retained in the memory of Judah was not a record of exceptional prowess . . . but rather a victory brought about . . . by the Lord himself" (*The Politics of Jesus* [2nd ed.; Grand Rapids: Eerdmans, 1994] 80). Compare 2 Chr 16:7–10.

spears? Relying on a promise from God, Gideon's men put their lives on the line. In the context of war, the definition of faith is forged: faith is the casting of one's destiny on God who spoke the word of promise. Faith is less a cerebral process than it is a life/death commitment based on an unshakable confidence in the veracity of Yahweh's word (consider David's words before approaching Goliath, 1 Sam 17:45) and purpose. Wars in the Bible address humans who are slow to hear and even slower to believe, to instruct them on the meaning of faith. The problem that God commanded war is not easily resolved, but the problem is partly recast when war (inevitable among nations, asserts P. C. Craigie) becomes a pedagogical tool.

The message of these God-directed wars for Israel is *not* that war is the divinely sanctioned means for setting matters right. The kerygma of the Yahweh wars expresses a different message: pithy, down-to-earth experiences to illustrate what we abstractly call "incarnation" or define as faith.

Wars sanctioned by the Lord Yahweh, with the destruction they brought, must be appraised in light of who God is—namely, a God of holiness. This holiness is expressed by a justice that is both hard edged and compassionate. This means that evil is resisted and destroyed through hard justice; it also means that God enters the fray of violence as an overture to the incarnation and pedagogically makes clear what is meant by trusting him. Christians, remembering the asymmetry that exists between themselves and God, do well to leave the righting of wrongs to God. Believers do, however, have a mandate to work toward justice, understood as honorable relationships, but they may not establish it coercively. Their responsibility is quite the opposite. Believers cannot participate in precipitating violence. Their calling is to absorb violence.

Violence Directly Associated with God

Thus far, I have isolated two kinds of violence: (1) the ubiquitous human violence in various forms that is attributable to the human bent to sin (the solution to which is a transformed heart) and (2) the violence precipitated in response to a divine command. This God-sanctioned violence is best understood from the standpoint of God's holiness expressed through justice, both the hard-edged justice of punishment and the soft-edged justice of compassionate self-revelation.

A third category of violence is the most problematic of all: the violence of which God is more directly the author. The Bible does not shrink from attributing to God activities that bring injury, harm, and death and are characterized by violence. Indeed, Scripture opens and closes with grim scenes of violence initiated by divine action. Early in human history, God engineered the Flood, which destroyed life worldwide (Genesis 6–9). The Bible ends with depictions of violence in the book of Revelation: at the sound of successive trumpets God will destroy a third of earth's vegetation with hail and fire (Rev 8:7); by means of a star falling from heaven, a third of earth's rivers and springs of water will be poisoned (8:10); and with the release of locusts, humans who do not have the seal of God on their foreheads will be tortured (9:3–5). One whose name is Word of God rides on a white horse in this vision. "From his mouth comes a sharp sword with which to strike down the nations. . . . He will tread the wine press of the fury of the wrath of God the Almighty" (19:11–15).[43] Between these brackets, the Flood and end-time devastation, are prophetic oracles of God depicted as coming in wrath, for example, against Babylon, where utter destruction will render the place uninhabited (Jer 50:13). Several psalms focus on a violent God,[44] and in the New Testament, Paul relates that the Lord Jesus will be "revealed from heaven with his mighty angels in flaming fire, inflicting vengeance . . . on those who do not obey the gospel of our Lord Jesus" (2 Thess 1:7–9).

Destructive actions by a hostile God do not fit the picture of a God who cozies up to earth's mortals, eliciting from them a response that forms a "bonding relationship." But in faithfulness to the text, an interpreter must not trivialize these difficulties by explaining them away. Can these scenarios of God's violence be explained? Are not the twin themes of God's wrath and God as a warrior embarrassing and scandalous?[45] An initial response must be humility. The mystery of God's operations are beyond human comprehension. The clay, as Isaiah observes, does not interrogate the potter (Isa 45:9). Brueggemann, who doubts that the violence of Yahweh can be rationalized, writes: "Israel's countertestimony makes it clear that Yahweh is a God capable of violence, and indeed the texture of the Old Testament is deeply marked by violence. In the end, a student of the Old Testament cannot answer for or

---

43. Schwager skirts the book of Revelation because of its imagery, but he is hardly on solid textual ground when he asserts: "Indeed, this book [Revelation] does not contain any statement ascribing violent deeds to God himself" (*Must There Be Scapegoats?* 218).

44. See Erich Zenger, *A God of Vengeance? Understanding the Psalms of Divine Wrath* (Louisville: Westminster John Knox, 1996).

45. Regarding God's wrath, in addition to Bible dictionary articles and theologies of the Old Testament, see Bruce Baloian, *Anger in the Old Testament* (New York: Peter Lang, 1992); Paul Raabe, "The Two 'Faces' of Yahweh: Divine Wrath and Mercy in the Old Testament," in *And Every Tongue Confess: Essays in Honor of Norman Nagel on the Occasion of His 65th Birthday* (ed. Gerald S. Krispin and Jon D. Vieker; Dearborn, MI: Nagel Festschrift Committee, 1990) 283–310. On God as a warrior with annotated bibliography: Gerhard von Rad, *Holy War in Ancient Israel* (trans. Marva Dawn; Grand Rapids: Eerdmans, 1991); Millard Lind, *Yahweh Is a Warrior*; Patrick D. Miller, "God the Warrior: A Problem in Biblical Interpretation and Apologetics," *Int* 19 (1965) 39–46; repr. in Patrick D. Miller, *Israelite Religion and Biblical Theology: Collected Essays* (JSOTSup 267; Sheffield: Sheffield Academic Press, 2000) 356–64; and Tremper Longman III and Daniel Reid, *God Is a Warrior* (Grand Rapids: Zondervan, 1994).

justify the violence, but must concede that it belongs to the very fabric of faith."[46] A full explanation of God's anger will elude us, though it helps to be reminded, in the context of God's holiness, that his anger, unlike human wrath, is not sullied by unholy motivations.

Two biblical metaphors—God as king and God as warrior—offer considerable help in coming to terms with a violent, wrathful deity. The metaphor of God as king is informed by the fundamental issue of sovereignty and the maintenance of righteousness (cf. Ps 97:1, 99:1; Jer 21:11; 22:3, 15). Divine sovereignty means that the forces of chaos and evil are under God's control. It is both God's prerogative and within his power to arrest the incursion of evil. The Flood story makes clear that evil will not continue forever unchecked (compare the Sodom and Gomorrah story and Revelation 19). The huge catastrophe was brought on precisely because of violence on the earth. "Now the earth was corrupt in God's sight, and the earth was filled with violence (*ḥāmās*)" (Gen 6:11). God responded with righteous violence. The downward spiral of evil continues only so far; God intervenes. Descriptions of the Day of the Lord reinforce the claim that the evil committed by nations will be arrested: "Egypt shall become a desolation, and Edom a desolate wilderness" (Joel 3:19); or again: "I have heard the taunts of Moab and the revilings of the Ammonites" (Zeph 2:8), in response to which God promises to move with retribution, so that "Moab shall become like Sodom and the Ammonites like Gomorrah" (Zeph 2:9). The triumph of the good comes at the expense of the defeat of the evil. God vindicates himself and the just by bringing down the oppressor. Evil will not have the last word, for God is sovereign.[47]

Closely related to the metaphor of God as king is the metaphor of God as warrior, an image that is introduced at the exodus event ("The Lord is a warrior; the Lord is his name" [Exod 15:30]) but that metamorphosed by the time of the New Testament. This and other images signal that God will overpower evil and set matters right. The message communicated by this image of God as warrior is hope. On the Day of the Lord, a concept traced by von Rad to the

---

46. Brueggemann, *Theology of the Old Testament*, 381. Elsewhere, Brueggemann mentions "Yahweh's profound irrationality" (p. 383) and expresses the wish that this dimension of Yahweh had been expunged from the record. Hubert Frankemölle comments, "Accordingly, the 'God of peace' (cf. Rom 15:33, 16:20; 2 Cor 13:11) is at the same time always also the 'God of wrath' (cf. Rom 3:5f, 5:9; 1 Thess 1:9f.). It is impossible to devise a logical, noncontradictory theology system, for reality is itself contradictory" ("Peace and the Sword in the New Testament" in *The Meaning of Peace: Biblical Studies* [ed. Perry Yoder and Willard M. Swartley; Louisville: Westminster John Knox, 1992] 227).

47. "Probably the most important thing we can say about God is that the world and history belong to *God* and it is *God* who has the last word about history, as its 'judge'" (E. Zenger, *A God of Vengeance?* 63; emphasis in original). See Brueggemann, who says that violence "belongs to the enforcement of sovereignty" (*Theology of the Old Testament*, 381).

holy war tradition[48] but that functions as the "Day of the Big Audit"—wrongs will be righted. Hence, Zechariah counsels: "Therefore wait for me, says the Lord . . . for my decision is to gather nations, to assemble kingdoms, to pour out upon them my indignation, all the heat of my anger" (Zeph 3:8). John Goldingay explains, "Yahweh is not essentially war-like," but as a corollary of his being involved with Israel, the Old Testament "accepts wholeheartedly the warring activity of Yahweh. . . . If he is to be the God of all of life, he must be a God of war."[49] George E. Wright makes the same point even more forcefully: "[If] God is Lord he must also be warrior. Unless he is, there is no ground for hope."[50] Thus, to hold that God is indeed a warrior who, in holy wrath, eradicates evil by bringing harm and destruction is not a reality about which to be embarrassed. Instead, it is a reality to be embraced.

One of the reasons for downplaying the motif of God as warrior is the assumption that to embrace this portrait of God results in a community that is warlike. In reality, the opposite is true, as Millard Lind has shown.[51] People who confidently cast themselves on a God who will oppose the oppressor decisively need not precipitate violence. Consider Israel's role at the Red Sea and at Jericho. Moses instructs the people when they are threatened by the oncoming Egyptians, "The Lord will fight for you, and you have only to keep still" (Exod 14:14). At Jericho, it is God who brings down the walls (Josh 6:1–21). The fact that coercion and human force is not the answer is memorably illustrated in the story of Gideon. Following God the warrior fully in faith does not have the effect of grooming warlike followers. That God is a warrior means the opposite—that his people need not be warlike. "Indeed it is precisely because God is so forcefully resistant that the people of God can be nonresistant."[52] Hope is engendered through the conviction that God will right the wrongs, even if he does so later rather than sooner. The resurrection is proof of this fact. It is because of this eschatological reality that it makes sense to "turn the other cheek" and to love the enemy (Matt 5:38–48).[53]

---

48. Gerhard von Rad, *Old Testament Theology* (2 vols.; New York: Harper & Row, 1965) 2:119–25.

49. John Goldingay, *Theological Diversity and the Authority of the Old Testament* (Grand Rapids: Eerdmans, 1987) 65.

50. G. E. Wright, *Old Testament and Theology* (New York: Harper & Row, 1969) 147.

51. Lind, *Yahweh Is a Warrior.* William D. Barrick justifies a Christian's participation in war on the basis of Christ's engagement in end-time bloodshed (Rev 19:11–21) ("The Christian and War," *MSJ* 11 [2000] 224–25). This argument can hardly stand in light of the larger biblical presentation.

52. Thomas Yoder Neufeld, "Resistance and Nonresistance: The Two Legs of a Biblical Peace Stance," *The Conrad Grebel Review* 21 (Winter 2003): 60.

53. Richard Hays states, "Thus, from Matthew to Revelation we find a consistent witness against violence and a calling to the community to follow the example of Jesus in *accepting* suffering rather than *inflicting* it" (*The Moral Vision of the New Testament: A Contemporary Introduction to New Testament Ethics* [San Francisco: HarperSanFrancisco, 1996] 332; italics his). Commenting on

It is instructive to follow the trajectory of the image of God as warrior: God the warrior becomes God the martyr. W. H. Brownlee has traced this development, observing especially what transpires in intertestamental times, notably against the background of 1, 2, and 4 Maccabees.[54] Some, such as Matthias, faced with an invader's atrocities, resisted the Syrians by force. But the mode of resistance sometimes took an alternate, nonviolent form. The most telling incident of atonement based on the suffering of martyrs is related in 2 Maccabees, in which seven sons submit to martyrdom while their mother watches (chap. 7). The heroes in the books of Maccabees are the martyrs who "fight" against the opponent, not by taking up arms but by laying down their lives. The implicit theology, namely, that to suffer martyrdom is to engage in holy war, is made explicit in 4 Maccabees, in which credit for the victory over the enemy is given to the martyrs (17:20–22; compare 6:28–29, 18:4).[55]

This trajectory of the warrior reaches its destination in the life of Jesus, who battles the cosmic forces of evil. Jesus defeats demonic forces. "His exorcisms inaugurate a holy war which climaxes in the victory of his death and resurrection."[56] When the 70 return from their mission reporting that, by the name of Jesus, even the demons submit to them, Jesus can say, "I watched Satan fall from heaven like a flash of lightning" (Luke 10:18). He portrays himself as the victor. "You will see the Son of Man seated at the right hand of the Power, and coming with the clouds of heaven." Christ engages in the battle and is the victor, but it is a victory purchased with martyrdom, death on a Ro-

---

the "focal lens" of the "new creation," Hays asserts that "such action ["turning the other cheek"] makes sense only if the God and Father of Jesus Christ actually is the ultimate judge of the world and if his will for his people is definitely revealed in Jesus" (ibid.).

54. "It is our intention now to show that in this capacity [human martyr], also, Jesus was a holy warrior" (W. H. Brownlee, "From Holy War to Holy Martyrdom," in *The Quest for the Kingdom of God: Studies in Honor of George E. Mendenhall* [ed. H. B. Huffmon, F. A. Spina, and A. R. W. Green; Winona Lake, IN: Eisenbrauns, 1983] 286).

55. Brownlee summarizes, "We move from the institution of Holy War, with its *ḥerem* of total destruction of the enemy, to the divine-human Warrior, Who gives His life for the salvation of the whole world, including His own enemies" (ibid., 291). New Testament scholars, such as Bruce Stevens, have examined the connection between the expression *Son of Man* and the divine warrior. Stevens offers some background from Ugarit. Baal is the warrior god who defeats Mot (death) and receives an everlasting kingdom from El. In Dan 7:9–14, 27, the "Ancient of Days" recalls Ugaritic El, and the "Son of Humanity (Man)" is reminiscent of the Ugaritic victorious warrior who overcame the enemy (Death) and was given a kingdom. Already in Daniel, this kingdom is associated with the suffering of the "saints of the Most High. " So the "Son of Humanity (Man)" motif, while having warlike associations, also has associations with suffering. Stevens's article, "The Divine Warrior in the Gospel of Mark" (*BZ* 31 [1987] 101–9), is summarized by Willard Swartley (*Israel's Scripture Traditions and the Synoptic Gospels: Story Shaping Story* [Peabody, MA: Hendrickson, 1994] 109–10).

56. Ibid., 147.

man cross. As Willard Swartley concludes, "God's victory path for Jesus [as divine warrior] is through the cross."[57] Coercion through violence is not the answer; that way lies the myth of redemptive violence.[58] Instead, the final solution to violence, which is ultimately made clear in the paradox of the warrior turned martyr, is the absorption of violence.[59] The warrior is Christ on the cross. Through the cross, peace is established. Love has trumped wrath. Shalom has trumped violence by absorbing it.

Based on these two images of God as king (sovereign) and warrior (victor over evil), several ethical conclusions follow, only one of which I will discuss. Christians need not—should not—engage in violence. The fact that Yahweh our God is a powerful warrior, whose passion for holiness and justice is intense and who will deal decisively with evil, means that his followers can afford to leave the righting of wrongs in God's hand. Both testaments emphatically affirm this point. Moses asserts in the name of God, "Vengeance is mine" (Deut 32:35). Paul, in urging a peaceable lifestyle, tells his audience in Rome: "Never avenge yourselves, but leave room for the wrath of God, for it is written, 'Vengeance is mine, I will repay, says the Lord'" (Rom 12:19). God is completely able to deal with the inequities and the violence in the world without our help. Habakkuk, whose book opens with the complaint that the "law becomes slack and justice never prevails," is particularly instructive regarding the believer's stance. The book's centerpiece, that the just shall live by faith, bears directly on how to deal with violence, for the third chapter depicts a majestic theophany in which God comes to set matters right. So what does it mean for the just to live by faith? It means that they are guided by the vision that the Almighty will settle the score. To believe God is to leave the redress of evil to

---

57. Ibid., 111. For the connection between Jesus as Son of Humanity and the divine warrior motif in Mark, compare his discussion (pp. 109–11) and the articles referred to there, especially Stevens, "The Divine Warrior," 101–9. For a further connection between God as warrior and the cross, see B. C. Ollenburger, who describes the way that Menno Simons in the 16th century linked the cross and the conviction that God is a warrior who comes to the aid of the suffering righteous ("The Concept of 'Warrior God' in Peace Theology," in *Essays on Peace Theology and Witness* [Occasional Papers 12; ed. Willard Swartley; Elkhart, IN: Institute of Mennonite Studies, 1988] 112–27).

58. For a discussion of the myth of redemptive violence, see Walter Wink, *Engaging the Powers: Discernment and Resistance in a World of Domination* (Minneapolis: Fortress, 1992) 13–31.

59. W. T. Cavanaugh says, "Martyrs offer their lives in the knowledge that their refusal to return violence for violence is an identification with Christ's risen body and an anticipation of the heavenly banquet" (quoted in Juhnke, "American History," 131). Richard Bauckham notes, "Christians are called to participate in his war and his victory—but by the same means as he employed: bearing the witness of Jesus to the point of martyrdom" (*Bible in Politics*, 233ff.; quoted in *Kingdom Ethics: Following Jesus in Contemporary Context* [ed. Glen H. Stassen and David P. Gushee; Downers Grove, IL: InterVarsity, 2003] 153).

God. People who believe that God can be trusted refuse to add to the violence by participating in it.[60] They do more, of course; they participate in God's project of peacemaking and peace-building.[61] But at a minimum, they operate with the conviction that the cross shows the way to deal with violence: absorb it. Break the cycle.[62]

So we end where we began: at the cross. The hard truth that God addresses the evil of the world with holy hostility, even violence, must not be minimized. But this wrathful action must be viewed in the full context of God's revelation in Christ. God's method of dealing with this unrighteousness is that God himself, in the person of his Son, takes on his own body the sin of humanity. A passionate love trumps a passionate anger. Christ's word to those who those who nailed him to the cross is "Father forgive them for they know not what they do" (Luke 23:34). Forgiveness, fashioned out of love, breaks the stranglehold that violence has on the world.

Conclusion

The argument in this essay is about the priority of shalom, a shalom that is achieved not through coercion but through the sacrifice of self-interest. God's road to peace runs through the cross. The human-to-human violence depicted in the Scriptures is solved by the transformation of the heart. Essential to this

---

60. This was the conviction of the early church for the first three centuries. As late as A.D. 295, Maximilianus, a 21-year-old Numidian Christian was killed by the proconsul of Africa for refusing military service. He stated, "I cannot serve as a soldier; I cannot do evil. I am a Christian" (W. C. Placher, *Jesus the Savior* [Louisville: Westminster John Knox, 2001] 195). For a classic biblical/theological statement, see Yoder, *The Politics of Jesus*; a more popularly formulated argument is found in John D. Roth, *Choosing against War: A Christian View* (Intercourse, PA: Good Books, 2002).

61. The emphasis in this essay is on one facet of peacemaking: absorbing the hostility. Active peacemaking is an extension of this initial conviction. A vision for a peaceable kingdom calls for the exercise of imagination for potential peacemakers. For the role of imagination in theology, see, for example, Stanley Hauerwas's essay, "On Keeping Theological Ethics Imaginative," in *Against the Nations: War and Survival in a Liberal Society* (Notre Dame, IN: University of Notre Dame Press, 1992) 51–59. On constructive nonviolence, see Glen Stassen, *Just Peacemaking: Transforming Initiatives for Justice and Peace* (Louisville: Westminster John Knox, 1992); or more recently, idem, "Jesus and Just Peacemaking Theory," in *Must Christianity Be Violent?* (ed. Chase and Jacobs; Grand Rapids: Brazos, 2003) 135–55. See also Walter Wink, "Engaging the Powers Nonviolently," in *Engaging the Powers: Discernment and Resistance in a World of Domination* (Minneapolis: Fortress, 1992) 175–257. For a series of anecdotes, including a description of Christian Peacemaker Teams, see Ronald J. Sider, *Nonviolence: The Invincible Weapon?* (Dallas: Word, 1989). See Titus Peachey and Linda Gehman Peachey, eds., *Seeking Peace: True Stories of Mennonites around the World* (Intercourse, PA: Good Books, 2003).

62. "Nonviolence is an integral part of the gospel message, because its basic teaching is the absolute value of love" (Hamerton-Kelly, *Sacred Violence*, 14). See also Desmond Tutu, *No Future without Forgiveness* (New York: Doubleday, 1999).

transformation is forgiveness, the opposite of reprisal and vengeance. The violence that is the result of God's directives is intended to restrain evil. God involves himself in the human mess, and believers can afford to let God do the fighting, a point even more forcefully made by the series of biblical texts that depict God as warrior and emphasize his wrathful vengeance. By following the divine warrior, who suffers martyrdom and who through his sacrificial death interrupts the violence cycle, believers act on the principle that bringing shalom demands the absorption of violence.

CHAPTER 4

Impulses toward Peace in a Country at War: The Book of Isaiah between Realism and Hope

M. DANIEL CARROLL R.

A Personal Pilgrimage

War became a theological problem for me during my years in Guatemala (1982–96). Living and ministering in that long-suffering country during those years forced me to begin to consider what may be an appropriate evangelical response to what that Central American nation was experiencing. The war had been going on in the mountains for three decades, and the way it was waged by both sides of the political divide pushed me to embrace a pacifist position. The political hypocrisy and the brutality of the Left and Right (although the sheer scale of the army's viciousness far outstripped the viciousness of the guerrillas),[1] even as each group championed its cause in the media and had its defenders in the battle for world opinion, confirmed for me that nonviolence was the only possible ethical option for Christians. For quite some time, Liberation Theology had been processing the possibility of justifying a certain kind of violence to overthrow unjust regimes (some even appealed to the just-war tradition);[2] on the other hand, many evangelical

---

1. The magnitude of the human rights violations was not fully apparent until the publication of REMHI, *Guatemala: Never Again!* (trans. Gretta Tover Siebentritt; Maryknoll, NY: Orbis, 1999). More information is available in documents of the United Nations and different Christian denominations, *testimonio* literature, anthropological studies, and historical novels. Of course, it is important to evaluate these sources. On the Latin American military, see (although these books have different theoretical constructs) Brian Loveman and Thomas M. Davies Jr., eds., *The Politics of Antipolitics: The Military in Latin America* (2nd ed.; Lincoln: University of Nebraska Press, 1989); Richard L. Millett and Michael Gold-Bliss, eds., *Beyond Praetorianism: The Latin American Military in Transition* (Miami: North-South Center Press, University of Miami, 1996).

2. See José Míguez Bonino, *Toward a Christian Political Ethics* (Philadelphia: Fortress, 1983) 106–13; Enrique Dussel, *Ethics and Community* (trans. R. R. Barr; Tunbridge Wells, U.K.: Burns &

59

Christians tended either to default to support of the government (based on a reading of Romans 13 and the conservative ideology that had accompanied the Christian tradition they had received from North American missionaries) or to avoid the topic of war and revolution altogether.[3]

My being an Old Testament professor made the theological problem more acute. The Old Testament often has been characterized as a violent book and the God of the Old Testament as a violent God. Of course, the Old Testament does contain descriptions of weaponry, tactics, and battle. Combatants appear in all kinds of situations as well—as valiant heroes, cruel murderers, or tricksters. Wars themselves are given various explanations and evaluations: some are seen as a means of divine judgment, others as necessary to defend the people of God; several are condemned as the campaigns of conquering empires and greedy nations; in a few cases, some are presented as opportunities to witness the incomparable power of Yahweh. Raising even more theological questions is the Song of the Sea, with its assertion that "Yahweh is a warrior" (Exod 15:3).[4] Nevertheless, even in the Old Testament, war is not God's final word: the promise of universal peace is a fundamental part of the text's eschatological hope. How best to understand all of the Old Testament's data and its relevance for war in the here and now has been a bone of contention among Christians for two millennia. I had wrestled with the dilemma of war in Latin America in several publications before returning to the United States in the summer of 1996,[5] but in this country my thinking would be challenged from another quarter.

Not long after my arrival at Denver Seminary, I approached our chancellor, Vernon Grounds, about the possibility of meeting on a regular basis. He announced that our project would be to read Reinhold Niebuhr's *Faith and His-*

Oates, 1988) chap. 16; I. Ellacuría, "Trabajo no-violento por la paz y violencia liberadora," *Concilium* 25 (1988) 85–94. Jon Sobrino, "Apuntes para una espiritualidad en tiempos de violencia: Reflexiones desde la experiencia salvadoreña," *RLT* 29 (1993) 189–208.

3. Much has been written about the ideology of evangelicals in Latin America at that time. Caution, however, should be exercised in consulting sources. Some have misunderstood or distorted the reasons for and extent of this conservative tendency to the point of proposing, for instance, that this stance was partially the fruit of a conspiracy of the U.S. government to penetrate and manipulate evangelical groups. Note the more balanced reports in David Stoll, *Is Latin America Turning Protestant? The Politics of Evangelical Growth* (Berkeley: University of California Press, 1990); Paul Freston, *Evangelicals and Politics in Asia, Africa, and Latin America* (Cambridge: Cambridge University Press, 2001).

4. For the wide range of topics related to war in the Old Testament, note T. Raymond Hobbs, *A Time for War: A Study of Warfare in the Old Testament* (OTS 3; Wilmington, DE: Michael Glazier, 1989); and Susan Niditch, *War in the Hebrew Bible: A Study in the Ethics of Violence* (New York: Oxford University Press, 1993). These works take different perspectives on the relevance of the Old Testament material than does this essay.

5. See below, nn. 44 and 49.

tory.[6] We began to meet once a week to read and discuss this classic reflection on the meaning of history and the nature of Christian responsibility within the perplexing and often tragic situations of our world. That exposure to this great social theologian of a previous generation prompted me to reread *Moral Man and Immoral Society* (a volume I had obtained years before but had never read) and also to peruse his most famous work *The Nature and Destiny of Man.*[7]

Having come from Guatemala, where I had been frustrated by what seemed to me to be the inadequate theological analyses of both Liberation Theology and the more conservative circles within which I had ministered, I found Niebuhr's "Christian realism" compelling in many ways. Obviously, this essay is not the proper context in which to summarize the breadth and depth of his thought,[8] but several observations are in order. Niebuhr recognized humanity's inherent will to power and noted that it plays itself out in destructive ways, both within and between nations. His thinking also corroborated what I had witnessed in Latin America: it would not do to reduce socioeconomic and political problems to issues of personal salvation and sanctification (the propensity of not a few evangelical thinkers) or to propose that the solution to the ills of society lies primarily in structural change (Liberation Theology's socialist alternative). Niebuhr understood the pervasiveness of sin in society and politics. Clearly, no social ethic can afford to have an inadequate anthropology or a naïve view of history. The corollary to these facts, according to Niebuhr, is the unavoidable necessity of occasionally having to use coercion— sometimes to the point of waging war—to maintain and establish at least a modicum of justice in this unjust world. He felt that this perception of the true condition of humanity and the insights into the meaning of history, grounded as they were in the basic narratives of the Bible (which Niebuhr called its "myths"), provided the best explanation for the state of affairs in the past and today. In his view, these insights were one of the unique contributions of Christianity.

In many ways, Reinhold Niebuhr tests me still. I continue to appreciate much of his view of sin at societal and international levels; nevertheless, his claim that, as Christians, we must be willing to accept the necessity of violence to accomplish justice has troubled me. How might a pacifist respond? Niebuhr himself was quite critical of the pacifists of his day, citing their ingenuous

6. Reinhold Niebuhr, *Faith and History: A Comparison of Christian and Modern Views of History* (New York: Scribner's, 1949).

7. Reinhold Niebuhr, *Moral Man and Immoral Society* (New York: Scribner's, 1960); idem, *The Nature and Destiny of Man: A Christian Interpretation* (2 vols.; New York: Scribner's, 1951).

8. The bibliography on Niebuhr is immense. Two sources that I have found helpful are Dennis P. McCann, *Christian Realism and Liberation Theology: Practical Theologies in Creative Conflict* (Maryknoll, NY: Orbis, 1981); and Langdon Gilkey, *On Niebuhr: A Theological Study* (Chicago: University of Chicago Press, 2001).

attempts to apply religious ideals to the rough-and-tumble problems of collective life. Two books that I have read recently appeal to Niebuhr in our post–September 11, 2001 world for this very reason. Jean Bethke Elshtain of the University of Chicago calls for a return to the vision of Niebuhr. War, she says, may be the only sensible response to the terrorism that threatens this country and the best concrete way to express our love for the "weaker brother" in the international community.[9] Veteran war correspondent Chris Hedges decries the unimaginable ugliness of combat and the destructive self-deceptions of war, but he also invokes Niebuhr when he states that the horrors of armed conflict cannot keep us from carrying out an "ethics of responsibility."[10]

Over the last few years, I have found the ethicist Stanley Hauerwas to be a partner in my dialogue with Niebuhr.[11] Hauerwas argues, I believe rightly, for another starting point in the debate over whether Christians as individuals and the Church as an institution should support and be involved in war. Niebuhr began his reflections by exposing the extent of human sin in society and between nations and then sought to understand how best to establish relative justice in this sinful world. In his mind, coercion and conflict are evils that must be accepted as necessary, even inescapable, means to achieve this end. Hauerwas, however, approaches the problem from a very different angle. He says, "Christians refuse to allow their understanding of nonviolence to be determined by the world. . . . Christians do not choose nonviolence because we can rid the world of war, but rather *in a world of war we cannot be anything but nonviolent as worshipful followers of Jesus the Christ.*"[12]

In these words, two crucial foundational issues come to the fore. First, we must answer the question "Who are we?" This is the issue of *identity.* Are we ultimately mere citizens of the nation-states within which we live, or are we ulti-

---

9. Jean B. Elshtain, *Just War against Terrorism: The Burden of American Power in a Violent World* (New York: Basic Books, 2003) 99–111. Helpful summaries of Niebuhr's and Elshtain's arguments are presented by J. Daryl Charles and his defense of just-war theory in his *Between Pacifism and Jihad: Just War and Christian Tradition* (Downers Grove, IL: InterVarsity, 2005) 67–70 and 78–81, respectively.

10. Chris Hedges, *War Is a Force That Gives Us Meaning* (New York: Anchor, 2002) 16–17.

11. Stanley Hauerwas has engaged Niebuhr so extensively because Niebuhr's views serve as a helpful foil to clarify his own stance. See Stanley Hauerwas, "Tragedy and Joy: The Spirituality of Peaceableness," *The Peaceable Kingdom: A Primer in Christian Ethics* (London: SCM, 1983) 135–51; idem, "Can a Pacifist Think about War?" *Dispatches from the Front: Theological Engagements with the Secular* (Durham: University of North Carolina Press, 1994) 116–35; "Whose 'Just' War? Which Peace?" ibid., 136–52; Stanley Hauerwas (with Michael Broadway), "The Irony of Reinhold Niebuhr: The Ideological Character of 'Christian Realism'" in Hauerwas, *Wilderness Wanderings: Probing Twentieth-Century Theology and Philosophy* (Boulder, CO: Westview, 1997) 48–61; idem, *With the Grain of the Universe: The Church's Witness and Natural Theology* (Grand Rapids: Brazos, 2001).

12. Hauerwas, "Can a Pacifist Think about War," 131 (emphasis added).

mately a people shaped by the person and work of Jesus Christ?[13] The answer to this question determines where our deepest loyalties lie. The second question, which follows from the first, is "What are we to do?" This question pertains to the issue of *mission*. Must we commit ourselves to the defense of these nation-states and to accomplishing agendas defined by their policies, even if this may entail participating in a web of violence in contradiction to the values of Jesus Christ and his kingdom? Or are we called to sacrificial and faithful service to this kingdom—that has a different set of claims on our lives and that strives for goals that are quite distinct from the goals of our governments? In the end, Hauerwas claims, a nonviolence stance is inseparable from the person of Jesus, the confession that his kingdom has come, and the alternative practices of the community that confesses him as Lord. In light of this perspective, we do not ask, "How may we best protect the sociopolitical and economic culture we cherish?" but instead, "How may we testify to the *other kingdom* amid the violence and death of this fallen world?"

I turn to the Old Testament and the quest to comprehend its place within this set of convictions. This essay engages in conversation with a particular prophetic text, the book of Isaiah, in order to continue to grapple with how believers in Jesus Christ may approach the debate on war. The historical context of my study is the end of the 8th century, the Assyrian invasion of Judah by Sennacherib in 701 B.C. The following discussion is divided into three parts. How the prophet evaluates the pragmatic policies of Hezekiah and his policy makers in preparation for this war is the topic of the first section. In other words, how does Isaiah assess the "realism" of Judah's leaders? The second section explores the prophet's hope for a different sociopolitical order that lies beyond the conflict with the Assyrian Empire. The final section considers how contemporary believers may appropriate Isaiah's words in the formulation of a view on war.

Prophetic Reflections on the Preparations for the Assyrian Invasion

The Archaeological Data

Sargon II died unexpectedly in battle in 705 B.C.[14] He was the first Assyrian king to die in combat, and his death shocked an empire that was proud of its

---

13. This, of course, has been a major point in the work of John Howard Yoder, most famously in *The Politics of Jesus* (2nd ed.; Grand Rapids: Eerdmans, 1994). Hauerwas appreciatively cites Yoder as a major influence on him in this area. For them and for me, the most important starting point in this discussion is *Christology*.

14. For the historical background of this section, see especially these recent studies: William R. Gallagher, *Sennacherib's Campaign to Judah: New Studies* (SHCANE 18; Leiden: Brill, 1999);

historic military might and the prowess of its rulers. His death, coupled with other recent pressing problems (such as Assyria's serious economic problems and the epidemic of 707 B.C.) signaled the vassal states that this was a propitious time to revolt. When Sennacherib succeeded his father as king, he was obliged to respond to the rebellions that broke out in various parts of the empire. His first action was to move to the southeast against Merodach-Baladan, who had taken control of Babylon. Merodach-Baladan had gathered a large coalition of Elamites, Chaldeans, Arameans, and Arabs to face the Assyrian attack that was sure to follow his usurpation. Most likely, it was at this time that Merodach-Baladan made contact with Hezekiah in Judah in order to coordinate this rebellion with another rebellion in the west. The visit by the Babylonian envoys is recounted in Isaiah 39. The Judean king played a prominent role among the other nations in the west that joined the revolt (Tyre, Ammon, Moab, Edom, and Ashkelon), to the point of imprisoning Padi, the pro-Assyrian king of Ekron, in Jerusalem.

These vassals who had decided to turn against the empire were dealt a devastating blow when Merodach-Baladan and his allies suffered a decisive defeat at the battle of Kish in 704 B.C. Although he himself was able to escape the debacle, Merodach-Baladan's forces were destroyed. Any expectation that Babylon would cripple the new Assyrian king and thus portend success elsewhere was dashed.[15] Sennacherib now would turn his attention to Phoenicia and Syria–Palestine and bring to bear the full weight of his armies against the seditious states there.

Whether Hezekiah began the fortification of Judah after the defeat at Kish or earlier, when he initially had decided to withhold tribute and rebel with Babylon's encouragement, is hard to determine. But work he did to ready his people for what was to come. The narrator says that Jerusalem's walls were reinforced and the water supply secured (Isa 22:8–11; cf. 2 Kgs 20:20; 2 Chr 32:3–5, 30). Archaeology has confirmed both of these activities. Nahman Avigad unearthed a wall 20 feet thick on the western hill of the Old City, which probably can be attributed to these efforts to strengthen the city's defenses.[16]

K. Lawson Younger Jr., "Assyrian Involvement in the Southern Levant at the End of the Eighth Century B.C.E.," in *Jerusalem in Bible and Archaeology: The First Temple Period* (ed. A. G. Vaughn and A. E. Killebrew; SBLSymS 18; Atlanta: Society of Biblical Literature, 2003) 235–63. For more on the various scholarly debates (such as the stages of Sennacherib's campaign; whether there was more than one Assyrian campaign into Judah; the role of Egypt; and the relationship between the Assyrian and biblical accounts in 2 Kings and Isaiah), see L. L. Grabbe, ed., *'Like a Bird in a Cage': The Invasion of Sennacherib in 701 BCE* (JSOTSup 363; ESHM 4; London: Sheffield Academic Press, 2003).

15. In addition to the sources in n. 14, see Louis D. Levine, "Sennacherib's Southern Front: 704–689 B.C.," *JCS* 34 (1982) 28–58.

16. N. Avigad, "Excavations in the Jewish Quarter of the Old City," in *Jerusalem Revealed: Archaeology in the Holy City 1968–1974* (Jerusalem: Israel Exploration Society, 1975) 41–51, esp. 41–44.

The most famous find is what is now called Hezekiah's Tunnel, an ambitious project that cut some 1,750 feet beneath Ophel Hill in order to bring water from the Gihon Spring into a reservoir (the Siloam Spring) within the city walls.[17] Archaeology also has demonstrated that at this time Lachish was fortified in an impressive manner. The remains of hundreds of *lammelek* 'for/of the king' storage jars at Lachish also may be evidence of the collection of food supplies there for Judah's armies as they prepared for the Assyrian onslaught.[18] Its fall in 701 B.C. was considered such an impressive feat that it was celebrated on reliefs on the walls of Sennacherib's palace in Nineveh.[19] Judah had sought a pledge of military support from Egypt as well, although the extent of its actual involvement in the war against Assyria is debated.[20]

In all of this, we see a series of pragmatic decisions of the king of Judah and his advisors to organize for war. This is an example of "Realpolitik" that the coming of Sennacherib's armies seemed to require. Internal preparations had been made, and international agreements had been secured. Nevertheless, these measures failed. The Assyrian accounts of Sennacherib's "Third Campaign" describe his devastation of Judah.[21] He began his invasion by subduing Phoenicia. Eight other western kings quickly capitulated and presented tribute to him at Ushu (located on the coast opposite Tyre). Subsequently, the Philistine cities of Ashkelon and Ekron were defeated, their leadership punished, and spoils sent back to Assyria. Whatever attempt Egypt did make on behalf of the coalition obviously had not succeeded. Every fortified town fell to the Assyrians—even the seemingly impregnable Lachish. Hezekiah stood alone and exposed, without any human hope of relief. Jerusalem was spared, although, of course, the Assyrian and biblical versions give different reasons for Sennacherib's withdrawal.

---

17. Amihai Mazar, *Archaeology of the Land of the Bible—10,000–586 B.C.E.* (ABRL; New York: Doubleday, 1992) 483–85. For the Siloam inscription, see *COS* 2.28:145–46.

18. David Ussishkin, "Lachish," in *OEANE* 3:317–23; cf. Mazar, *Archaeology of the Land of the Bible*, 430–34.

19. For these reliefs, see Julian Reade, *Assyrian Sculpture* (Cambridge: Harvard University Press, 1998) 65–71. The reliefs now reside in the British Museum in London.

20. Note James K. Hoffmeier, "Egypt's Role in the Events of 701 B.C. in Jerusalem," in *Jerusalem in Bible and Archaeology* (ed. Vaughn and Killebrew) 219–34; and J. J. M. Roberts, "Egypt, Assyria, Isaiah, and the Ashdod Affair: An Alternative Proposal," ibid., 265–83.

21. The various Assyrian accounts (for example, on the Chicago and Taylor Prisms, the Rassam Cylinder, and several Bulls) are conveniently presented in W. Mayer, "Sennacherib's Campaign of 701 BCE: The Assyrian View," in *'Like a Bird in a Cage'* (ed. L. L. Grabbe; London: Sheffield Academic Press, 2003) 168–200, esp. 186–200. Also note *COS* 2.119:300–305.

The Prophetic Evaluation

In addition to the evidence from archaeology, the book of Isaiah dedicates several chapters to the events surrounding Sennacherib's invasion in 701 B.C. Indeed, Assyria casts a long shadow over the first half of the book of Isaiah, even before this specific crisis. The presence of Assyria in the region due to the Syro-Ephraimite War of 734 B.C. is foretold (Isaiah 7–8), and the attack of Sargon II on Ashdod in 712 B.C. is noted (Isaiah 20). The terminology of several passages also reflects an awareness of imperial propaganda and aims at subverting the power of its images.[22] It is Sennacherib's invasion and siege of Jerusalem, however, that especially occupies the prophet's attention. In chaps. 21–23[23] and 28–33, he sharply condemns the government's efforts to get ready to confront the empire's armies. The lack of quality leadership and the corruption of the ruling elite are recurring themes in the book (e.g., 1:10, 23; 3:1–4, 13–15; 5:8–24; cf. 2:12–17; 3:16–4:1). The devastation of 701 B.C. particularly exposed this weakness, with disastrous consequences.[24] The siege itself and related events are described in Isaiah 36–39.

The character flaws in the leadership manifested themselves in two fatal foreign policy decisions, the military treaties with Babylon and Egypt. As I pointed out earlier, the first failed miserably. The strategy to deal simultaneous blows to Sennacherib from both ends of the empire, which at the time seemed eminently reasonable, had overestimated the resources of Babylon and the resolve of Merodach-Baladan's cohorts. The prophet voices his displeasure to Hezekiah over not having been informed of this arrangement beforehand and chastises the king's pride in showing off his wealth to the emissaries from Babylon, who apparently had slipped in unannounced. Now that Babylon had fallen, all Judah could do was to try to defend itself against overwhelming odds and do the best it could to survive (Isaiah 39).

---

22. Note esp. Isa 10:5–19. See Peter Machinist, "Assyria and Its Image in the First Isaiah," *JAOS* 103 (1983) 719–37; Gallagher, *Sennacherib's Campaign to Judah*, 75–87, 169–216.

23. For the 701 B.C. dating of chaps. 21–23, see especially Gallagher, *Sennacherib's Campaign to Judah*, 22–74. Many commentators relate this passage to the defeat of Babylon ca. 540 B.C. For example, Otto Kaiser, *Isaiah 13–39* (trans. R. A. Wilson; OTL; Philadelphia: Westminster, 1974) 120–29; Ronald E. Clements, *Isaiah 1–39* (NCBC; Grand Rapids: Eerdmans, 1980) 176–79. Scholars who favor the 701 B.C. dating include John N. Oswalt, *The Book of Isaiah Chapters 1–39* (NICOT; Grand Rapids: Eerdmans, 1986) 389–90; Christopher Seitz, *Isaiah 1–39* (Interpretation; Louisville: John Knox, 1993) 162–68; and Brevard S. Childs, *Isaiah* (OTL; Louisville: Westminster John Knox, 2001) 148–51. Each, in his own way, suggests views incorporating a combination of both dates. Some also relate the descriptions in other passages, such as Isa 1:5–9, to 701 B.C.

24. Note Edgar W. Conrad, *Reading Isaiah* (OBT; Minneapolis: Fortress, 1991) 122–30; Andrew Davies, *Double Standards in Isaiah: Re-evaluating Prophetic Ethics and Divine Justice* (Biblical Interpretation Series 46; Leiden: Brill, 2000) 59–84. Cf. Scott M. Thomas, "Isaiah's Vision of Human Security: Virtue-Ethics and International Politics," *Faith and International Affairs* 4 (2006) 21–29.

To Isaiah, it was clear that the demise of Merodach-Baldan would soon result in the arrival of Assyria and the inevitable downfall of Judah. He laments
the suffering that he knows will come. Upon hearing the news of Babylon's defeat (21:2, 9), Isaiah cries out:

> At this my body is racked with pain, pangs seize me like a woman in labor;
> I am staggered by what I hear, I am bewildered by what I hear.
> My heart falters, fear makes me tremble;
> The twilight I longed for has become a horror to me. . . .
> "Babylon has fallen, has fallen!
> All the images of its gods lie shattered on the ground."
> O my people, crushed on the threshing floor,
> I tell you what I have heard from the LORD Almighty, from the God of Israel.
>   (21:3–4, 9b–10, NIV; cf. 21:10, 22:4)

Judah's chariots and horsemen, the weapons in the central armory, and all the
work to strengthen the walls of Jerusalem and safeguard the water supply
would come to naught. Isaiah's grief, however, is laced with anger. He reveals
a problem deeper than simply the success or breakdown in logistical preparations to solidify the defenses of the nation's cities. These efforts masked
something that was fundamentally much more problematic for a people that
professed to be followers of Yahweh. It is the character of the leadership, the
prophet declares, that is to blame for Judah's ruin. Even as they lead the country to its ruin with their wrongheaded decisions, they callously revel in eating
and drinking at banquets (21:5; 22:12, 13; cf. 28:3, 7–8). There is no sincere pursuit of God in this time of peril. The nation's policy-makers are arrogant and
senseless. The steward Shebna, a prime example of these attitudes, comes under explicit condemnation (22:15–19).[25]

The agreement with Egypt receives more extensive treatment. Isaiah's criticisms appear in a sequence of six woes (Isaiah 28–33).[26] The initial woe complex
(28:1–29) describes the pact with Egypt as a "covenant with death" (28:15).[27] In

---

25. Commentators wrestle with how to coordinate this information about Shebna's and
Eliakim's status with what is related in Isaiah 36–37. Seitz holds that there are actually two men by
the name of Shebna (*Isaiah 1–39*, 160); others believe that the name is a secondary insertion (Clements, *Isaiah 1–39*, 187–88). A more natural reading, however, sees no need for these suggestions.
The textual data suggest a complex character who responds in different ways at different points
of the crisis and whose status changes. His show of faith in Isaiah 36–37 could very well follow the
prophet's reprimand in Isaiah 22.

26. Scholars disagree over the extent of this unit (whether it extends through chap. 35). For
careful literary readings, see Gary Stansell, "Isaiah 28–33: Blest Be the Tie That Binds (Isaiah Together)," in *New Visions of Isaiah* (ed. Roy F. Melugin and Marvin A. Sweeney; JSOTSup 214; Sheffield: Sheffield Academic Press, 1996) 68–103; Seitz, *Isaiah 1–39*, ad loc.

27. We label these passages "woe complex" because they combine more formal woe material
with other messages of judgment and deliverance. At first glance, Isa 28:1–13 may seem out of place
because it is directed at Samaria and the Northern Kingdom. Whatever its historical provenance,

other words, with this political agreement Judah has signed its death sentence. If the leaders had only believed,[28] then this arrangement might never have been made (28:16). Defeat is assured, because the treaty will prove useless (28:17–19). They who made it are scoffers, foolish, and unjust (28:14, 22; cf. 28:1, 7–8). They have not understood that the awful events that will unfold come from God's own hand: Yahweh must do his "strange work," an "alien task" of cleansing his people by utilizing Assyria as his instrument of judgment (28:19–20; cf. 28:2–6). This pattern with Assyria had been established decades before in the Syrian-Ephraimite conflict (7:17–8:10; cf. 10:5–19). If the leaders had been able to read the signs of the times (even as a farmer appreciates the tasks of plowing and planting and orders his steps, 28:23–28; cf. 28:9–13) and grasped the ways of their God, they would have recognized that Yahweh is the true source of wisdom and made different policy choices (28:29).

The second woe (29:1–14) again announces that Yahweh *Ṣĕbā'ôt* 'the LORD Almighty' (NIV) is the one who will judge his people by means of this invasion (29:1–4), even while it also underscores that God will defeat the enemies who would besiege Jerusalem (29:5–8). There is no need to turn to someone else for help. However, Isaiah sees that the people have no genuine interest in hearing a true word from God. The nation has sought counsel elsewhere, but the "wisdom of the wise" will come to no account (29:9–14). The third woe (29:15–24) continues the attack on the leadership. Isaiah denounces them for conceiving their plans apart from the Holy One of Israel and his prophet.[29] They hid their plans from God. It is as though they had said, "How can Yahweh help? It may be well and good to claim faith in him and pray, but what the country really needs are specific, practical military and political measures to stop the

---

however, it serves as an introduction to what follows. The thematic and lexical links are many, and the "therefore" of 28:14 makes the connection explicit. Judah should have learned from the fate of Israel, but instead it has repeated the same sins of reckless arrogance and misguided plans. Writers who take the phrase "covenant with death" to refer to the treaty with Egypt include Clements, *Isaiah 1–39*, 229–30; Childs, *Isaiah*, 208; John Goldingay, *Isaiah* (Peabody, MA.: Hendrickson, 2001) 155; J. J. M. Roberts, "Double Entendre in First Isaiah," *CBQ* 54 (1992) 39–48. Others interpret it as an occult agreement with the underworld: Kaiser, *Isaiah 13–39*, 251–52; Oswalt, *The Book of Isaiah*, 516–17; Seitz, *Isaiah 1–39*, 210; Joseph Blenkinsopp, *Isaiah 1–39: A New Translation with Introduction and Commentary* (AB 19; New York: Doubleday, 2000) 393–94. Note the condemnation of necromancy in Isa 8:19–22, 57:8–9 (cf. 2:6, 29:4).

28. The verb here is *'āman* (Hiphil participle). This verb also appears at another crucial time during an earlier siege (Isa 7:9). It is helpful to coordinate it with the verb *bāṭaḥ* (see below, n. 33).

29. See J. J. M. Roberts, "Blindfolding the Prophet: Political Resistance in First Isaiah's Oracles in the Light of Ancient Near Eastern Attitudes toward Oracles," in *Oracles et Prophéties dans l'Antiquité: Acts du Colloque de Strasbourg 15–17 juin 1995* (ed. J.-G. Heintz; Travaux du Centre de Recherche sur le Proche-Orient et la Grèce Antiques 15; Strasbourg: Publications de l'Université de Strasbourg II, 1997) 135–46. See William McKane, *Prophets and Wise Men* (London: SCM, 1983) 65–85.

Assyrians!" (29:15–16). They remembered Isaiah's opposition to Ahaz's political solution to the crisis of 734 B.C. (7:1–17)—was it not conspiracy against the crown? (8:12)—and how he had dramatically expressed God's censure of the regional revolt against Assyria in 712 B.C. (20:1–6). They may have wondered, "What encouragement could this prophet give in this time of exceptional need? How can we rely on him now, when he has spoken out against the king so often in the past?" Once again, Isaiah describes them as mockers, as ruthless and unjust (29:20–21). Their choices will bring shame upon Judah (29:22). In the future, however, the humble and the contrite will see the salvation of God (29:17–19, 22–24).

It is only after this prolonged diatribe against the faithlessness of Judah's "realistic" leaders in the first three woes that Isaiah specifically mentions the treaty with Egypt in the fourth and fifth woes (Isaiah 30–31). The portrait thus far of the leaders' character leads the reader to expect that this treaty has been misconceived from the beginning. Their plan does not find its source in Yahweh and is formulated in deceit (30:1, 2, 8–11, 15–17). Egypt, designated "Rahab the Do-Nothing," proves to be "utterly useless" (30:7). To make matters worse, the only message that Judah wanted from Yahweh was a word that would bolster patriotic fervor and support national policy (30:8–14). They had ignored the One who "longs to be gracious" (30:18) and who had the power to effect deliverance (30:19–33); they did not see that to lean on Pharaoh would yield only disgrace (30:3, 5, 12). The subsequent woe reinforces the condemnation of the leaders' decision not to seek Yahweh in their efforts to finalize an alliance with Egypt (31:1). The confidence in chariots and horsemen is irrational, Isaiah says, because the Egyptians are but flesh. Yahweh, though, is God. He alone is wise (31:2); he alone can defeat Assyria (31:3–9), a conviction eloquently celebrated in the sixth woe of chap. 33.[30]

Judah's leaders had made up their minds to follow their own calculations of the best way to face the threat from Assyria. They refused to see that the nation had brought this disaster upon itself and that the solution lay with Yahweh. They were so absorbed with their own strategies that they could not perceive that Yahweh had a strategy, too.[31] It is revealing to trace the theme of God's "plan" (*ʿēṣâ* [noun]; *yʿṣ* [verb]) in the book of Isaiah, because we discover that Yahweh, in his incomparable sovereignty, had always intended the defeat and humiliation of Assyria. Yahweh *Ṣĕbāʾôt* had sworn:

---

30. The identity of the "destroyer" of Isa 33:1 depends in large measure on what date is assigned to the passage. The literary-historical context leads us to consider this sixth woe to be the climactic declaration of Assyria's defeat. It anticipates Isaiah 36–37. Some date the chapter to the time of the Exile and a few even later, to the Maccabean age.

31. Conrad, *Reading Isaiah*, 52–82.

Surely, as I have planned, so it will be,
and as I have purposed (yā'aṣtî) so it will stand.
I will crush the Assyrian in my land;
on my mountains I will trample him down.
His yoke will be taken away from my people,
and his burden removed from their shoulders.

(14:24–25, NIV)

This outcome had already been set in motion. The events of chap. 37 would prove that the miraculous victory was not pious wishful thinking but instead an unbelievable marvel that would leave no doubt that Yahweh, not Sennacherib, was the "great king" (36:4, 13).

This plan also was not a recent invention of God. Long ago he had purposed Assyria's rise and fall (25:1, 37:26), even its final redemption (19:23–25)! In addition, his plan envisioned much more than just the fate of the Assyrian Empire. It included the nations of the earth and encompassed all of history itself and would not—indeed could not—be thwarted (14:26–27; cf. 40:13, 46:8–11, 47:13). Others may plot against the people of God, but it would be to no avail (7:5–6, 8:9–10). This supreme plan would expose the emptiness of the machinations of Egypt's wise men (19:2–4, 11–12, 16–17).[32] Why then did Judah's leaders pursue a plan other than the plan of the Holy One of Israel—especially in cooperation with Egypt? Why devise plans "in darkness," which was sin against Yahweh (29:15–16, 30:1–2; cf. 5:18–19), who, the prophet proclaims, is "wonderful in counsel ('ēṣâ) and magnificent in wisdom" (28:29)? Ironically, the Assyrians mock the "realistic" strategies of Judah's leadership (Isaiah 36). It had not succeeded in slowing the advance of the empire's armies, so at the walls of Jerusalem the field commander (the Rab-šāqēh) taunts Hezekiah's representatives, saying, "You say you have strategy ('ēṣâ) and military strength—but you speak only empty words" (36:5 NIV). How right he was!

The appropriate response to the plan of God would have been trust. This verb (bāṭaḥ) is another key term in the book of Isaiah.[33] It is particularly

_____

32. It is difficult to date Isaiah 19. The similarities with Isaiah 30–31 can incline the interpreter to correlate it with 701 B.C., but the repeated phrase "in that day" and its descriptions (19:16–25) appear to refer to something beyond that time. This juxtaposition, however, is not an uncommon stylistic feature of the book of Isaiah. Current events are presented as a type of what is to come. See the comments below concerning the king of Isaiah 32.

33. J. W. Olley, "'Trust in the LORD': Hezekiah, Kings, and Isaiah," *TynBul* 50 (1999) 59–77; David Bostock, *A Portrayal of Trust: The Theme of Faith in the Hezekiah Narratives* (Paternoster Biblical Monographs; Milton Keynes, U.K.: Paternoster, 2006), esp. 167–204; cf. Gary N. Knoppers, "'There Was None Like Him': Incomparability in the Book of Kings," *CBQ* 54 (1992) 411–31, esp. 418–25. What the text does not reveal is exactly what kind of alternative action based on this "trust" that Isaiah would have supported. Some scholars believe that he wanted the nation to do nothing except watch Yahweh's miraculous action. We cannot be sure. See below, n. 42. For a

prominent in the Assyrian field commander's words. He repeatedly ridicules the objects of Judah's trust: "On what are you basing this confidence of yours? (*mâ habbiṭṭāḥôn hazzeh ʾăšer bāṭāḥtā*; lit., 'What is this trust that you trust?') On whom are you depending (*ʿal-mî bāṭaḥtā*) that you rebel against me?" (36:4b, 5b NIV). Neither Egypt (36:6, 9) nor the god of Judah himself (36:7, 15; cf. 37:10) could save this tiny vassal's capital from defeat. The *Rab-šāqēh* was again correct but, in this case, only in part. Yes, they had trusted in Egypt and had been sorely disappointed, but they had not trusted in Yahweh. They had trusted in (NIV: "relied on") oppression and deceit instead (30:12) and had depended on their own tactics. To believe that Egypt could be their "refuge" or "shade" was to cling to a "lie" (28:15, 30:2). How different everything could have turned out, says Yahweh: "In repentance and rest is your salvation, in quietness and trust (*biṭḥâ*) is your strength, but you would have none of it" (30:15; cf. 28:12). Trusting Yahweh was the lesson to learn in this process. It was the goal for which the people of God should strive and that they would one day proclaim to be a wondrous blessing (see 12:2, 26:4; cf. 8:17).

In summary, the prophetic evaluation of Judah's preparations for war is extremely negative. These measures appeared to the people in charge to be sensible and necessary, but in actuality, they were self-deluding and, in the end, self-destructive. They were based on a series of decisions made by people who valued pragmatism over proper faith and whose character guaranteed that their foreign policy would be flawed. Nevertheless, Isaiah's message is not merely judgment. In addition to the negative tone concerning the leaders' "realism," there is at the same time a word of hope for the people of God that lies beyond the affliction that would soon befall them.

The Hope beyond the Disaster:
A Different Kind of King (Isaiah 32:1–8)

Wedged between the fifth and sixth woes of chaps. 31 and 33 is a passage of hope. The pericope Isa 32:1–8 is not the only prophecy of deliverance in this long section (note, for example, 28:5–6, 16–17; 29:17–24; 30:18–33), but it is different from what had been said to this point in that it mentions a king.[34]

This picture of the future begins with a focus on character: the king "will reign in righteousness," and his "rulers will rule in justice" (Isa 32:1). There could not be a more stark contrast to Judah's leaders! The combination of

---

complex reading of the trust theme in Isaiah, see Mark Gray, *Rhetoric and Social Justice in Isaiah* (LHBOTS 432; New York: T. & T. Clark, 2006) 179–234.

34. For exegetical details and scholarly views, see especially Paul D. Wegner, *An Examination of Kingship and Messianic Interpretation in Isaiah 1–35* (Lewiston, NY: Mellen Biblical Press, 1992) 175–301.

"righteousness" and "justice," so important to Isaiah's theology, now characterizes individuals who one day will lead the nation.[35] No mocking or arrogance or oppression can be detected here. As a result, the people of God will enjoy peace instead of war and shelter instead of the horrors of a siege (32:2). Their eyes will see and their ears will hear (32:3)—a wonderful reversal of the blindness and deafness that they had experienced under Ahaz (6:9–10) and under the present regime (cf. 29:9–10, 18–19). No longer will they suffer the rash and ill-fated decisions of ungodly fools; in the new order, things will be as they should be under the "noble man" who plans (*yāʿaṣ*) "noble deeds," not evil (32:4–8).

This good news raises the question, "Who is this king?" Basically, there are three interpretive answers: (1) this is a description of a model king; (2) the king is an actual historical figure of Isaiah's day; and (3) this person is the future Messiah. Each of these views does contain an element of truth, but, as we shall see, a more complete answer is found in a combination of the three.

First, the Hebrew reads simply "a king" (32:1). There is no article to alert the reader that a particular person necessarily is being identified. In addition, the description in 32:1–8 echoes very closely the theme and vocabulary of Prov 8:15–16, which says:

> By me *kings reign* and rulers make laws that are just;
> by me *princes govern*, and *nobles*, all who rule on earth.[36]

The "me" in these two verses is the wisdom of God. This connection to the wisdom tradition (also note Prov 16:10, 12, 13; 20:8, 26; 25:4–5; 29:4) suggests that these verses present a general picture of the values and virtues of a good king.[37] The ideal of a just king was common in the ancient Near East and was a key component of the royal ideologies of that time.[38] It is not surprising that Judah had the same aspirations (see Psalms 45, 72).

Nevertheless, the text does not limit itself to this first option. Within the literary flow of the book of Isaiah, a specific righteous king does come to the fore. As others have pointed out, the predicted child (7:14–17) finds a degree of fulfillment in the person of Hezekiah (Isaiah 36–38).[39] There are too many

---

35. For these themes, note Thomas L. Leclerc, *Yahweh Is Exalted in Justice: Solidarity and Conflict in Isaiah* (Minneapolis: Fortress, 2001); for Isaiah 28–33, see pp. 73–86.

36. The shared terminology is in italic.

37. H. G. M. Williamson, *Variations on a Theme: King, Messiah, and Servant in the Book of Isaiah* (Carlisle: Paternoster, 1998) 62–72.

38. K. W. Whitelam, *The Just King: Monarchical Judicial Authority in Ancient Israel* (JSOTSup 12; Sheffield: JSOT Press, 1979); Dale Launderville, *Piety and Politics: The Dynamics of Royal Authority in Homeric Greece, Biblical Israel, and Old Babylonian Mesopotamia* (Grand Rapids: Eerdmans, 2003).

39. Conrad, *Reading Isaiah*, 34–51; Seitz, *Isaiah 1–39*, ad loc. I add that the lexical similarities between Isa 7:14–17 and 8:3–18 suggest an earlier tentative fulfillment in Maher-Shalal-Hash-Baz.

lexical connections between these two texts to deny this conclusion. In both settings there is an encounter with the prophet at "the aqueduct of the Upper Pool, on the road to the Washerman's Field" (7:3, 36:2). Hezekiah, unlike his father Ahaz, does respond to the prophetic exhortation, "Do not fear" (7:4–9, 37:6–7) and in faith receives Yahweh's sign (7:10–16; 37:30–32; 38:7, 22). Ahaz's lack of belief had brought Assyria upon Judah as judgment (7:13–25). In contrast, Hezekiah is able to save the city from the Assyrian threat in 701 B.C. by his prayer (37:14–20), and the remnant that resides in Zion is amazingly spared (37:31–32). Sennacherib's invasion, of course, forms the historical backdrop to chaps. 28–33, and so a natural reading of 32:1–8 in this literary context would conclude that Hezekiah is likely this righteous king. These verses, therefore, in some fashion anticipate the deliverance that comes in chaps. 36–37. Hezekiah also accomplishes some of the things spoken of in chaps. 9 and 11. Is he not a descendent of David who has shattered the yoke that Judah bears and who reigns in righteousness (cf. 9:4–6[5–7])? He does not capitulate to the taunts of the *Rab-šāqēh* and to what his eyes see but instead seeks Yahweh's face (cf. 11:3). The Deuteronomistic History says of Hezekiah: "There was no one like him, either before him or after him" (2 Kgs 20:5; cf. 2 Chr 32:32). Only Josiah is given a higher commendation (2 Kgs 23:25).

Yet this very context, historical and literary, disqualifies him from being the final fulfillment of Isaiah 32. The words of the prophet do find an initial referent in Hezekiah, but then they point beyond him. He is not the total embodiment of the hope. To begin with, Hezekiah possibly was included in Isaiah's condemnation of the nation's leadership, because he probably would have been party to the political misadventures that the prophet criticized. This involvement may explain why Hezekiah said nothing to Isaiah of the arrival of the Babylonian representatives (Isaiah 39). In this context as well, he fell prey to the sin of pride that so easily characterizes human rulers. Hezekiah had not sought the counsel of Yahweh until all seemed lost and the city was surrounded. In other words, while chap. 32 does find some measure of fulfillment in Hezekiah, the reader must press on to try to discover another king who brings the peace and justice that everyone desires.

The recognition that in the final analysis Hezekiah cannot be the king described in Isa 32:1–8 also reveals that he cannot finally fulfill all the expectations of chaps. 9 and 11. We observe that the royal figure of these three passages is not given a name. Chapters 40–66 expand on this portrait of the Messiah, but the anonymity continues. To the description of the king is added

---

It is tentative because Isa 9:1–6[2–7] makes clear that the son of promise must be of the royal line. Another historical referent that has been suggested is Josiah. See Clements, *Isaiah 1–39*, 259; Marvin A. Sweeney, *King Josiah of Judah: The Lost Messiah of Israel* (New York: Oxford University Press, 2001) 248–52.

the striking dimension of the Servant of Yahweh. This individual, this Messiah, therefore, will be a Servant-King who will be exalted through suffering.[40] This revelation, of course, anticipates the announcement in the New Testament that Jesus is this One. What is important for my purposes, however, is the realization, first, that the Messiah would be greater than any human king that Judah had ever seen. The people of God would have to wait for his coming. Second, it is evident from a careful reading of the book of Isaiah that Yahweh himself is ultimately the sovereign king of Judah and Israel and the nations of the world. From Isaiah's confession at his commissioning, "My eyes have seen the King, Yahweh *Şĕbā'ôt*" (6:5) to the final chapter, in which God sits on a heavenly throne (66:1), Yahweh reigns supreme (cf. 24:23, 41:21, 43:15, 44:6). He mediates this rule through Judah's kings and will do so especially through the Messiah, but the divine King is their greatest judge and lawgiver, their truest leader, in whom Judah must place its absolute trust (33:17–22).[41] He is the nation's Creator and Redeemer, who in the present saves the remnant from annihilation by the Assyrians and who will deliver them from the new and future enemy, the Babylonians. Yahweh will purge sinful Jerusalem of its rebellious ways. By the close of the book, he has promised to transform Zion into a holy city that will sing his praises to the ends of the earth.[42] His glorious kingdom will have come.

This hope for a king in 32:1–8 is the second element of Isaiah's denunciation of Judah's leadership. The first indictment was their lack of integrity and trust in God. This passage underscores that a lasting peace lies beyond all of the calculations for the war against Assyria and beyond the character and

---

40. Richard Schultz, "The King in the Book of Isaiah," in *The Lord's Anointed: Interpretation of Old Testament Messianic Texts* (ed. P. E. Satterthwaite, R. S. Hess, and G. J. Wenham; Tyndale House Studies; Carlisle: Paternoster / Grand Rapids: Baker, 1995) 141–65.

41. See J. J. M. Roberts, "The Divine King and the Human Community in Isaiah's Vision of the Future," in *The Quest for the Kingdom of God: Studies in Honor of George E. Mendenhall* (ed. H. B. Huffmon, F. A. Spina, and A. R. Green; Winona Lake, IN: Eisenbrauns, 1983) 127–36.

42. For the Zion theme in Isaiah, see B. C. Ollenburger, *Zion the City of the Great King: A Theological Symbol of the Jerusalem Cult* (JSOTSup 41; Sheffield: Sheffield Academic Press, 1987) 107–29; B. G. Webb, "Zion in Transformation: A Literary Approach to Isaiah," in *The Bible in Three Dimensions: Essays in Celebration of Forty Years of Biblical Studies in the University of Sheffield* (ed. D. J. A. Clines, S. E. Fowl, and S. E. Porter; JSOTSup 87; Sheffield: Sheffield Academic Press, 1990) 65–84; C. R. Seitz, *Zion's Final Destiny: The Development of the Book of Isaiah: A Reassessment of Isaiah 36–39* (Minneapolis: Fortress, 1991). An older but still useful treatment is found in Gerhard von Rad's *Old Testament Theology*, vol. 2: *The Theology of Israel's Prophetic Traditions* (trans. D. M. G. Stalker; New York: Harper & Row, 1965) 147–75. Von Rad grounds the Zion theme in the holy war tradition and sees echoes in the Songs of Zion in the Psalter (e.g., Psalms 46, 48, 76). Although there certainly are connections along these lines, my reading argues that the movement within the text itself points beyond this tradition to a different reality and politics determined by the Messiah, when war is no more. I am grateful to Walter Moberly for bringing von Rad to my attention.

capabilities of the men who have governed Judah. This hope resides in one even greater than Hezekiah. He was a good ruler in many ways, yet in the end he was also flawed. There can be peace only with Messiah in a different kind of kingdom that Yahweh himself will bring.

Lessons from Isaiah for the Contemporary Debate on the Christian and War

What do the prophet's words to Judah in the 8th century have to say about our current struggle to understand what may be the appropriate posture of Christians and the Christian church regarding war? I suggest that there are at least three lessons that one may draw from Isaiah's two-pronged prophetic critique of the situation of his day.

First—and this perhaps is the simplest conclusion to draw—it is prudent to probe the good judgment of the decisions that lead a nation to war. More precisely, it is wise to explore the values and attitudes of those who make the policy choices. Character does matter. Of course, this is the type of issue in relationship to the conflict in Iraq that is being debated in the current election year. This is a salutary, first-level lesson to learn from the biblical text, but I do not believe that it reaches the heart of the matter. The importance of evaluating motives and hidden agendas in war is clear, but to search this prophetic book for insights regarding a present-day nation (in this case, the United States) is to fall into Reinhold Niebuhr's mire—that is, the drive to ascertain how nation-states should best respond to and limit conflict in the world.

The question that needs to be asked is not "what should *this country* take from Isaiah?" but instead "what should *Christians* learn about faith in God in the context of war from these prophetic texts?"[43] This second question returns to the two fundamental issues that were raised in the introduction: Who are we (*identity*)? What are we to do (*mission*)? This leads me to two additional lessons that I feel the people of God must learn from the prophet.

To begin with, we see that believers are called to trust in the absolute power of Yahweh to deliver. One may protest, "This is naïve. It will not work.

---

43. There are some significant voices that have recently been raised advocating the importance of reading the Old Testament as Christian Scripture. This theological commitment has implications for the use of the OT for moral reflection. This is why the goal cannot be simply to draw a few timeless principles unrelated to our confession of Jesus and the centrality of the Gospel narratives. For thoughtful engagements of this theological-ethical challenge, note Francis Watson, *Text and Truth: Redefining Biblical Theology* (Grand Rapids: Eerdmans, 1997); Christopher R. Seitz, *Word Without End: The Old Testament as Abiding Theological Witness* (Grand Rapids: Eerdmans, 1998); R. W. L. Moberly, *The Bible, Theology, and Faith: A Study of Abraham and Jesus* (Cambridge Studies in Christian Doctrine; Cambridge: Cambridge University Press, 2000).

All the prayers and calls to believe in God cannot save us from enemy attack! We have to be responsible, pragmatic, and prepare our defenses." How much we sound like the Judah of Isaiah's day! The prophet's point was that Yahweh was able to save. To depend on horses and chariots and mortar and brick is to rely on human cunning and the weakness of flesh. These will fail us, sooner if not later. Yahweh also had sent Assyria to judge the sins of his people. This observation could raise another set of issues for our time, but they lie outside the purview of this essay. In our passages, the more fundamental point involves the integrity of the faith of the people of God, and this is the focus of the second lesson from the book of Isaiah. Would Judah be like all the other peoples, who trusted in their arms and their gods of war? Would they fight for the same kinds of social, economic, and political goods that others warred to own? Would they join the spiral of violence and themselves employ the tactics of the empire that they both feared and despised?

To legitimate any conflict in Yahweh's name too easily is to miss Isaiah's and other prophets' declarations that Yahweh humbles the military pretenses of the nations of the world, even Israel's.[44] Human aspirations to power are destructive and self-deceiving (Isa 10:12–19, 14:3–23). The kings of Assyria and Babylon boast of their unmatched military might, but they will share the fate of all humanity: they will lose their power and die. In addition, arrogance breeds contempt. Thus, it is not surprising that the prophets show us that this pride often is accompanied by oppression and the neglect of the poor.

More seriously, in their view, to sanctify war can result in the reshaping of Yahweh in our national image; it is to worship an idol of our own making. In Isaiah's mind, this people know and worship a unique God; therefore, they should espouse a different kind of leadership and a different kind of politics.[45] To do otherwise is to betray Yahweh himself. In New Testament terms, we must first understand the person and work of Jesus Christ. Once this understanding is established, we are able to appreciate more fully the meaning and significance of our *identity* as Christians. How should the ethics of Jesus and our being in Christ shape our view of war? I suggest that they lead to a stance of nonviolence and love for our enemies. Can participating in war contribute to the *mission* to make disciples of every nation? I think not. To achieve these goals requires envisioning an uncommon sociopolitical presence, a unique (and very different!) set of "responsible" actions committed to

---

44. See my "Prophetic Text and the Literature of Dissent in Latin America: Amos, García Márquez, and Cabrera Infante Dismantle Militarism," *BibInt* 4 (1996) 76–100.

45. This is the argument of Millard C. Lind regarding Old Testament historical narratives. It holds true for the prophetic literature as well. See his *Yahweh Is a Warrior: The Theology of Warfare in Ancient Israel* (Scottdale, PA: Herald, 1980). Cf. J. Gordon McConville, "Law and Monarchy in the Old Testament," in *A Royal Priesthood: The Use of the Bible Ethically and Politically* (ed. C. Bartholomew, A. Wolters, and J. Chaplin; Grand Rapids: Zondervan, 2002) 69–88.

a distinct mode of being in the world and for the world that can point the world beyond itself and its self-destructive ways.[46]

The third and final lesson that I offer for consideration is grounded in Isaiah's eschatological hope. In this essay, I have briefly examined Isa 32:1–8. The eschatological component is crucial because it communicates that war is not what ultimately defines human existence. One day it will end. Regarding the future, Isaiah proclaims: "He [that is, Yahweh] will judge between the nations and will settle disputes for many peoples. They will beat their swords into plowshares and their spears into pruning hooks. Nation will not take up sword against nation, nor will they train for war any more" (Isa 2:4, NIV). This is an important point that we must grasp in order to respond to critics who argue that the text is locked into ancient views on war and that to believe an Old Testament perspective is to become its theological and ideological captive.[47] Has not the Old Testament been used to justify all kinds of atrocities in history?

My point is that, when using the Old Testament in discussions about war, we dare not neglect its proclamation concerning the future. Yes, the Old Testament has been appropriated for nefarious ends, but to sever what it says about the realities of war in Israel from these visions of the future and of Messiah's reign is to miss what I call its "impulses toward peace" that take us past the limitations of that time. These visions should also shape our moral imagination and point us beyond our horizons. I am, of course, appealing to the work of Walter Brueggemann.[48] This standpoint allows us to break free from the way the rest of humanity sees the world and determines its affairs. It equips us to unmask the limited ideologies that mold us and that appeal to mores opposed to our calling. We can envision a different kind of future and

---

46. Responsible *to what* and *to whom* becomes a primary question. To claim, as some have, that Yoder, Hauerwas, and others encourage withdrawal from engaging in society and lack of constructive participation in the democratic process is to misinterpret their (and my) stance. Rather, we advocate rethinking how politics should be understood and practiced by Christians so that it is not captive to prevailing ideologies. See John H. Yoder, *For the Nations: Essays Public & Evangelical* (Grand Rapids: Brazos, 2004); Stanley Hauerwas, *With the Grain of the Universe*; idem, *Performing the Faith: Bonhoeffer and the Practice of Nonviolence* (Grand Rapids: Brazos, 2004); note especially the postscript (pp. 215–41), in which Hauerwas responds to the criticisms of J. Stout's *Democracy and Tradition* (Princeton: Princeton University Press, 2004).

47. Among recent publications, I mention Hobbs, *A Time for War*, 193–98; James Barr, *Biblical Faith and Natural Theology* (Oxford: Oxford University Press, 1993) 199–221; Carol J. Dempsey, *Hope Amid the Ruins: The Ethics of Israel's Prophets* (St. Louis: Chalice, 2000); Cyril S. Rodd, *Glimpses of a Strange Land: Studies in Old Testament Ethics* (OTS; Edinburgh: T. & T. Clark, 2001) 185–206; and John J. Collins, "The Zeal of Phinehas: The Bible and the Legitimation of Violence," *JBL* 122 (2003) 3–21. For the ethical dilemma in Isaiah itself, see Davies, *Double Standards in Isaiah*; Gray, *Rhetoric and Social Justice in Isaiah*.

48. See Walter Brueggemann, *The Prophetic Imagination* (2nd ed.; Minneapolis: Fortress, 2001); idem, *Theology of the Old Testament* (Minneapolis: Fortress, 1997).

work toward its realization.[49] The words that complete the passage just cited are "Come, O house of Jacob, let us walk in the light of the LORD" (Isa 2:5, NIV). Let us walk in peace.

The hope in Isa 32:1–8 centers on the Messiah and his kingdom. The New Testament proclaims that the Messiah has come. The future is now; the kingdom has been inaugurated. This fact, I believe, should determine—I return to my twin emphases—our ethical identity and actions.[50] It is true that we do not now see the fullness of the kingdom of the Prince of Peace, but we do participate in its reality nonetheless. In the interim, in the time between the times, in this era between the first and second coming, how should we live? Do we adopt the stance of Niebuhr and order our lives according to the fallenness of the world, accepting the inevitability and necessity of its violence? Or do we imitate the life of Jesus and give ourselves so that others may have life? Herein lies the challenge of Isaiah's eschatology, his impulses toward peace in a country at war. This is the challenge of being a disciple of Jesus Christ and a member of another people. Do we participate in war or do we commit ourselves to peacemaking?[51] The better path is peacemaking, because with Isaiah we anticipate Messiah's day: "The fruit of righteousness will be peace; the effect of righteousness will be quietness and confidence forever" (Isa 32:17, NIV).

---

49. Most of my own work has been in Amos. See my "Reflecting on War and Utopia in the Book of Amos: The Relevance of a Literary Reading of the Prophetic Text from Central America" in *The Bible in Human Society: Essays in Honour of John W. Rogerson* (ed. D. J. A. Clines, P. R. Davies, and M. D. Carroll R.; JSOTSup 200; Sheffield: Sheffield Academic Press, 1995) 105–21; idem, "Living between the Lines: A Reading of Amos 9:11–15 in Postwar Guatemala," *R&T* 6 (1999) 50–64; idem, "The Power of the Future in the Present: Eschatology and Ethics in O'Donovan and Beyond " in *A Royal Priesthood* (ed. C. Bartholomew, A. Wolters, and J. Chaplin; Grand Rapids: Zondervan, 2002) 116–43.

50. In addition to the works cited in nn. 11, 13, and 46, see Richard B. Hays, *The Moral Vision of the New Testament* (New York: HarperSanFrancisco, 1996) 317–46; Glen H. Stassen and David P. Gushee, *Kingdom Ethics: Following Jesus in Contemporary Context* (Downers Grove, IL: InterVarsity, 2003) 149–58. Interestingly, Stassen and Gushee note the importance of Isaiah for their work.

51. Ibid., *Kingdom Ethics*, 158–74.

CHAPTER 5

Distinguishing Just War from Crusade: Is Regime Change a Just Cause for Just War?

Daniel R. Heimbach

In this essay, I will not address the pacifists' question whether war is ever morally right. I respect Christian pacifists but do not agree with their view on war. I hold the view that, beginning with the time of the New Testament, what we call the *just-war* approach to the ethics of war and Christians' participating as soldiers in war has always been the teaching of the majority of the church. I believe the just-war approach is totally faithful to Scripture and is not a corruption of biblical morality, as pacifists often claim. But I say this only to clarify my stance in the general debate among Christians over the morality of war.

My purpose is not to address a pacifist question, but a just-war question. I will address how we should properly interpret *just cause* for morally permissible war, a question that is particularly relevant in view of many conflicting statements that have been made recently justifying or criticizing the war with Iraq in 2003 (see appendix, pp. 90–92). I am convinced that there are indeed times when the first and most urgent moral obligation of a government in the face of evil is to stop the evil, by waging war if necessary, and my remarks are addressed to individuals who agree. In other words, I am engaging in an in-house debate between proponents of the just-war ethic. Therefore, if you are a pacifist, I beg your indulgence and invite you to listen. My narrow focus is the line dividing just war from crusade: I distinguish the two based on how each justifies going to war. I have one objective, which is to present the reinterpretation of the just-cause principle in the just-war moral tradition by transforming just war into crusade.

Controversy over Just Cause for War with Iraq

The problem I am addressing is illustrated by comparing recent statements made in debate over whether invading Iraq in 2003 was or was not justified according to just-war tradition. President George W. Bush initially justified using force to remove Saddam Hussein's regime by citing the threat he posed to peace and safety both in the United States and around the world. He first focused on Iraq's refusal to meet terms of surrender at the end of the Persian Gulf War. Then he shifted increasingly to justifying war with Iraq to remove fear of a *future* threat—a *potential* threat that had not yet materialized.

In a speech delivered at West Point, President Bush said, "War on terrorism will not be won on the defensive. . . . The only path to safety is the path of action. . . . Our security . . . will require preemptive action."[1] In his State of the Union address of January 2003, President Bush asked this of the American people: "Imagine . . . [terrorists] armed by Saddam Hussein. . . . Some have said we must not act until the threat is imminent. . . . If this threat is permitted to fully and suddenly emerge, all actions, all words all recriminations would come too late. . . . If Saddam Hussein does not fully disarm for the safety of our people, and for the peace of the world, we will lead a coalition to disarm him."[2] A month later, he said war with Iraq was needed because "dangers of our time must be confronted actively and forcefully, before we see them again in our skies and in our cities."[3] Then, finally, in announcing war with Iraq on March 19, 2003, President Bush said that invasion was justified because "the people of the United States and our friends and allies will not live at the mercy of an outlaw regime" that could someday threaten our own peace and safety "with weapons of mass murder."[4]

In contrast to the words of President Bush, critics have made statements that said there could never be a just cause for preemptive war, no matter what happens. On September 23, 2002, one hundred Christian ethicists issued a declaration saying, "As Christian ethicists, we share a common moral presumption against a preemptive war on Iraq by the United States." Paul Casey of Wesley Theological Seminary, who helped lead this effort, said the signers were concerned because just cause has usually been limited to self-defense, and "the Bush administration has repeatedly said . . . preemptive force against Saddam Hussein would be morally legitimate."[5] More recently, Tom Teepen, a

---

1. George W. Bush, "President Bush Delivers Graduation Speech at West Point," delivered June 1, 2002; text issued by the White House on June 1, 2002; available at http://www.whitehouse.gov/news/releases/2002/06/20020601-3.html.

2. Idem, "State of the Union Speech," delivered January 29, 2003; text issued by the White House on January 29, 2003; available at http://www.cnn.com/2003/ALLPOLITICS/01/28/sotu.transcript/.

3. Idem, "Remarks to the American Enterprise Institute," delivered February 26, 2003; text issued by the White House on February 26, 2003.

4. Idem, "Speech Announcing War with Iraq," delivered March 19, 2003; text issued by the White House on March 19, 2003.

5. Scott McLemee, "100 Christian Ethicists Challenge Claim Pre-Emptive War on Iraq Would

writer for Cox Newspapers, has said, "The Bush administration . . . went to nail down a disturbing new American policy that asserts a U.S. right to start preventive wars wherever an administration sees a potential threat."[6]

In addition to President Bush and his critics, there has been a third group consisting of evangelicals who give moral justification, not only for what the administration is doing but (especially) for the President's claim to have just cause for attacking Iraq before Saddam Hussein could actually threaten or be able to attack us. In October 2002, Richard Land of the SBC Ethics and Religious Liberty Commission, Chuck Colson of Prison Fellowship, Bill Bright of Campus Crusade, James Kennedy of Coral Ridge Ministries, and Carl Herbster of the American Association of Christian Schools sent a joint letter to President Bush. They began by explaining that "in just war theory only defensive war is defensible." But the writers then went on to say that they were sure "using military force if necessary to disarm Saddam Hussein and his weapons of mass destruction" already had just cause without waiting for Iraq actually to threaten the United States or its allies. War was justified, they thought, as a way of "defend[ing] freedom and freedom-loving people" from what amounted to the risk of a future attack.[7]

Chuck Colson elaborated in *Christianity Today*, arguing that the concept of just cause in just-war moral theory should be "stretched." He understood that, "historically, the doctrine's requirement of just cause has been defined as responding to an attack." But, he said, "I think this reflects too narrow an understanding of just war" and argued, "Out of love of neighbor . . . Christians can and should support a preemptive strike . . . to prevent an imminent attack."[8] Richard Land, who studied under Paul Ramsey at Princeton, also believed there was legitimate just cause for attacking Iraq before they took action against us. He said, "Most Americans sense grave danger with the Iraqi government . . . [and] the nightmare I fear is that we wake up one day and discover that Saddam Hussein has fissionable material he can use to threaten those who oppose his attempts to impose his own hegemony in the Middle East."[9] With this in mind, Land concluded that there "can be a just cause of war if the regime is evil enough."[10]

Be Morally Justified," *Chronicle of Higher Education, Daily News*, September 23, 2002, n.p. Online: *http://chronicle.com/daily/2002/09/2002092302n.htm.*

6. Thomas Teepen, "Good Catch," *News and Observer (Raleigh)*, December 19, 2003.

7. Richard Land et al., "Letter to President Bush," n.p. Online: *http://erlc.com/article/the-so-called-land-letter.*

8. Charles Colson, "Just War in Iraq," *Christianity Today*, December 9, 2002, 72.

9. Quoted in Dwayne Hastings, "Land Says President on Solid Grounds," *For Faith and Family*, November 18, 2002.

10. Quoted in Jason Hall, "Fighting a Just War in Iraq," *SBC Life* (April 2003) 8.

So here are moral advisers making opposing statements on just cause for war in the just-war tradition and a president using terms offered by individuals supporting what he senses he must do. But who, if anyone, correctly defines *just cause* in just-war moral theory, and was there a legitimate just cause for invading Iraq? To answer, we must understand that the problem is deep, has been around a long time, and divides notable scholars.

Conflict over Just Cause in Just-War Tradition

In the current debate, George Weigel of the Ethics and Public Policy Center has sharply opposed Bishop Wilton Gregory, President of the United States Conference of Catholic Bishops. In September 2002, Bishop Gregory wrote President Bush, saying, "We find it difficult to justify extending the war on terrorism to Iraq, absent clear and adequate evidence of Iraqi involvement in the attacks of September 11th or of an imminent attack of a grave nature." This was because *"The Catechism of the Catholic Church* limits just cause to cases in which *the damage by the aggressor on the nation or community of nations* [is] *lasting, grave and certain."* [11] But directly opposing the position taken by Bishop Gregory and the Conference of Catholic Bishops, George Weigel, himself a Catholic scholar, in an article published in the January 2003 issue of *First Things*, argued that, even though "in the classic just war tradition, just cause was understood as defense against aggression, the recovery of something wrongly taken, or the punishment of evil," he believed that "new weapons capabilities and outlaw or rogue states require a development of the concept of defense against aggression." Weigel said, "The mere possession of weapons of mass destruction" should now be treated as an act of aggression, and therefore "preemptive military action to deny the rogue state that kind of destructive capacity would not, in my judgment, contravene the defense against aggression concept of just cause." [12]

The same division arose between Robert Tucker and Paul Ramsey in the 1960s at the height of Cold War tension between the United States and the Soviet Union. Tucker took the historic view on just cause, saying that "preventive war is . . . unjust" because it condones "resort to war by a state in circumstances other than those of self or collective defense against armed aggression." He concluded, "Preventive war must . . . be condemned, whatever the circumstances that are alleged to condition its initiation." [13] For Tucker, even the advent of nuclear weapons "has not had the effect of changing the central

---

11. Wilton Gregory, "Letter to President Bush"; dated September 13, 2003 (italics mine); available at http:// www.nccbuscc.org/sdwp/international/bush902.htm.
12. George Weigel, "Moral Clarity in a Time of War," *First Things* (January 2003) 24–25.
13. Robert Tucker, *The Just War: A Study in Contemporary American Doctrine* (Westport, CT: Greenwood, 1960) 15.

tenet of the American just war doctrine, that the just war is first and foremost the war fought in self or collective defense against armed aggression."[14]

But Ramsey disagreed, saying that the historic interpretation of just cause in just-war tradition was insufficient and needed to be enlarged. Instead, Ramsey proposed what he called "the constructive thesis . . . that a truer doctrine of the just war cannot avoid asserting in its doctrine the possibility of a just initiation of armed force."[15] Ramsey held that "the distinction between defense and offense is notoriously difficult to make," and, given the consequences of nuclear war, nations should no longer "be required to delay responding to serious threats until the point where the peace has been breached."[16] In arguing this way, Ramsey knew he was denying the historic just-war view and was taking a position more in line with a crusade war ethic. Indeed, he admitted that, "apart from a purely pacifist position, . . . the only theory of war which finds itself obliged to reject what we nowadays call *preventive* war" was the historic just-war position that he considered inadequate.[17] In other words, Ramsey realized that his view on war aligned with crusade and against the historic just-war view.

Because there has been a great deal of division over what just cause means, the line distinguishing just war from crusade has sometimes been so confused that some writers have actually classified historic just war as a form of crusade, while others have classified historic crusade as a form of just war. For example, Harold O. J. Brown, in *War: Four Christian Views*, uses the best-known reason for historic just war to define what he calls "crusade." He says, "We can define crusade as a war that is begun . . . as an attempt to set right a past act," or "a crusade . . . may be defined as a war waged to remedy a past atrocity," or "a crusade . . . is a war fought to undo something that no one had the right to do in the first place."[18] In direct contrast to Brown, John Kelsey, in *Islam and War*, claims that Islamic wars of religious aggression—holy wars, wars of jihad—now should be included in "a new, more inclusive just war tradition" because they pursue a vision of ideal justice interpreted as conquering the world for Islam.[19] In fact, Brown and Kelsey have both interpreted just cause incorrectly, but they have confused the difference between just war and crusade in precisely opposite ways.

---

14. Ibid., 97–98.

15. Paul Ramsey, *Just War: Force and Responsibility* (New York: Scribner, 1968) 61.

16. Ibid., 207.

17. Ibid., 61.

18. Robert G. Clouse, ed., *War: Four Christian Views* (Downers Grove, IL: InterVarsity, 1981) 155–56, 158.

19. John Kelsey, *Islam and War: The Gulf War and Beyond* (Louisville: Westminster John Knox, 1993) 46–55.

Throughout the history of just war tradition, the main body of this tradition has always limited just cause to wrong actually inflicted by one state or nation on another. But this restriction has long been disputed by proponents of justifying war in pursuit of their own notions of improved safety or ideal social order. While there are parallels in the Bible, specific development of classic just-war tradition began among the Greek city-states well before Augustine. For centuries before the rise of Alexander the Great, just cause for war among the Greeks was strictly limited to redressing acts of aggression—defending against or correcting an *actual* wrong inflicted by one state on another. It did not allow war to enlarge territory or to improve the security between states. Then, with the rise of Alexander, followed by Rome, the original, strictly limited view of just cause was severely challenged.

First, Aristotle, who educated and advised Alexander, interpreted just cause to allow attacking others whom he said were destined by nature to be ruled as slaves.[20] Then, with the rise of Rome, the philosopher Cicero (106–43 B.C.), a close friend and advisor to Julius Caesar (100–44 B.C.), declared that "defending" the honor of Rome by conquering weaker nations and spreading Roman civilization to vanquished people was certainly a just cause. In fact, the historian Roland Bainton says Cicero transformed the just-war ethic developed under the Greek city-states "into a code for conquerors—an ethic for empire."[21] Cicero claimed that "a war is . . . undertaken by the ideal state . . . in defense of its honor," and he was sure that Caesar with his legionaries had "gained dominion over the whole world" justly, saying, "Do we not observe that dominion has been granted by nature to everything that is best, to the great advantage of what is weak?"[22] According to Cicero, "The only excuse for going to war is that we [Romans] may live in peace unharmed . . . [and] among our countrymen justice has been observed so conscientiously . . . that generals who conquer nations through war become . . . the patrons of those states. . . . [W]ar for supremacy and glory must start from these motives."[23]

So when Augustine (A.D. 354–430), as a Christian bishop, justified morally legitimate war, he specifically worked to correct the crusading distortion of just cause generated by Aristotle for Alexander the Great and by Cicero for the Roman Empire under Julius Caesar. Augustine, who was schooled in the original meaning of just cause according to Plato and early Greek tradition and who combined their philosophy with careful study of the Bible, restored the original meaning of just cause by again limiting it to a response to actual

---

20. Aristotle, *Politics* 1.1256B.21–26.
21. Roland Bainton, *Christian Attitudes toward War* (Nashville: Abingdon, 1960) 41.
22. Cicero, *De republica* 3.23, 25.
23. Cicero, *De officiis* 1.35, 38.

wrongdoing. He was especially opposed to claiming just cause for wars waged merely in fear of *potential* wrong. Augustine said:

> Those wars are generally defined as just which avenge some injury (*ulcisci injurias*), when a nation or state is to be punished for having failed to make amends for wrong done by its members, or to restore what it has seized unjustly.[24]
>
> Does it displease good men . . . to provoke with voluntary war neighboring kingdoms [though most wicked] who are peaceable and do no wrong [to neighboring kingdoms], as a way to enlarge one's own kingdom? If good men feel this way, they are right and I praise them.[25]
>
> Your wishes are bad, when you desire to conquer a ruler you merely hate or fear.[26]
>
> It is the wrong doing [actual, not potential] of the opposing side which compels the wise man to wage just wars.[27]
>
> When we wage a just war, our adversaries must be sinning [actually, not potentially].[28]

From this survey, it is absolutely clear that just-war tradition that is faithful to its origins is strongly opposed to stretching just cause beyond redressing wrong that is actually suffered. I will now show why we must not expand just cause beyond actual wrongdoing based on the nature of just-war moral theory and on the Bible.

Why Just-War Theory is Incompatible with Crusade

First, consider why the nature of just-war moral theory is completely incompatible with stretching the definition of just cause to allow preventive war—going to war before an enemy actually does something that is considered evil. The problem is that, when just cause is stretched beyond addressing actual wrong to include notions of *ideal* justice, just war becomes an ethic of crusade, and this transformation begins with allowing war to prevent atrocities before they happen. Stretching just cause to allow preventive war renders the nature of just cause for war incompatible with every other *ad bellum* principle in just-war theory. This single change destroys the whole just-war ethic as a moral approach distinct from the ethic of crusade. In just-war moral theory, the *ad bellum* principles must be completely consistent because every one of them must be met before war is allowed. Therefore, if one *ad bellum* principle is incompatible, the whole just-war approach falls apart.

---

24. Augustine, *Quaestiones in Heptateuchum*, 6.10.
25. Augustine, *City of God,* 4.14.
26. Ibid., 4.15.
27. Ibid., 19.7.
28. Ibid., 19.15.

In properly functioning just war theory, the *ad bellum* principles *restrain* decisions about going to war. They serve as barriers that must be overcome and are not incentives driving nations to war. But, if just cause is stretched to allow preventive wars that pursue notions of ideal safety or social order, it is no longer a *barrier* to war but becomes an *incentive* for war. In addition, changing the nature of just cause this way goes far beyond justifying limited war for limited objectives and justifies instigating wars that can never truly end. No ideal can ever be fully realized in this life. Thus, using war to remove all potential evil results in justifying a perpetual state of war. This is the essence of crusade and is utterly incompatible with the nature of just-war theory as a whole.

Furthermore, stretching just cause to allow preventive war causes it to be especially contrary to the *ad bellum* principle of *last resort*, because preventive war aims at stopping *potential* evil, whereas last resort aims at stopping or correcting *actual* evil. Preventive war assumes that conflict is inevitable before it actually occurs, whereas last resort never assumes conflict is inevitable *until* it is actual. In addition, preventive war seeks to act *as soon as* strategically possible, whereas last resort seeks to wait *as long as* strategically possible.

Stretching just cause to allow preventive war would mean that Aristotle and Cicero were right to redefine just war as an ethic of empire and that Augustine was wrong to correct them. Stretching just cause to allow preventive war would mean agreeing with Kelsey that Islamic jihad—Muslim holy war—is a legitimate form of just war. Stretching just cause to allow preventive war would shift the moral question from "Is going to war justified?" (a just-war question) to "Is avoiding war justified?" (a crusade question). Stretching just cause to allow preventive war would mean ceasing to distinguish just war from crusade and claiming that just-war morality allows crusade.

Of course, the pacifist denies that there is any difference between just war and crusade. To the pacifist, all ways of justifying war are bad; if just war is associated with crusade, it only becomes easier to dismiss them both. But just-war ethicists must defend the difference zealously—the just-war ethic is not the crusade ethic. If the barrier is breached in the name of achieving a higher view of social order or greater security between states, the distinction between the just-war ethic and the crusade ethic is destroyed. We then are left with only crusade or pacifism. If this happens, just-war scholars could no longer criticize the morality of terrorism. They would instead employ this very morality and be reduced to quarreling over proper application.

Now consider the biblical case against stretching just cause beyond responding to actual wrong. The Old Testament states that God "holds victory in store for the upright . . . for he guards the course of the just" (Prov 2:7–8). But God also expresses great anger at nations that war with others that have done no actual wrong against them. He condemns Tyre for "disregarding a treaty of brotherhood" (Amos 1:9). He condemns Edom for "pursuing his brother with a sword" and "stifling all compassion" (Amos 1:11). And he condemns the Ammonites for attacking a neighboring nation simply to "enlarge their borders" (Amos 1:13). According to the New Testament, government has the power of the sword to restrain "those who do wrong," and a ruler is defined as "an agent of wrath to bring punishment on the wrongdoer" (Rom 13:3, 4). Biblical justification for rulers' use of the sword addresses actual, not potential, wrongdoing.

It is common knowledge that the Bible, in both Old and New Testaments, includes morally approved wars of crusade—wars of regime change aimed at removing actual and potential evil, wars to establish and advance a higher, more-ideal social order. The war of God's vengeance against the Midianites and Israel's conquest of Canaan are in this category. So also is the battle of Armageddon described in Revelation. But wars of crusade are moral in the Bible only under three conditions. First, God himself orders them directly; they are never allowed at human initiative. Second, God's order is verified by everyone called to participate; wars of crusade are not authorized by men merely alleging to speak for God. Finally, crusades are moral in the Bible only when God himself leads the army in battle; God himself is the ultimate commander, not a human general acting in place of God. In fact, the Bible *never* permits human rulers to initiate wars on their own merely to pursue improved conditions but only to redress wrong actually suffered at the hand of the attackers. In the Bible, human rulers are not allowed to initiate wars for fear of *possible* evil never *actually* perpetrated.

Conclusions about Justifying War with Iraq

How does the above apply to just cause for invading Iraq in 2003? I believe that the war with Iraq was indeed justified, that there was legitimate just cause. But, in explaining how it was justified, President Bush and others included one reason with which I do not agree. The only morally appropriate reason for this war was to enforce the terms of the 1991 surrender. The just cause for the Persian Gulf War (the invasion of Kuwait) still pertained. In just-war terms, continuing a war already justified is not the same as justifying a new war. In moral and political terms, President Bush was not starting from scratch.

But, if this is set aside, the United States' invasion of Iraq in 2003 is very difficult to justify. It was not easy to justify the invasion as a new war without changing the meaning of just cause to allow preventive war in fear of possible evil, transforming just war into crusade. Evidence of an actual connection with terrorists' attacks on the United States would have justified starting a new war, but the evidence was not clear or convincing. An actual declaration of war against the United States would have justified starting a new war, but

Iraq never declared war. Launching an actual attack on the United States would have justified starting a new war, but Iraq never attacked. Intercepting actual plans to attack the United States would have justified starting a new war, but no plans were discovered. Responding to a call for aid in the midst of an actual uprising inside Iraq would have justified joining a new war to help, but no one requested aid.

By the properly understood historic meaning of just cause for just war, invading Iraq merely due to fear of something that never actually happened is what Augustine called a "bad wish."[29] Regime change can result from a properly justified war. But regime change to remove fear of what *may* happen cannot be used to justify war without its becoming a crusade. Excusing wars of aggression for a perceived improvement of circumstances is crusade thinking, which is incompatible with the fundamental nature of just-war moral theory. Fear of what a nation, however wicked, *may* do, though it has not committed any actual wrongdoing against the attacker, is outside the proper meaning of just cause that legitimizes war according to genuine just-war tradition, in secular philosophy and in the Bible.

Based on the above argumentation, I did not agree (and still do not agree) with stretching and thereby changing interpretation of the just-cause principle. However, in just-war terms, I also thought (and still think) that invading Iraq was a totally justified enforcement of the terms of the 1991 surrender. Iraq did actual wrong by invading Kuwait without provocation, and Iraq again did actual wrong by refusing to meet the terms for ending the Persian Gulf War. President Bush had a serious moral duty to enforce the 1991 terms of surrender, even by military means, and acting on this duty did not require justifying a new war. It was a continuation of a war already justified by Iraq's invasion of Kuwait.

I am thankful for the leadership of President Bush, and I am thankful that the wicked regime of Saddam Hussein has been removed. However, while I am thankful for what President Bush did and believe it was entirely justified, I also believe that he was poorly advised in some cases to speak as though he were justifying a new war that could only be allowed by erasing the difference between just war and crusade. I would have advised the president to deny firmly that he was justifying a new war, to remain silent regarding Saddam Hussein's potential for evil, and instead to argue that the United States was invading to enforce terms of surrender that Iraq had accepted to end the Persian Gulf War but had resisted for 12 years. Furthermore, while I disagree with justifying invasion of Iraq as a new war, I do not commend the one hundred Christian ethicists who sent the statement to President Bush denying just cause for preemptive war. If they had in mind a broad definition of *preemptive*,

29. Ibid., 4.15.

the wording of their statement may have been acceptable.[30] But whether it was acceptable or not, issuing the statement at that time in that particular setting implied that invading Iraq was not justified at all, and this was not so. Invading Iraq was completely justified—not as a new war but as the completion of the Persian Gulf War.

Concerning just cause, President Bush was on the right track at the beginning of his State of the Union address in January 2003:

> Twelve years ago, Saddam Hussein faced the prospect of being the last casualty in a war he had started and lost. To spare himself, he agreed to disarm all weapons of mass destruction. [Yet] for the next 12 years, he systematically violated that agreement. He pursued chemical, biological and nuclear weapons even while inspectors were in his country. Nothing to date has restrained him from his pursuit of these weapons: not economic sanctions, not isolation from the civilized world, not even cruise missile strikes on his military facilities.

This was the only warrant needed for invading Iraq. It did serious harm to just-war tradition to say (as did George Weigel, Chuck Colson, and others) that developments in military technology and the rise of rogue states now require changing the definition of just cause to allow war that preempts actual wrongdoing.

Readers should remember that I affirm the morality of the just-war ethic. I believe it is biblical. I believe it is the correct Christian ethic of war. I believe there are indeed times when waging war is morally legitimate. I am profoundly grateful that the world no longer fears the regime of Saddam Hussein in Iraq. And, though I disagree with one explanation of how it was justified, I believe President Bush did the right thing.

---

30. In 1842, Daniel Webster defined *preemptive war* as "a necessity of self-defense . . . instant, overwhelming, leaving no choice of means, and no moment for deliberation" (quoted in D. W. Bowett, *Self-Defense in International Law* [New York: Praeger, 1958] 59). Michael Walzer says that this definition only allows "respond[ing] to an attack *once we had seen it coming* but before we had felt its impact" (*Just and Unjust Wars* [New York, Basic Books, 1977] 74). Walzer goes further by defining *preemptive war* as a response to "states and nations that are already . . . *engaged in harming us* (and who have already harmed us by their threats even if they have not yet inflicted any physical injury)." This requires "a degree of active preparation" that makes "manifest intent to injure . . . a positive danger" but does not include "mere augmentation of power" (ibid., 81, italics his). These definitions are consistent with historic just-war interpretation of just cause because both limit *preemption* to responding to harm perpetrated by an enemy and do not allow war to eliminate fear of what an enemy may do. As defined by Webster or Walzer, preemptive war is consistent with historic just-war tradition, but statements by Bush, the 100 ethicists, and Colson regarding just cause for invading Iraq in 2003 all used the term *preemptive war* in ways that went beyond the use of Webster and Walzer. All applied it to Iraq's attempt to augment its power with weapons of mass destruction and to the Western world's fear of what Saddam Hussein may have done. According to Webster and Walzer, this war can be classified as "preventive," not preemptive, an approach contrary to historic just-war tradition.

Of course, one should not minimize the real sense of fear and vulnerability experienced when dealing with a rogue state. There was good reason to fear what Saddam Hussein could have done with nuclear, biological, or chemical weapons. Americans should not give up trying to make the world a safer, freer, and otherwise more ideal home for the greater human family. But faithful interpretation of just-war tradition has never allowed nor should it ever allow war to be an instrument serving this enterprise. Nothing beyond redressing *actual* wrong inflicted by one state or nation on another can ever be a legitimate just cause for war in the just-war moral tradition.

I fear that anyone who redefines just cause to allow preventive war aimed at regime change to ease fear of potential evil or to enlarge a notion of ideal social order not only fails to understand the true meaning of just cause within just-war tradition but is, in fact, destroying the whole just-war approach by transforming it into an ethic of crusade. We must reject this notion, no matter how good the incentive or spectacular the goal.

Appendix:
Conflicting Statements on Just Cause

On limiting just cause to responding to *actual* wrong done by one state to another	On expanding just cause beyond responding to *actual* wrong done by one state to another
"Thus says the LORD: . . . I will not turn back my wrath from Edom because he attacked his brother with a sword. . . . I will not turn back my wrath from Ammon because he . . . [went to war] to extend his borders." (Amos 1:11–13)	"It is according to nature . . . that war must be used . . . against such men as are by nature intended to be ruled over but resist. That is the kind of warfare which is by nature just." (Aristotle, *Politics* 1.1256B.21–26)
"It is better to suffer wrong than to inflict it." (Plato, *Gorgias* 489)	"War is . . . undertaken by the ideal state . . . in defense of its honor." (Cicero, *De republica* 3.23, 25)
"[War is approved] till the innocent have done justice upon the guilty who plague them." (Plato, *The Republic* 471)	"[Romans] have gained dominion over the whole world. . . . [And] do we not observe that dominion has been granted by nature to everything that is best, to the great advantage of what is weak?" (Cicero, *De republica* 3.23, 25)
"[A ruler] does not bear the sword without cause. He is . . . an agent of wrath to punish the wrongdoer." (Rom 13:4)	"A truer doctrine of the just war cannot avoid asserting in its doctrine the responsibility of a just initiation of armed
"Those wars are generally defined as just which avenge some injury, when a nation or state is to be punished for having failed to make amends for wrong done by its	

members, or to restore what it has seized unjustly." (Augustine, *Quaest. Hept.* 6.10)

"Does it displease good men . . . to provoke with voluntary war neighboring kingdoms [though most wicked] who are peaceable and do no wrong [to neighboring kingdoms], as a way to enlarge one's own kingdom? If good men feel this way, they are right and I praise them." (Augustine, *City of God* 4.14)

"Your wishes are bad, when you desire to conquer a ruler you merely hate or fear." (Augustine, *City of God* 4.15)

"It is wrong doing of the opposing side which compels the wise man to wage just wars." (Augustine, *City of God* 19.7)

"When we wage a just war, our adversaries must be sinning." (Augustine, *City of God* 19.15)

"A just cause is . . . namely, that those who are attacked, should be attacked because they deserve it on account of some fault." (Aquinas, *Summa Theologica* II.II.Q.40.1)

"Preventive war is . . . unjust . . . [and] must therefore be condemned, whatever the circumstances that are alleged to condition its initiation." (Robert Tucker, *The Just War: A Study in Contemporary American Doctrine*, 15)

"*The Catechism of the Catholic Church* limits just cause to cases in which 'the damage by the aggressor on the nation or community of nations [is] lasting, grave and certain.'" (Wilton Gregory, "Letter to President Bush")

"As Christian ethicists, we share a common moral presumption against a preemptive war on Iraq by the United States." (Statement by 100 Christian Ethicists)

"I fear anyone who changes just cause to allow preventive war aimed at regime

force." (Paul Ramsey, *Just War: Force and Responsibility*, 61)

"Nations cannot be required to delay responding to serious threats until the point where the peace has been breached." (Paul Ramsey, *Just War: Force and Responsibility*, 207)

"I shall argue . . . Islamic tradition suggests that holy war . . . [should] lead to a new, more inclusive just war tradition." (John Kelsey, *Islam and War*, 44, 55)

"War on terrorism will not be won on the defensive . . . the only path to safety is the path of action. . . . Our security . . . will require preemptive action." (President Bush, "Graduation Speech at West Point")

"Historically, the doctrine's requirement of just cause has been defined as responding to an attack. . . . But I think this reflects too narrow an understanding of just war. . . . Christians can and should support a preemptive strike . . . to prevent an imminent attack." (Charles Colson, "Just War in Iraq," 72)

"New weapons capabilities and outlaw or rogue states require a development of the concept of defense against aggression. . . . Can we not say that, in the hands of certain kinds of states, the mere possession of weapons of mass destruction constitutes an aggression?" (George Weigel, "Moral Clarity in a Time of War," 25)

"I think just cause can be a just cause of war if the regime is evil enough." (Richard Land, *SBC Life* [April, 2003] 8)

"The dangers of our time must be confronted actively and forcefully, before we see them again in our skies and in our cities." (President Bush, "Remarks to the American Enterprise Institute")

change to ease fear of potential evil or to enlarge some notion of ideal social order not only fails to understand the true meaning of just cause within just war tradition but is, in fact, destroying the whole just war approach by transforming it into an ethic of crusade." (Daniel Heimbach, "Remarks at Denver," 7 February 2004)

"I would argue that true international justice is defined as the equal claim of all persons [individuals, not states], whatever their political location or condition, to having coercive force deployed in their behalf if they are victims of one of the many horrors attendant upon radical political instability. . . . This is an ideal of international justice whose time has come." (Jean Elshtain, *Just War against Terror: The Burden of American Power in a Violent World* [New York: Basic Books, 2003] 168)

CHAPTER 6

Noncombatant Immunity and the War on Terrorism

TONY PFAFF

*The views expressed in this paper are those of the author and do not reflect
the official policy or position of the Department of Defense of the U.S. Government.*

Shortly after the United States began conducting military operations in
Afghanistan, an article appeared in the *Los Angeles Times* claiming that the
military's overwhelming concern for avoiding noncombatant casualties ham-
pered its ability to find Osama Bin Laden and end the war quickly. The article
pointed out that this paradoxically lengthened the war and led to more noncombatant casualties.[1] The military has not only been criticized for excessive
concern, however, but also for excessive carelessness. After the accidental
bombing of an Afghan wedding party, many commentators accused U.S.
forces of not taking enough risks to avoid this sort of tragedy. Furthermore,
some questioned the justice of a war in which, by some reports, more Afghan
civilians were killed by U.S. air strikes than American civilians were killed in
the terrorist attacks that precipitated them.

In the wake of September 11, 2001, many are concerned that the United
States is using excessive force and disregarding the legal and moral norms of international politics. They argue that it is inappropriate to treat this conflict as
a war and would prefer to see terrorists pursued as criminals, as they have been
in the past.[2] Prior to September 11, 2001, the war on terror was fought primarily by law enforcement agencies. Even after the attack on the USS *Cole*, teams
of FBI agents, not light infantry divisions, were dispatched to Yemen to pursue the terrorists. And while the United States has launched military strikes in
the past to retaliate against or destroy terrorist facilities, the strikes have for
the most part been carried out in such a way as to avoid, though not always successfully, noncombatant casualties. However, the invasion of Afghanistan represents a *qualitatively* different approach. There, military force was not only

---

1. William Arkin, "Fear of Civilian Deaths May Have Undermined Effort," *Los Angeles Times*,
January 16, 2002.

2. Michael Howard, "What's in a Name," *Foreign Affairs* (January/February 2002) 8–13.

used to attack terrorists and the people who support them, but it was also used in a way that noncombatants were knowingly, though unintentionally, harmed.

These two approaches, which I will refer to as the "criminal" and "war" models, respectively, represent two distinct practical and ethical ways of conceptualizing the use of force by the state. Each evolved within a particular context and in response to a particular threat, but both represent ways states use force to maintain civil order and prevent violations of their political sovereignty and territorial integrity. While I do not imply a neat dichotomy between the two approaches, the criminal model most often applies when civil order is threatened, and the war model applies when civil society itself is threatened.

The most salient difference between the two is the degree of allowance for civilian casualties. In the criminal model, police are not permitted to engage in courses of action in which innocent civilians will knowingly be harmed, but soldiers are permitted to do this in war. In the criminal model, the protection police owe civilians is nearly absolute, but in the war model, soldiers have greater permission to put civilians at risk. Police are obligated to use the least force possible; soldiers are obligated to use the greatest force permissible. This may seem to be a subtle difference, but when it is applied to the current war on terrorism, it yields a difficult ethical problem.

If terrorists are simple criminals, then acting in a way that will lead to civilian deaths, even if unintentional, is morally impermissible. However, in the post–September 11 environment, limiting the ability to respond to this threat in a way that may endanger civilians of enemy nations seems to put the lives of one's own innocent civilians needlessly at risk. Thus, the U.S. government's obligation to protect its own citizens comes into direct conflict with the more general obligation not to harm innocents. Instead of being a true moral dilemma, however, this ethical problem arises out of a misunderstanding of the kind of threat certain terrorists pose.

Political and technological developments of the late 20th and early 21st centuries have enabled terrorists to engage in what is known as fourth-generation or asymmetrical warfare, in which small, often nonnational groups represent a disproportionate threat. These developments thus pose a new kind of threat that cannot be neatly categorized as either criminal or enemy. But by borrowing from both of these models, I will show that, while pursuing terrorists under the criminal model is morally preferable, certain terrorists under certain conditions represent the kind of threat that permits pursuing them under the war model.

Noncombatant Immunity

It is a nearly universally accepted moral principle that it is wrong to harm innocent people intentionally. However, states are obligated to protect their citizens from harm, and individuals vested with this responsibility sometimes find it necessary to risk violating the moral principle in order to uphold the civil principle. Soldiers sometimes must attack enemy military targets located near civilian residences. Police sometimes put bystanders' lives at risk when they pursue criminals. The application of these principles is further complicated by the fact that soldiers intentionally kill enemy soldiers, many of whom are innocent of any act of aggression, and police sometimes pursue and use force against suspects who are innocent.

The Bible says little directly regarding the protection of noncombatants in war. In fact, many passages in the Old Testament seem to argue against it. "However, in the cities of the nations the LORD your God is giving you as an inheritance, do not leave alive anything that breathes" (Deut 20:16, NIV). This seems counterintuitive to many Christians, who note that the Bible also proclaims the sanctity of human life. While it is beyond the scope of this essay to reconcile fully the above passage from Deuteronomy with the absolute value of human life, it is important to distinguish between wars that God personally authorizes and wars authorized by human authorities. Even though God had his reasons for his instructions to the Israelites, he also has instructions for us and how we are to regard human life.

Most secular philosophers argue that the state's obligation to protect its citizens derives from the right to life, a value that conforms to and arguably derives from the Christian value of the sanctity of human life. Furthermore, both secular and Christian thought justifies the use of force by the state in order to preserve the lives and well-being of citizens. As Paul notes in Romans 13, Christians must submit to the authority of the state, which, on God's behalf, does not "wield the sword" for no reason but to punish wrongdoers. "But if you do wrong, be afraid, for he [the authority] does not bear the sword for nothing. He is God's servant, an agent of wrath to bring punishment on the wrongdoer" (Rom 13:4, NIV). This passage seems sufficient to justify the force used by the state to protect the lives and well-being of its citizens. But the problem remains—what should the government do when protecting its own citizens puts other citizens at risk?

In the context of war, this issue is resolved in the distinction between combatants and noncombatants, which is roughly analogous to the distinction between the guilty and the innocent. But this distinction is imperfect. Most soldiers are not guilty of the crime of war, though some civilians are. So even though soldiers do not bear moral guilt for war, they do represent the means by which the responsible parties carry out their threat. For this reason, they may be targeted, while noncombatants, regardless of their stance toward the war, may not be. The restriction against targeting civilians is called "noncombatant immunity" and is central to Christian thinking on just war. Without this constraint on military necessity, there would be no barrier to total war, and the Christian value of the sanctity of human life would be fatally under-mined. In a total war, no particular target and no particular weapon would be prohibited. Thus, it seems contradictory to commit oneself to the sanctity of human life and then reject the right to life of civilians in an enemy country simply because of where they reside. However, this injunction does not pre-clude taking action, even when it is likely or certain that noncombatants will be harmed. But this harm must be limited.

As St. Thomas Aquinas notes, the prohibition against killing the innocent is absolute. Quoting Exod 23:7, he states, "It is written, 'Innocent and just per-son thou shalt not put to death.'"[3] But he also notes that killing in war is per-mitted, though not without restrictions.[4] One restriction worth noting here is the Golden Rule, "So in everything, do to others what you would have them do to you, for this sums up the Law and the Prophets" (Matt 7:12, NIV). Aquinas then debates whether this principle can be used as an objection to conducting ambushes in war. "Now our enemy is our neighbor. Therefore, since no man wishes ambushes or deceptions to be prepared for himself, it seems that no one ought to carry on war by laying ambushes."[5] Ultimately, he accepts the Golden Rule as a constraint, but he dismisses the "objection" on the grounds that ambushing does not require doing something that one does not want to undergo (in this case, lying). He further notes that the thing we would not want done to us (lying) would always be impermissible.

It is beyond the scope of this paper to explicate Aquinas's thinking on de-ception fully, but applying the same process to noncombatant immunity, we do arrive at meaningful restrictions. Take, for example, the Allies' bombing in World War II. When bombing targets in France, the Allies engaged in preci-sion bombing against German targets, keeping civilian casualties to a mini-mum. When they bombed targets in Germany, they often bombed entire cities, without regard for noncombatant casualties. By considering the Allies' citizens' lives to be more valuable than German lives, it appears that the Al-lies' bombing practices violated the Golden Rule.[6]

With the importance of noncombatant immunity firmly established as a critical part of Christian just-war thinking, international law prohibiting sol-diers from intentionally killing citizens of enemy states if they are not directly involved in the fighting makes moral as well as legal sense.[7] In this view, citi-zens are immune from harm because they do not represent an immediate

---

3. Thomas Aquinas, *Summa theologica* II.II.Q.64, a6.

4. Ibid., Q. 40.

5. Ibid., Q. 40.a3.

6. John Finnis, "Catholic Natural Law Tradition," in *The Ethics of War and Peace* (ed. Terry Nardin; Princeton: Princeton University Press, 1996) 27.

7. 1923 Hague Rules of Aerial Warfare, Article 22; 1949 Geneva Convention IV, Article 3.

threat to the ability of military forces to prosecute the war. Because they do not represent an immediate threat, their deaths are not *necessary* in order to achieve the goals of the war. Thus, in the context of fighting wars, the law and morality of war typically distinguishes between noncombatants and combatants. Noncombatants may never be targeted, and combatants may be targeted. When targeting combatants, however, noncombatant casualties may be permitted given the constraint of proportionality. These distinctions are necessary because soldiers, as St. Ambrose famously pointed out, are moral equals, and though they represent a threat, they are innocent of any act of aggression, whereas some civilians are guilty of it.[8] David, Ambrose notes, accepted Abner as a moral equal for the way he waged war, independent of the moral correctness of the war. Furthermore, David lamented the treacherous nature of Joab's actions against Abner, which he viewed as worthy of punishment. "May the LORD repay the evildoer according to his evil deeds" (2 Sam 3:39, NIV). This reading further suggests that, when soldiers are no longer a threat, such as soldiers who have surrendered or are wounded and no longer capable of fighting, they are entitled to immunity from harm. Further, some civilians, such as munitions factory workers at work, because they are engaged in an activity that is logically inseparable from fighting the war, are subject to harm.[9]

Because police do not typically fight wars, it may seem odd to discuss noncombatant immunity in this context; but, because they also deal with threats to the peace, similar notions apply. For police, only civilians who have somehow demonstrated themselves to be a violent threat may be killed. And even then, police must make reasonable attempts to apprehend them first.[10] Thus, in the context of the pursuit of criminals we can make a distinction between (1) innocent civilians, who are not a violent threat and are not subject to harm and (2) suspects, who may have committed a crime but who must be given the opportunity to surrender first. In the second category, police may use deadly force only after they have offered the suspect a chance to surrender and then only to prevent the suspect from fleeing or to stop someone from committing a violent crime. Typically, police do not use deadly force against nonviolent criminals.

Pursuing Criminals and Fighting Enemies

Police and soldiers are obligated to take risks in order to fulfill their respective functions. But because this often involves the use of deadly force, they sometimes put others at risk as well. Their functions, however, limit whom

---

8. P. Christopher, *The Ethics of War and Peace: An Introduction to Legal and Moral Issues* (2nd ed.; Trenton, NJ: Prentice Hall, 1999) 25, quoting Ambrose, *Duties of the Clergy*, 2.7.33, p. 49.

9. Michael Walzer, *Just and Unjust Wars* (New York: Basic Books, 1992) 138–75.

10. John Kleinig, *The Ethics of Policing* (Cambridge: Cambridge University Press, 1996) 110.

they may put at risk and the kinds of risks they may take. *By enforcing laws, police maintain peace; by fighting wars, soldiers establish it.* But whether enforcing laws or fighting wars, the only morally appropriate use of deadly force is to establish or maintain a just peace.[11] For the soldier, this most often means establishing peace between the society he serves and other societies; for the police officer, this most often means detaining and, under certain circumstances, killing someone who represents an immediate threat to the peace that the society currently enjoys.[12]

If we are going to argue that the application of military force differs depending on whether a state of peace exists, we must be clear about what this state looks like in order for this idea to have any practical application. First, a future peace must be more secure than the peace before the war was fought. This means that it must be a peace in which parties in conflict can and want to resolve their differences nonviolently. Thus, while an absence of fighting is a necessary condition for peace, it is not sufficient as a permanent solution. Parties in conflict must have available to them peaceful means to resolve conflicts of interest. This not only means that, at the end of a war, the warring parties must be able to coexist peacefully but that the citizens within each state must be able to do so as well, and this requires a just and stable political system.

Establishing political stability is dependent on the restoration of civic peace, which is the kind of peace necessary to attain and secure fundamental human goods, including security and distributive justice. The war convention includes a set of strictures about combat; it insists that means must be proportional to ends and that combatants must be distinguished from noncombatants.[13] The purpose of these strictures is to establish the conditions necessary for civic peace and, once these conditions are met, to preserve it.[14] The effort to establish peace between states means that there are moral limits on the use of force, but it also means that the foreseen but unintended deaths of noncombatants are permissible. However, once peace is established, these deaths are no longer justified because they undermine, rather than preserve,

---

11. Walzer, *Just and Unjust Wars*, 121. It is important to note that, in both contexts, what justifies the use of force is correcting or preventing an injustice. The state of affairs that leads to injustice is unstable. Thus if force only returns the state of affairs to its original state, it has served no moral purpose. Therefore, when considering whether to permit soldiers or police to resort to force, one must consider how this will result in a more stable peace in which injustices are less likely to occur.

12. See my *Peacekeeping and the Just War Tradition* (Carlisle, PA: Strategic Studies Institute, U.S. Army War College, 2000).

13. Jean Bethke Elshtain, "International Justice as Equal Regard and the Use of Force," *Ethics and International Affairs* 17 (Fall 2003) 65–67.

14. Ibid.

the establishment of civic peace, which is necessary if the just aims of the war are to be achieved.

Therefore, this set of conditions must be present for a state of peace to exist:

1. The enemy must be defeated or contained.
2. Institutions necessary for law enforcement must be functioning, including police, courts, and prisons.
3. These institutions must be credible; that is, people must be willing to rely on them to resolve disputes.

Because the use of force represents, to some degree, an absence of peace, it makes no sense to use any more force than is necessary to maintain or establish peace. This means that police are obligated to use the *least force possible* so that they do not disrupt the peace any more than is necessary to restore it. Soldiers, on the other hand, are permitted to use the most force possible, given the restrictions of the law and morality of war, because their aim is to establish a peace that does not currently exist.[15] The following example from the Los Angeles riots in 1992 demonstrates this difference. "Police officers responded to a domestic dispute, accompanied by Marines. They had just gone up to the door when two shotgun birdshot rounds were fired through the door, hitting the officers. One yelled 'cover me!' to the Marines, who then laid down a heavy base of fire."[16] This example is instructive because it shows that, even in the same situation, police and members of the military have different understandings of how much force is minimally necessary. Even though they had been attacked, the police did not feel that they or anyone else were in immediate danger. In their view, it would have been better to ascertain if there were nonviolent ways to resolve the issue. As far as the Marines were concerned, they were under fire; thus, it was morally appropriate to respond with any degree of force that eliminated the threat while not putting civilians at any more risk than necessary. The two different reactions were due to the way each perceived the threat. For the police, the threat was a criminal whom they had to apprehend in order to minimize the disruption to the peace that the crime represented. The Marines perceived the threat to be a direct attack on themselves. Because the use of violence represents a further disruption of the peace, police always attempt to use the *least force possible*. But Marines are trained to defeat enemies, who must be killed if there is to be peace. They always attempt to use the *most force permissible*.

---

15. See my *Peacekeeping*, 17–18.

16. James D. Delk, *Fires and Furies: The L.A. Riots, What Really Happened* (Palm Springs, CA: ETC, 1995), quoted in Christopher M. Schnaubelt, "Lessons in Command and Control from the Los Angeles Riots," *Parameters* (Summer, 1997) 1.

This is not to say that police are prohibited from taking risks that *may* place civilian lives in danger. For example, police are permitted to engage in high-speed pursuits even though these pursuits have resulted in accidents in which innocent bystanders have been killed. But police are not permitted to engage in these pursuits or any other activity if they know civilians will be killed or seriously injured,[17] whereas there are many conditions under which actions of this sort would be permissible for soldiers. Thus, if it were permissible to pursue terrorists only as criminals, it would never be permissible to do so in a way that civilians would knowingly be harmed.[18]

This is not to say that there are no limits to the danger in which soldiers may place noncombatants. The deadly force that circumstances sometimes require soldiers to employ is justified by the fact that their role is to defend innocents against aggression, thus fulfilling in part the moral obligation states have to protect their citizens. But if the defense of innocents is a moral imperative, then the *intentional* taking of innocent life must be morally prohibited. Thus, while soldiers have the positive duty to protect their own civilians, they also have the negative moral duty not to harm civilians of other nations intentionally.

By virtue of accepting their role, soldiers obligate themselves to accept risks that noncombatants do not.[19] However, this obligation is limited by the sometimes-competing obligation to accomplish missions that were properly assigned. If there were no limits of this sort, then moral constraints on the use of force would undermine the ability of soldiers to accomplish their missions. For example, it would make the use of human shields attractive to the enemy because the likelihood of harm to civilians would preclude any military operations.[20] Thus, a prohibition against any civilian deaths would encourage immoral behavior on the part of the enemy and render the obligation to defend innocent life illogical and morally self-defeating. Thus, soldiers are not obligated to take so much risk that the mission will fail, nor are they obligated to take so much risk that their unit will not be able to continue the war effort.[21]

Because the amount of risk soldiers are obligated to take is limited, it is then permissible for them to engage in courses of action in which they may unintentionally but knowingly harm civilians. But this liberty has its limits. Judgments about what sort of risk may lead to mission failure are notoriously

---

17. Kleinig, *Ethics of Policing*, 118–22. See also my *Peacekeeping*, 13–20.

18. Kleinig, *Ethics of Policing*, 118–22.

19. James M. Dubik, "Human Rights, Command Responsibility, and Walzer's Just War Theory," *Philosophy and Public Affairs* 11 (1982) 355.

20. This has been, in fact, a feature of the Taliban strategy against the United States. By placing military equipment and other military targets in the vicinity of civilian populations, they have hoped to compromise U.S. attacks by turning public opinion against the U.S.

21. Christopher, *The Ethics of War and Peace*, 93.

difficult to make. Thus, if the military's ethical obligations ended with ensuring the success of the mission, the potential for abuse would fatally undermine the entire concept of noncombatant immunity because even well-meaning soldiers would be hard pressed to determine reasons to take the safety of noncombatants into account.

Even this permission has its limits, defined by the doctrine of double effect, one of the more restrictive features of the just-war tradition. This doctrine was first formulated by St. Thomas Aquinas as a response to St. Augustine's moral prohibition against self-defense and recognizes that, in the pursuit of a moral good such as self-defense, there may be unintended but foreseeable harms.[22] It also recognizes that it is important not to allow the moral harms one may commit to undermine the moral good one is pursuing.

According to this doctrine, it is permissible to perform a good act that has bad consequences if other specific conditions hold. These conditions are: (1) the bad effect is proportional to the desired military objective; (2) the bad effect is unintended; (3) the bad effect is not a direct means to achieving the good effect; and (4) the soldiers take actions to minimize the foreseeable bad effects resulting from any course of action, even if it means accepting an increased risk to themselves. I will return to the application of this doctrine to the war on terror below.

Criminals, Enemies, and Terrorists

The criminal and war models provide members of law enforcement and military organizations with the moral frameworks within which they may judge practical plans, practices, and methods for confronting different kinds of threats. Most of the disagreement regarding the pursuit of terrorists is over which, if either, model is the most appropriate to apply. The difference between the two models is how each perceives the threat to which it is responding. Resolving the disagreement will depend on determining the precise kind of threat the terrorists represent.

There is a great deal of debate regarding the best definition of terrorism. The Federal Bureau of Investigation (FBI) defines terrorism as "the unlawful use of force or violence against persons or property to intimidate or coerce a government, the civilian population, or any segment thereof, in furtherance of political or social objectives."[23] If we accept this definition, then it is clear that terrorism is a crime, at least to the extent that it is a violation of the laws of the states in which these acts take place. But for it to be permissible for military or law enforcement officials to harm noncombatants, acts of terrorism must be

---

22. Ibid., 52.
23. Code of Federal Regulations, 28 CFR §0.85.

defined more broadly than mere crimes; they must be defined as "acts of war." This is an important point because it suggests that, while the current response to al-Qaeda may be justifiable, it may not always be appropriate. Some terrorists are more like criminals, and to pursue them as enemies risks doing more moral harm than good.

Some critics reject the idea that the current terrorist threat represents a new kind of security concern. In a recent book on the war on terrorism, former career diplomat Charles Hill claims that the idea that this is a new kind of conflict is a myth that must be dispelled. He points out correctly that many nations have been fighting terrorism, including Islamic terrorism, for a number of years. He also accurately notes that this war consists mostly of the assassination of government officials and the hijacking and destruction of commercial means of transportation, resulting in the deliberate killing of civilians when they are most vulnerable.[24] But what Hill fails to observe is that there is a qualitative, not simply quantitative, difference between even the most destructive of these events, such as the bombing of PanAm flight 103 over Lockerbie, Scotland, in which more than 300 people died, and the events of September 11, 2001. In the airplane bombing, terrorists destroyed a commercial aircraft in order to instill fear in a target population and thereby force political change. On September 11, terrorists used modern communications and civilian aircraft to coordinate and conduct a direct attack on the political, military, and economic institutions that are indispensable to the United States' exercise of its political sovereignty and preservation of its territorial integrity. This ability to threaten political sovereignty and territorial integrity makes the current war on terror *qualitatively* different from earlier wars. In what Hill describes as the "first war on terrorism," the terrorists simply were not capable of waging war, only of committing crimes. This changed on September 11, 2001.

What has changed is that technology has greatly increased the effectiveness of weapons and the speed and distance over which forces can move and communicate. Additionally, globalization has made many nations of the world vulnerable in new ways. More powerful weapons, better global communication systems, and greater opportunity to divert nonweapon technologies to destructive ends have dramatically increased the ability of small groups to pursue their goals, regardless of the political support they may have.[25] The ability to leverage these developments to wage war makes the threat terrorists represent disproportionate to their size or power base. By waging this kind of asymmet-

---

24. Charles Hill, "A Herculean Task: The Myth and Reality of Arab Terrorism," in *The Age of Terror* (ed. Strobe Talbott and Nayan Chanda; New York: Basic Books, 2001) 83–85.

25. Thomas Homer-Dixon, "The Rise of Complex Terrorism," *Foreign Policy*, January/February 2002, 54.

ric warfare, terrorists can do more than instill fear in the civilian population; they can also attack and destroy the institutions that administer and defend the United States or any other state. The terrorists' well-publicized attempt to obtain weapons of mass destruction underscores this point.[26]

Thus, while terrorists certainly are criminals, and much of their activity, depending on the group, is best regarded as criminal, their ability to wage asymmetric warfare suggests that some may be more appropriately regarded as enemies, given the magnitude of the threat they represent. In previous periods, the power to wage war on a state rested solely in the hands of other states. Now it can also rest in the hands of a few dozen highly motivated people with cell phones and access to the Internet. This means that certain terrorist organizations represent a *new category* of threat that is characterized by an ability and willingness not only to terrorize civilians but to violate the political sovereignty and territorial integrity of sovereign nations in order to achieve their political ends. Their capabilities distinguish them from mere criminals. This makes resolving the moral tension created by treating criminals as enemies difficult and complex.

In view of these changes, both the criminal and war models are inadequate to account fully for the moral obligations, permissions, and prohibitions that law enforcement officials and members of the military have regarding innocents and noncombatants in the conduct of the war on terror. They are inadequate because the threats they are designed to respond to are not the kind of threat represented by the terrorists. However, in determining our moral obligations toward noncombatants, we do not need to develop new concepts because terrorists are both criminals and enemies.

Pursuing Enemies:
The War on Terrorism

In response to the seriousness of the threat that the al-Qaeda terrorists represent, some, such as noted strategist Ralph Peters, argue that even normal moral restraints should be ignored in order to pursue the terrorists. Peters further argues that, in the wake of the attacks of September 11, 2001, any concern about noncombatant casualties that constrains military action is best considered misguided "diplomatic table manners" and an allegiance to "outdated conventions."[27] He even argues that the intentional targeting of noncombatants in many cases is necessary to successfully wage the war against terror. While this seems extreme, it is reasonable to question past prohibitions on

---

26. For excellent resources regarding fourth-generation warfare, see http://www.d-n-i.net/ second_level/fourth_generation_warfare.htm.

27. Ralph Peters, "Civilian Casualties: No Apology Needed," *The Wall Street Journal*, July 25, 2002, A10.

harming noncombatants in light of the past permissions and prohibitions on the pursuit of terrorists.

Many other critics of the United States' war against terrorism would prefer, in the words of Prof. Michael Howard, "a police operation conducted under the auspices of the United Nations on behalf of the international community as a whole, against a criminal conspiracy whose members should be hunted down and brought before an international court, where they would receive a fair trial and, if found guilty, be awarded an appropriate sentence."[28] These critics see a disconnect between U.S. claims to value law, order, and stability in the world and what they consider a blatant disregard for these ideals in pursuit of the terrorists.[29]

Howard likens the current conflict with al-Qaeda to conflicts that the British fought to protect their interests in Malaysia, Cyprus, Palestine, and Ireland.[30] In these conflicts, which the British called "emergencies," police and intelligence services were given "exceptional powers" and were reinforced by the armed forces when necessary. "If force had to be used, it was at a minimum level and so far as possible did not interrupt the normal tenor of civilian life."[31] Howard makes several important points. The current war against terrorists is not the first time a major power has faced a smaller and potentially dangerous adversary. He is also correct to point out that it will be necessary to use the combined efforts of police, intelligence, and military forces in order to prevent al-Qaeda from achieving its goals. The military will not be able to do it alone. Furthermore, Howard is right to say that it is important to use the minimum force necessary in pursuing these terrorists. But words such as "necessary" and "possible" are notoriously vague, and one may plausibly argue, given the different senses that "necessary" can have, that the United States is in fact conforming to the above criteria.

The terrorists who struck the United States on September 11, 2001, have the intent and capacity to violate the political sovereignty of the United States in ways not previously experienced. Thus they are, in the sense discussed above, enemies. However, their acts of violence do not represent an act of aggression by a state, and thus for the United States to commit an act of aggression against another state is problematic. Killing innocent citizens of another state is even more dubious.

---

28. Howard, "What's in a Name?" 9.

29. It is worthwhile also to ask to what extent may the United States, in accordance with the new doctrine emphasizing preemptive strikes, commit acts of aggression by violating the political sovereignty and territorial integrity of other nations in pursuit of the terrorists. But to limit the scope of this essay, I will not address this question.

30. Ibid., 8.

31. Ibid.

If the criminal model were the appropriate model to apply, then it would never be permissible either to attack a sovereign state or to kill, even unintentionally, the innocent citizens of another state. Criminals may only be pursued within the framework of law. As Noam Chomsky, another critic of U.S. efforts, points out, "When IRA bombs were set off in London, there was no call to bomb West Belfast. . . . Rather, steps were taken to apprehend the criminals, and efforts were made to deal with what lay behind the resort to terror." Chomsky also wonders why there were no calls to bomb Idaho and Michigan in response to the bombing of the Federal Center in Oklahoma. [32] In this view, to pursue the terrorists under the war model would itself be an act of terror.

But Chomsky's objection misses the point. The al-Qaeda terrorists do not only attempt to achieve political goals by means of instilling terror in civilian populations. They have also demonstrated the capability of destroying and willingness to destroy the institutions that, in Howard's words, preserve the "normal tenor of civilian life" and that are the means by which a nation exercises its sovereignty and preserves its territorial integrity. Whether or not they actually achieve this goal is irrelevant; the fact that it is their goal and that they have the capability of carrying it out is what makes them enemies.

It may not be permissible to pursue every terrorist group as though it were an enemy. To warrant a response under the war model, capability and intent—evidenced by actual acts of terror—of violating the political sovereignty and territorial integrity of a particular nation are both necessary and sufficient conditions. If a particular terrorist group does not meet one of these conditions, it is not permissible to pursue it under the war model. The problem, of course, is that the interconnectedness of the world today makes it difficult to determine when this is the case.

Britain should not, by any estimation, bomb West Belfast, nor did the United States have the right to launch military strikes against Idaho, the home of the perpetrator of the Oklahoma bombing. This is the point at which the war model breaks down in the context of the war on terrorism. The citizens of West Belfast are British citizens. The citizens of Idaho are U.S. citizens. States have a positive obligation to protect their own citizens. It would be irrational and self-defeating, therefore, to violate this obligation in order to uphold it. Thus, within one's own borders, it would be immoral to pursue terrorists in a way that would knowingly harm civilians.[33]

---

32. Noam Chomsky, *9-11* (New York: Seven Stories, 2001) 24.

33. A possible counterexample may be if terrorists were about to detonate a weapon of mass destruction and authorities could only prevent this by bombing the neighborhood where the terrorists placed the weapon. In this case, the threat represented by the weapon *may* justify actions of this sort. See my *Peacekeeping*, 16–17.

However, terrorists operate outside the borders of the United States, sometimes with the support of other states but often without any support. When a state actively supports terrorists who commit acts of aggression, the state is also guilty of acts of aggression. Therefore, it may be attacked, and its citizens may be subject to unintentional harm. In this case, terrorists are state actors, and the state bears responsibility for their actions.

But many terrorist organizations operate in a number of states, often outside government control. This complicates matters because, as nonstate actors, terrorist organizations can make use of state resources without the state's bearing any responsibility. Similarly, the actions of the terrorists subject the noncombatant populations to unintentional harm in the areas in which they operate.

It is important to remember that noncombatants are not subject to unintentional harm because they somehow deserve it. Instead, they are subject to unintentional harm because they are citizens of a state against whose act of aggression the government must move in defense. The actions of the aggressor state have put them in harm's way.

However, this permission to risk civilian injury is severely restricted. It would be self-defeating to harm populations in states in which terrorists operate with impunity, because this act could compel the states to which these populations belong to initiate a just war *against* the United States. The moral obligation of states to protect their citizens from harm would compel them to defend their populations against unintentional but inevitable harm perpetrated by U.S. forces in the pursuit of terrorists. Thus, pursuing this sort of policy is morally irrational because it has the potential to widen the conflict unnecessarily and make pursuit of the terrorists more difficult.

For this reason, I conclude that it will *always* be preferable to pursue terrorists under the criminal model, because this model represents the least disruption of the peace and the least risk to noncombatants. But this restriction will have limits. Pursuing terrorists under the criminal model may pose the least risk to foreign noncombatants, but to the extent that this restriction impedes efforts to eliminate the terrorist threat, it poses the most threat to friendly noncombatants. Some states may not cooperate with terrorists, but they also may not cooperate with efforts to prevent terrorists from carrying out attacks. This can make it difficult to prevent terrorists from conducting future operations. While it is beyond the scope of this essay to explore fully the *jus ad bellum* implications of the war on terror, it is important to recall that, in war, the need to minimize the risk to noncombatants is limited by the need to defeat the enemy. Thus, in places where cooperation does not exist, as in Taliban-controlled Afghanistan, it is permissible to pursue terrorists in a way that may harm noncombatants; although, as noted earlier, this harm must be limited by the doctrine of double effect.

The Doctrine of Double Effect and Proportionality

As the *Los Angeles Times*'s article points out, "Some charge that obsessive attention to safeguarding civilians has undermined military effectiveness, fueled inter-service rivalries and hurt morale. Worse, these officials say, it has increased the likelihood of Al-Qaeda chieftains escaping because of its pervasive influence on U.S. strategy."[34] While this concern is legitimate, the fact that military leaders permitted fear of civilian casualties to so adversely affect morale as well as operations suggests that there is a great deal of confusion over what is morally obligated. What is needed is a modified proportionality.

Proportionality

The doctrine of double effect first requires that the harm done be proportional to the good achieved. This means first that the destruction done to civilian lives and property must be less than the good done by destroying the military target. It may seem on the surface that it is this provision that potential adversaries may use to limit U.S. and allied courses of action. By hiding among civilians, key leaders can avoid harm and thus continue their own operations because, even with precision weapons, some noncombatants will be harmed. This poses a serious problem in the context of asymmetric warfare, in which people are more important than equipment. Cell phones and other means of communication can be easily replaced. Conventional explosives and even some kinds of weapons of mass destruction are neither difficult to obtain nor difficult to conceal. What are more difficult to replace are people who have the willingness to use and capability of using these things in order to conduct terrorist operations. Because of this, Peters and other commentators argue that, while noncombatant deaths are regrettable, the United States should pursue courses of action without regard for civilian safety. What matters is winning the war at any cost, regardless of who pays.

Unfortunately, a commitment to the total war that Peters recommends not only violates the biblical proscriptions (see 2 Sam 3:39); it also violates the contractual obligation of members of law enforcement and the military to uphold treaties that the United States has signed,[35] as well as the moral commitment they make to the founding principles of this country, which recognize equal rights to life and liberty. However, even though disregarding the idea of noncombatant immunity is not an option if a state is to maintain its other moral and contractual commitments, it is still worthwhile to question whether the United States' application of this idea is appropriate in the current context.

---

34. Arkin, "Fear of Civilian Deaths May Have Undermined Effort."
35. Field Manual 27-10, *The Law of Land Warfare*, 6–7.

While relying on proportionality as the only criterion by which to judge courses of action would be morally prohibited, and to pursue this as a general policy would represent a violation of the law and morality of war, one must not fall into the trap of calculating success in terms of noncombatant lives lost versus enemy lives taken. What matters is how much closer an operation brings a state to victory. If key leaders are the terrorist organization's center of gravity, then military leaders may need to consider this reality when determining how best to pursue them. In this kind of asymmetric warfare, it does not matter that one may kill two, four, ten, or one hundred noncombatants in order to kill one terrorist. What matters is how much harm the targeted terrorists could do relative to the amount of collateral damage caused in pursuit of them. Given that, in this kind of war, a few people can cause a disproportionate amount of harm, the permissions associated with noncombatant casualties will be greater than in more conventional conflicts.

This does not mean that permissions will be unlimited. Some terrorists and terrorist cells are more dangerous or capable than others, and U.S. forces must take this into consideration when making judgments of proportionality. If the terrorist target in question is relatively inconsequential or incapable of committing an act of aggression, then proportionality requires U.S. forces to forego engaging it. It is never right to kill noncombatants in order to achieve inconsequential goals.

Furthermore, when applying the condition of proportionality, a state must remember that what is permissible as collateral damage depends on the types of weapons available. If there is a way to kill terrorists and destroy their facilities without killing noncombatants, military leaders are obligated to take it. However, this point is not as obvious as it sounds. As Michael Schrage notes, precision weapons pose a special moral dilemma for U.S. soldiers and airmen.[36] By fielding very precise weaponry, the United States builds up the expectation that the wars it fights will be "clean"—that is, largely devoid of noncombatant casualties. However, as this expectation is raised, adversaries will find it increasingly profitable to hide military facilities and equipment in civilian and other noncombatant facilities, such as hospitals, schools, prisoner-of-war camps, and residential areas, thus increasing the likelihood of noncombatant casualties.[37] In this way, potential adversaries can reap the political benefits of portraying the U.S. and its allies as immoral. In response, Schrage argues, it is necessary to reexamine the laws of war.

While this is an interesting and legitimate concern, the doctrine of double effect allows combatants to find a way to balance their moral obligations with

36. Michael Schrage, "Too Smart for Our Own Good," *Washington Post*, June 2, 2002, B3.

37. Ibid. These decisions will occur on many levels. Soldiers/pilots must make the decision based on what weapons they have and the mission they are supposed to accomplish. Higher-level leaders must take care to ensure that soldiers are armed with the most precise weapons practical.

the need to accomplish their missions. Furthermore, it allows political and military leaders to differentiate reasonable from unreasonable expectations clearly by separating acts that intentionally put noncombatants at risk, such as placing legitimate targets beside illegitimate targets, from acts that put noncombatants at unintentional but necessary risk that is a by-product of conducting legitimate military operations.

The Bad Effect Is Unintended

The second rquirement of the doctrine of double effect is that the deaths of noncombatants be unintentional. Peters argues that the United States must be "willing to pursue the terrorists through their families." By this, he means taking advantage of the value that Arabs place on their familial relationships in order to discourage terrorists. Intentionally targeting family, friends, or even the terrorists' home neighborhoods, in order to make participation in terrorist acts costly is not permitted under this provision of the doctrine of double effect. But what is permitted is targeting terrorists while they are with family, friends, or other noncombatants. If terrorists choose to pursue a strategy of hiding in civilian populations so that the only way to strike them involves harming civilians, part or all of the fault of the civilian deaths lies with the terrorists, not the U.S. and its allies. Noncombatant immunity needs to be taken seriously by both parties to the conflict. If terrorists are able to conduct their operations in a way that minimizes risks to their own noncombatants but actually do otherwise, then the responsibility for the noncombatant deaths lies with the terrorists, not with the state that opposes the terrorists.

The Bad Effect Is Not a Direct Means to a Good Effect

The third requirement is that a state may not use the deaths of noncombatants as the means to a good effect. If Peters's exhortation were pursued as a general policy, then it would also be preferable to target terrorists when they are with their families (as opposed to when they are not) because this would maximize the cost of becoming a terrorist. But if U.S. and allied forces choose to engage a terrorist when he is with family, friends, and neighbors even if they can wait until he is by himself, then they commit a moral wrong. However, if the U.S. and its allies pursue a general policy of engaging terrorists whenever they present themselves as targets, regardless of their company, keeping proportionality in mind, then no moral wrong is committed.

Taking Additional Risks

A fourth requirement is that U.S. and allied forces must take extra risks, if necessary, to minimize the harm to noncombatants. Not only does this mean, as noted above, that the most precise weapons available must be used, but it also means that combatants must take extra risks in order to maximize this precision. For a combatant, this may mean flying lower or maneuvering closer in order to separate combatants from noncombatants more clearly. This means that if there is any way to eliminate a terrorist without harming his family, combatants must take it. This also means that political and military leaders must consider the moral limits of risk when deciding how to organize and employ their forces. If infantry can provide more precision than stand-off weapons such as artillery or close air support, then leaders must consider using them. Further, this means that soldiers and airmen must be supplied with the most precise tools available to accomplish the mission. A modern war cannot be waged without harming civilians, but as long as combatant forces accept the greatest risk permissible to avoid noncombatant casualties, the moral fault of civilian deaths lies with the aggressor.

Some may argue that placing constraints of this sort on fighting a deadly enemy needlessly and irresponsibly restrains the U.S. and its allies from pursuing courses of action that allow them to protect their own populations effectively. This argument ignores what the doctrine of double effect does permit: the U.S. and its allies should pursue an aggressive policy by which they engage terrorists wherever and whenever they find them, employing means that can kill them without doing any more damage than is necessary. Furthermore, even if, in particular situations, conforming to moral obligations leads to restraint and perhaps missed opportunities, this may be the short-term price to pay in order to gain the long-term benefit that moral integrity brings.

In practice, following this doctrine is about making choices. It means choosing to engage terrorists when and where the fewest noncombatants will be harmed, even if choosing otherwise may bring some military advantage. It means choosing the least harmful means of killing the terrorists, though more harmful means may be less risky or otherwise preferable. Finally, it means that even though certain terrorists are able to take advantage of the opportunities to conceal their activities within civil society, they should be pursued to the furthest extent possible as criminals, because this involves doing the least harm possible. But because of the nature of the threat these terrorists represent, when it is not possible to pursue them as criminals, it is permissible to pursue them as enemies and to do the greatest harm permissible.

Conclusion

Whether the United States has taken the morally appropriate path in dealing with the al-Qaeda terrorists depends on what kind of threat they represent. As horrific as the attacks on September 11, 2001 were, the terrorists ultimately did not achieve their goals. The U.S. economy stabilized and is on the road to recovery, the Pentagon's ability to command U.S. forces all over the world was not interrupted, and the White House was not damaged. Thus, while they are capable of conducting devastating attacks, it is not clear from prior experience that the al-Qaeda terrorists can commit the kinds of aggression that warrant war. If this is the case, then Howard is correct in saying that the military operations in Afghanistan have whittled away the "immense moral ascendancy" that America has gained as a result of the terrorist attacks.

However, the threat the terrorists represent is in what they *can* do, not what they *have* done. The events of September 11, 2001, demonstrated that the al-Qaeda terrorists are able and intend to wage war on the United States. Though not a state themselves, they have developed the ability to gather resources from a variety of states and organizations and use them in a way that threatens the political sovereignty and territorial integrity of the United States. Thus, the United States may have whittled away its moral ascendancy, but it did not need to do so. This does not mean that the U.S. response is not without criticism. All terrorists are criminals, but not all represent the kind of threat that justifies the foreseeable-but-unintentional harming of noncombatants. If one categorizes all terrorists this way, one risks doing a great deal of moral harm.

The al-Qaeda terrorists are criminals. But they are also enemies. Because it is always preferable to do less harm than more, it will always be preferable to pursue them under the criminal model because this model risks the least harm to noncombatants. But because terrorists are enemies, when it is not possible to pursue them as criminals, it is permissible to conduct operations that will knowingly though not intentionally harm civilians, given the restrictions outlined above.

There are, of course, unresolved issues. I have not adequately addressed the permissions associated with violating the political sovereignty and territorial integrity of other states in order to pursue the terrorists. Supporting terrorism may make moral sense to some states, but if terrorists operate in states that are willing to eliminate them but cannot do so, discerning what is permitted is more complicated.

Furthermore, I have not adequately discussed how to treat detained terrorists. While it is permissible in some circumstances to attack them under the war model, they *are still* criminals. Thus, whether they should enjoy the rights of a criminal or the rights of a prisoner of war is another complex question that should be explored.

In the course of responding to the terrorists' act of aggression, it will be important for U.S. leaders to resolve the ethical issues raised by this new kind of conflict as well as the practical issues. This does not necessarily mean that the United States should restrain its efforts in fighting this war; but it does mean that the prosecutors of this war must remember that the United States is a member of a community of nations and that there are obligations to citizens in other states, even states that support the terrorists, that must be observed.

A state cannot rationally fight evil by committing it. Thus when political and military leaders ask themselves the question, "What should we do?" they must consider the moral, not only the pragmatic, aspects of this question. Certainly, in the midst of America's justifiable anger, its leaders must take care not to become like the enemy it opposes.

Chapter 7

Terrorism:
What Is It and How Do We Deal with It?

Ian G. C. Durie†

Some essays in this volume aggressively promote Christian pacifism. This essay assumes the correctness of the just-war doctrine. In view of this stark juxtaposition, an autobiographical note in defense of the just war is in order.

Writing as a former soldier and practitioner of war, I have always subscribed to the doctrine of just war and invoked it in my own participation in the first Gulf War, in 1991. But more serious study took place during my ministry in the Association for Christian Conferences and Teaching (ACCTS) Military Ministries International. It was at a theological college in England that, in answer to questions from soldiers about how to deal with coups d'état rather than interstate conflict, I returned to first principles to examine the roots of just-war doctrine and to see how the doctrine stood the test of any conflict. After studying both Scripture and literature from the writings of Augustine through Francisco de Vitoria, Dietrich Bonhoeffer to Reinhold Niebuhr, Millard Lind, Paul Ramsey, and John Howard Yoder, my conclusion was that the responsibility for justice, law, and order in society requires the state to be prepared to use force conditionally and in a closely controlled manner to deal with internal disorder and external aggression and that Christians have a duty to play their parts, although some may be called to pacifism as an individual stance. The results of that research are offered in my essay, "Justifiable Resistance?"[1] This essay addresses the situation of internal conflict and how to think about it.

In this context, questions are frequently asked about terrorism. Terrorism is one of the focuses of the 21st century. It has, however, always existed as a tool not only of resistance but also of government. The Romans often used it to subdue unruly opponents, who themselves frequently resorted to terrorist tactics to resist Roman rule. The British government used it in Ireland at the

---

1. See my "Justifiable Resistance? Can the Theory of the Just War Be Extended to Opposing Unjust Regimes?" *Anvil* 18 (2001) 165–79.

beginning of the 20th century to try to subdue the newly formed Irish Republican Army, which was using terror tactics to fight for Irish independence. An up-to-date catalog of post–World War II history demonstrates that terror tactics were very evident in the second half of the 20th century, used by both governments and by their adversaries.

However, since September 11, 2001, when, in response to the terrible and highly visible attacks in the eastern United States, the U.S. government "declared war on terrorism," questions have arisen over what terrorism is. It is important to recognize that it is not an ideology (such as communism); it is an instrument, not a movement. Questions arise whether it can ever be justified and how it may be defeated. Because a state cannot declare war on an instrument, it may be helpful to redefine "declaring war on terrorism" as a declaration of war on individuals or groups who resort to or threaten to use terrorism.

Defining Terrorism

What, exactly, is "terrorism"? To be objective, one may begin with the dictionary definition of terrorism: "the use of terror-inspiring methods of governing or of coercing government or community." "Terror" is defined as "extreme fear."[2] This definition clearly includes the potential use of terror by enemies of the state against legitimate as well as illegitimate targets and by governments. (I will return to the vital issue of whether terrorizing a group waging war against the state, by any means, morally and legitimately warrants return terrorism.) However, we generally think of terrorists as the "bad guys" who are attacking innocent targets and/or the righteous forces of law and order. Not surprisingly, one modern American dictionary uses another definition: "The *unlawful* [my emphasis] use or threatened use of force or violence by a person or an organized group against people or property with the intention of intimidating or coercing societies or governments, often for ideological or political reasons."[3] The use of the word *unlawful* in this definition reinforces the adage that "one man's 'terrorist' is another man's 'freedom fighter.'" This dichotomy will always challenge the objective commentator.

Words and language are very powerful; they have great philosophical, political, and theological weight. Note also that language is always developing. So these alternative definitions of terrorism immediately raise the question

---

2. *Concise Oxford English Dictionary,* 11th ed., s.v. "terrorism"; ibid., "terror."

3. *American Heritage Dictionary of the English Language,* 4th ed., s.v. "terrorism." But it is worth noting that another American dictionary, *Webster's Revised Unabridged Dictionary* (1913), uses another definition: "The act of terrorizing or state of being terrorized; *a mode of government* [my emphasis] by terror or intimidation." Similarly, a British dictionary, *Collins English Dictionary, Complete and Unabridged* (6th ed.), uses the definition, "the systematic use of violence and intimidation to achieve some goal."

whether it is a pejorative term or whether it can it be neutral—that is, can terrorism be simply another means or instrument of warfare? In other words, is terrorism always bad? Conversely, is it ever lawful for government to use terror ("extreme fear") as a means of warfare? One may argue for the appropriateness of the "lawful" use of terror by a lawful government as a means of restraining a section of its own or any other population that is bent on perpetrating unlawful acts of violence. We will return to this question and deal with it in the discussion of proportionality, but allow me to submit here that governments could legitimately consider using terror in the pursuit of enemies of the state and that the use of terror against enemies of the state cannot be redefined apart from the term *terrorism*. Many examples of government terrorism currently exist. Thus, we must recognize that terrorism is not only "what is done to me"; it is a neutral term.

At the same time, popular usage demands that we treat terrorism typically as an instrument or tool of a resistance struggle. Whether or not it is unlawful depends on how it is used. So the first question is: can terrorism ever be used as a legitimate weapon of justified resistance? The second question regards the way that the state responds to terrorism. In answering this question, I will consider whether state terrorism itself may ever be justified. This essay discusses when and where terrorism may be used as a weapon of justified resistance, attempts to determine the appropriate response by governments to any form of terrorism or threat of terrorism, and considers how to establish a climate in which unlawful and unjustified terrorist insurgency may be neutralized.

Is Terrorism Ever Legitimate?

A review of the principles governing the use of force is in order. The starting point for the long-established principles of the just-war ethic is that they are unashamedly Christian, on the confident assumption that this ethic reflects objective, not relative, truth and that these principles can stand exposure to the global ethic, if it exists. Christian pacifists may align themselves with humanist and other pacifist traditions. However, Christians who understand that the right to use violent force lies within the permissive will of God,[4] in strictly limited circumstances, within the equally stringent limits for the conduct of such force as the just-war doctrine insists on—these Christians cannot be proved wrong by adherents of other traditions or moral standpoints in establishing the rules of war.

In these circumstances, then, the development of the classic principles proposed elsewhere to justify armed insurrection or rebellion within a state

---

4. The permissive will of God contrasts with the direct will of God. The issue of war is not unlike divorce. God's direct will is that marriage should be permanent, but divorce is permitted in strictly limited circumstances.

against its government are a suitable starting point for potentially resorting to internal or international terrorism.[5] These developed criteria are discussed in the appendix (pp. 123–125). In the case of justified resistance, terrorism may be the appropriate method of fighting of a relatively powerless minority against a more powerful majority.

If these principles are valid for resistance against the state, then one may argue that terrorism ("extreme fear-inspiring methods of coercing government or community") may be a justifiable means of resistance against legitimate targets (a key issue that must be addressed), because this action may be the only possible method of righting internationally recognized extreme oppression. It is, however, difficult to call to mind any 20th-century terror campaign that has sought to fight within these rules, although, as one may suspect, even terrorists seem to recognize some rules as providing acceptable limits ("acceptable to whom?" one may ask). Nevertheless, there are no easily identified cases of justifiable resistance in which the insurgents did not strike inappropriate or illegitimate targets—illegitimate at least in the judgment of the powers being targeted. The reason for this "soft" targeting is that it is relatively difficult to terrorize well-prepared security forces and the agents of government that are characterized as legitimate targets by the insurgents. Furthermore, even this legitimate targeting is difficult without collateral casualties, instilling extreme fear in the surrounding "innocent" civilian population. The current situation in Israel/Palestine illustrates this point. The indiscriminate attacks of Palestinian suicide bombers attempt, at the very least, to coerce by terror the Israeli people into compelling their government to make decisions that will secure a better future for Palestine (or to win sympathy from their Arab neighbors or even to obliterate the Israeli state altogether, in a holy war). I will return to this situation as a case study.

It is noteworthy that, in the last half century, terror has been used as a weapon in the wars for independence from colonialism and imperialism, in the spread of communism by insurgency, and in racial, ethnic, and religious struggles within and between states (as in Kashmir, for example). In all these cases, I will consider very broadly and briefly (below) that there has often been a degree (sometimes a high degree) of justification for the cause. But even when the cause has been justified, it is difficult to find an example (though Museveni's struggle in Uganda may be an exception) in which the rebels have only terrorized the military capability of the ruling power by focusing on the oppressive instruments and people of government and have not also targeted "innocent" civilian populations. In many cases, one may argue for the justice of the cause and the intention, for the element of last resort, for a recognition of the right (the authority) of the insurrectionists to declare

---

5. See my "Justifiable Resistance," 168.

hostilities, for the limited ends for which they fought, for a degree of proportionality, and (as history shows) for a good probability of success. However, the rebel cause is almost always undermined in the eyes of neutral observers by their failure to protect the innocent. Furthermore, many times the terrorists' effective targeting of the innocent and the incapability of government to protect the civilian population as a whole has undermined the government's capacity and will to win.

As I have already proposed, terrorism as a method of fighting is the tactic of a relatively powerless minority against a more powerful majority. It may be argued that terrorism, including international terrorism, is no more and no less than another form of warfare and that, provided that it sticks to the rules, it may be a legitimate form of warfare. The problem is that history shows that terrorism does not stick to the rules. In other words, terrorism is not a tool of just insurrection because, when used legitimately, it does not work. Interestingly, most terrorists seem to draw the line somewhere (though the attack on the Twin Towers in September, 2001, may contradict this assertion).

It is equally difficult to see how the use of terror by government can ever be legitimized. The active rebel fighters and their immediate apparatus of rebel leadership/government, which might be legitimate targets, are not easily terrorized, and it is their families and the wider "innocent" population that are the real victims of terrorism by the forces of the state. This contravenes the principles of proportionality, the protection of noncombatants, and almost certainly the probability of success.

The current example of Mugabe in Zimbabwe, who is not facing revolt but merely opposition, and the actions of Mugabe's "war veterans" against activists and supporters of the Movement for Democratic Change (and against some white farmers and their workers) amounts to state terrorism. Equally, in Israel/Palestine it is difficult to argue that the proportionality and collateral-damages stipulations allow for the nonjudicial assassination of leaders of the Palestinian uprising or the destruction of Palestinian homes and buildings. These actions surely belong to the category of state terrorism. Both actions are unsupportable, and it is difficult to imagine that lawful states could ever justify, legitimize, or use state terrorism to achieve peace.

Resisting International Terrorism

I will now address the topic of international terrorism. What is it, where does it originate, and how can it be resisted and defeated? The current preoccupation with the use of terrorism and the need to resist it is highlighted by the events of September 11, 2001, and the consequent fighting against recognized terrorist groups in Afghanistan; by the continuing bloody conflict in Israel/Palestine; by the situations in Chechnya and elsewhere throughout the world. These examples illustrate how difficult it is for governments that are targets of terrorism to respond.

Setting aside the possible gangster/blackmail get-rich-quick element beloved by movie-makers, the roots of international terrorism are almost always a perceived or real grievance that cannot be rectified satisfactorily by other means. The aggrieved party believes that it can achieve its ends with minimum penalty by the use of terror, and it chooses terror because it is either too weak or cowardly to withstand an honorable fight.

The first thing that must be said about resisting terrorism is that the response itself must always be legitimate and must adhere to the internationally recognized rules for the use of force and warfare. In these matters, the careful use of words (with attention to their meaning and the way they are understood) is paramount. My earlier comment that a declared war on terrorism should be a war on groups that threaten to use or resort to terrorism illustrates the point. Many argue that the legitimizing of the al-Qaeda struggle by dignifying it with the term *war* was a mistake and that the better approach would have been to treat all terrorists as criminals who must be brought to justice, while at the same time being prepared to use carefully controlled, precisely directed lethal force in bringing the terrorists to justice and in defending government and civilian targets from their attacks. The British government has continually sought to use this approach in the recent armed struggle in Northern Ireland. Glen Stassen has pointed out that the Turkish government has sought to address grievances of its Kurdish population in the same way.[6] In the case of Afghanistan, because the United States has declared war on terrorism (remember the power of language), there is now a problem with designating the captured al-Qaeda soldiers "illegal combatants" when they must surely be "prisoners of war" (and treated accordingly). If war had not been declared on terrorism, they could instead have been treated as international terrorists being brought to justice, if the evidence could be produced.

Holding National Governments to Account

The absolute necessity for governments to behave legitimately and accountably must be constantly reinforced and checked. If a legitimate government behaves illegally, wrongly, unethically, or immorally, it undermines its own authority and legitimacy and provides a precedent for its opposition to do the same.

It is the duty of all in positions of influence to uphold the moral and legal principles governing relations between nations, and it is the duty of all citi-

---

6. See Glen H. Stassen's essay in this volume, "Just Peacemaking Reduces Terrorism between Palestine and Israel," 127–148.

zens to hold their government accountable to these principles. In particular, the church, individual members of the church, human rights groups, the judiciary, the academic community, and international human rights organizations must call governments to account. Likewise, it is the duty of the government to give its military legitimate orders and adequate means to execute the tasks it sets for them in pursuit of legitimate national interests. It is also the solemn duty of the government to give a proper account to its citizens of the actions that it is taking in their name. There will sometimes be a conflict between national security interests and the interests of openness, but governments have a duty to prove themselves trustworthy before they hide their actions behind a cloak of "security."

Recent history provides illustrations of governments, such as the Nazi regime in Third Reich Germany or the Stalinist regime in the Soviet Union, that are extreme examples of untrustworthy governments and of ineffectual accountability. But it is not only dictatorships and undemocratic authoritarian governments that have been known to mislead their people. It is now widely acknowledged that the British and French governments acted illegally and immorally at the time of the 1956 Suez crisis by misleading their people. The United States government's openness at the time of the 1963 Cuban missile crisis is a welcome and refreshing exception. The same government, however, sadly betrayed its people regarding many elements of the war in Indo-China from the late 1960s onward. The classic process, with the full sanction of the United Nations, by which the British government went to war for limited ends (to recover the Falklands) in 1982, has much to commend it, as did the United States–led United Nations coalition's operation to free Kuwait from Iraqi occupation in 1991. These operations contrast with the recent war: there are serious doubts in the U.S., England, and worldwide about the justification for what was, at best, an overhasty United States/United Kingdom invasion of Iraq. Furthermore, some elements of the military action by the United States in Afghanistan have led others, such as Russia in Chechnya and Israel in Palestine, to claim legitimacy for acts of repression that would otherwise be universally condemned as wholly unjustified.

Today, it is essential that Christians (and others who have the God-given responsibility to ensure that right prevails) seriously consider the relevant criteria (as well as at the international laws of war), establish the facts that are known, and establish what is being hidden. They must do this in order to determine whether the government is doing what is right and in the interests of peace and justice for all in its use of force and in its subsequent conduct of operations. It is wise also to remember that war is a degrading business and that, the longer a conflict endures, the more difficult it is to continue acting rightly. The propensity for brutality is also greater over an extended time: the examples are legion.

To repeat, governments must be held accountable so that they earn the trust and respect of their people and the world community.

Neutralizing Terrorism

Beyond accountability of government, how is insurgent terrorism be defeated? The first problem of terrorism, as outlined above, is that groups who resort to terrorism, even if their cause is justified, rarely follow the rules of war in the targets they choose to attack. The second problem is fanatical terrorists. For some, the grievance they perceive is so great that they are prepared to take desperate measures, to commit suicide in the fulfillment of their mission to attack their hated enemies. Religious zealots can seize on these desperate straits. For example, certain groups of Islamic fundamentalists, against the received instruction of most orthodox Islamic teaching and in the belief that their suicidal, self-sacrificial, reckless acts of terror will earn rewards in the next life, have sanctioned suicide bombings such as the attacks on the World Trade Center and in Israel. The same can be said of the Hindu Tamils, who, armed with an extremist interpretation of their religion, are engaged in the civil war in Sri Lanka. All fanatics of this sort are very difficult to combat.

In each of these categories, the challenge for nations facing an internal or external terrorist threat is to determine how to reduce the threat to manageable proportions. History shows that it is rare that increasingly repressive measures by the regime in power have the desired effect of addressing the underlying sense of grievance. Instead, the issues must be confronted and the criminals arrested (or killed in the attempt—I also note that declaring "war on terrorism" may legitimize the nonjudicial killing of terrorist suspects as enemies engaged in combat). Israel is suffering from a predictable bloody backlash against its increasingly oppressive reaction to terrorist outrages within its borders as it seeks to target Al Fatah and other resistance or terrorist groups in Palestine. This repression often raises more extremists who are willing, even eager, to become martyrs in the perceived cause of their religion, country, or community. All repression must be avoided in the conduct of the "war on terrorism."

More positively, it must be understood that the path of terrorism is not easy. Groups that resort to it are generally zealots who must rely on sympathy and support for their cause from their surrounding community in order to operate. In other words, the terrorist "fish" (or "shark") needs a "sea" of sympathizers and approval in which to swim. As individuals who have labored to contain or defeat terrorism well know, the key is government counteraction of the propaganda of the terrorists in order to win the hearts and minds of the population at large. The government must win its citizens over so that they understand and accept the rightness of the government's case, thus shrinking the sea in which the terrorist can hide. Of course, its efforts will only be effective if the government's case is valid.

What about addressing the cause? In the film about the 1963 Cuban missile crisis, *Thirteen Days That Shook the World,* a deputy secretary of state asks the question, "Why do other people hate America so much?" After September 11, 2001, the same question was being asked. The answer is oppression and, of course, envy. Oppression, real or perceived, has many potential dimensions: economic, diplomatic, military, ethnic, environmental, and religious. It is not only the United States that is seen as the oppressor by large sections of the "two-thirds world." The worldwide capitalist system and the G8 (Canada, France, Germany, Italy, Japan, Russia, the United Kingdom, and the United States), the richest nations in the world, dominate a world in which their own interests usually predominate—one side effect of globalization.

It is, however, recognized in every ethical system that the promotion of peace, security, prosperity, righteousness, and justice for all their people are the priorities for governments. Where there are world and regional cooperations of governance and security, these groups, many currently under the hegemony of the United States, must act on their values. These same values must prevail among the community of nations. Again, governments must be called to account.

In Christian terms, Jesus' dictum that from them "to whom much is given, much is required"[7] lays a solemn duty of responsibility on powerful nations and groups of nations whose actions have an impact around the world. In Old Testament times, God, speaking through the prophet Isaiah, berated the comfort and complacency of individuals and nations in power and their indifference to the injustice inflicted on the people they were oppressing by their attitudes and actions. God's challenge to the powerful is this:

Is not this the kind of fasting that I have chosen:
to loosen the bonds of injustice,
to undo the thongs of the yoke,
to let the oppressed go free,
and to break every yoke?
Is it not to share your bread with the hungry,
and bring the homeless poor into your house;
when you see the naked to cover them,
and not to hide yourself from your own kin?
(Isa 58:6–7, NRSV)

Thus, as governments deal with terrorists in a way that is legal and just, it is vitally important for them to recognize and address the roots of opposition

---

7. Luke 12:48.

from which the terrorism springs. In this context, Stassen's "Just Peacemaking Principles" apply.[8] People in power must return to just cause and recognize that, however unreasonable the cause may seem, there is often a valid underlying grievance that must be addressed. Besides perceived oppression of their religions, the poverty of the two-thirds world is a cause for much discontent that religious extremists can use to foment sympathy for their causes. Such poverty is a shame and a disgrace to the powerful nations who could surely ameliorate it by an active policy of equipping and helping the countries who are on the outside to become owners of their own futures. It is not my place in this essay to suggest how this should be done; I merely recognize the duty of world governments to "to loose the bonds of injustice, to undo the thongs of the yoke, to let the oppressed go free, and to break every yoke."

Terrorists will rarely be concerned about every requirement of just war in their struggle, but in response to terrorism, groups that are attacked must commit to doing what is right. The prophet Micah said that what God requires is "to act justly and to love mercy and to walk humbly with your God."[9] With this attitude and also using the principles of the just war, governments can undermine any terrorist cause, particularly in emphasizing the serious duty to seek peace, prosperity, and justice for all. They must not only do this but they must be seen to be doing it. If not, the sea in which the terrorist "fish" breeds and hides will continue to offer him a sanctuary from which to operate.

In summary, then, terrorism is a potentially legitimate form of warfare, but terrorists never use it legitimately, and this is why it is not a justifiable means of resistance.

- In responding to terrorism, governments have a duty to respond legitimately within the constraints of just-war doctrine and the international rules of war, taking care not to further the terrorist cause by repressive actions; and they must not themselves resort to terrorism.
- Governments should seek to address the causes of injustice throughout the world, thus negating the means by which terrorists justify their actions.
- Both governments and those who oppose them should be called to account by Christians and others who have the duty of responding to God's call for justice and freedom from oppression for all nations and peoples.

It has been said, "The best way to promote United States' interests is to promote United States' ideals and values."[10] Let us improve on this and say

---

8. See Stassen, "Just Peacemaking Reduces Terrorism," 133–134.

9. Mic 6:8, NIV.

10. L.K. Johnson, "On Drawing a Bright Line for Covert Operations," *American Journal of International Law* 86 (1992) 284–309.

that, to promote the interests of the kingdom of God, we must at all times conduct ourselves in accordance with kingdom values—acting justly, loving mercy, and walking humbly with God.

Appendix:
Criteria for Justified Resistance

1. Just Cause. *The only just cause for armed resistance is defense against violent (and unjustified) aggression.* This condition includes extreme injustice when this injustice may be classified as violent aggression. Even so, defining unjust violent aggression as it applies to sections of a population oppressed by a partisan, corrupt, or tyrannical government is extremely difficult. The difficulty will always be in perception. What one section of a population may regard as a violent and oppressive restriction of its fundamental human rights may, in the eyes of the government and other sections of the same population, be seen as just and good for the population as a whole. Partiality and sectional interests may distort the judgment of the people and groups who are most closely involved. There is, therefore, a clear requirement to ratify the justness of the case by appeal to international bodies (such as the United Nations or the World Council of Churches) as a basis for negotiation and to seek a mandate for the use of force if negotiations fail.

2. Just/Right Intention. *The only just intention is to restore (or achieve) justice for the whole community.* This criterion raises the question whether justice warrants disordering action, or order warrants the tragic permission of some injustice.[11] There are other considerable potential difficulties. Insurrection arising from the oppression of minorities may mean that tribalism or factionalism plays a significant part in the cause of violence. There must be no motive of revenge or retribution, and any rebellion must strive for justice *for all*. Clearly, any solution to the conflict that creates new oppressions is unacceptable.

3. Last Resort. *Recourse to armed resistance must be a last resort, after every other effort to resolve the situation has been exhausted and has failed.* Resistance groups must acknowledge the evil of war and the fact that it can only be the lesser evil when all other solutions have failed. This principle must be held as paramount. Furthermore, until an initial self-sacrificial campaign of nonviolent resistance has been crushed or otherwise exhausted without progress in addressing the injustice, the resort to violence is not a step of last resort. A further obstacle, however, is that a resistance movement may experience considerable difficulty in establishing a negotiating position with the government. It is possible that the government's refusal to meet and to treat fairly the representatives of resistance movements before they resort to insurrection could itself constitute the

---

11. Paul Ramsey, *The Just War* (Lanham, MD: University Press of America, 1983) 29.

exhaustion of other means of resolution, if honest and strenuous moves have been made to open and maintain negotiations.

4. Competent Authority / Official Declaration of Hostilities. *The decision to resort to armed resistance must be made by the highest representative of the oppressed party (recognized by the international authorities) and should be marked by an official declaration of hostilities.* The difficulty of defining lawful authority for rebellion is self-evident, and one commentator points out that, of all the just-war conditions, "this is the one that appears least applicable to Christian involvement in revolution."[12] Without legitimating features, violent resistance cannot be contemplated further. First, the principle is that the injustice should be widely recognized as genuinely intolerable, not only in the eyes of the victims but in a broad coalition of Christian communities within and across national boundaries, seeking to know the will of God. Second (although I am not diminishing the difficulties inherent in gaining this recognition), groups intending to conduct violent resistance must be recognized as proper representatives by the groups whom they are seeking to free from oppression and must be capable of showing that they represent the best interests of the people as a whole. If negotiations fail, it is clear that there must be an official declaration of hostilities, stating the goals of the campaign and denoting proper channels of communication if negotiations are to be reopened.

5. Limited Ends. *Armed resistance must be waged for limited ends only — sufficient to repel aggression and to redress its injustice.* There is little to add to this deceptively simple clause, other than acknowledging the difficulty of putting it into practice.

6. Proportionality. *The means used to conduct armed resistance must be proportional to the offense and the end intended.* The problem of all war, revolutionary or conventional, is what Ellul calls "the law of violence."[13] Violence, on both sides, tends to be escalatory, and the danger is that the proponents of a campaign of violent resistance cannot fully foresee or may tend to underestimate the full horrors of the campaign as it develops. The British Army's principle of "minimum necessary force" legitimately applied must be the first and absolutely limiting principle. While not normally the case in unconventional wars, clearly there should be strictly articulated rules of war that are at least as stringent as the rules that govern international conflict, closely controlled by properly authorized rules of engagement.

7. Protection of Noncombatants. *Armed force must only be directed against enemy combatants. Noncombatants must be protected from direct or intentional attack.* As in conventional war, the difficulty of distinguishing combatants from noncombatants is evident. The "law of violence" tends to degrade people's judg-

12. J. G. Davies, *Christians, Politics and Violent Revolution* (London: SCM, 1976) 168.
13. J. Ellul, *Violence: Reflections from a Christian Perspective* (London: SCM, 1970) 93.

ments in this, and "freedom fighters" can all too easily become deserving of the label "terrorists" as they become less discriminate in their targeting of violence and broaden their definition of their enemies. The rebel leaders must carefully and legitimately define their targets as those who perpetrate oppression. The weakness of rebel/resistance forces will always make the "soft" target (uncommitted civilians and their property) an easier option than the legitimate target.

8. <u>Probability of Success</u>. *If a just peace cannot be achieved, then the additional suffering caused by the war serves no purpose. And because armed resistance may only be undertaken when there is a reasonable chance of success, it must be discontinued if this chance diminishes.* This condition poses the most severe test for parties proposing revolutionary violence. By its very nature, the uprising of an oppressed minority, driven by the perception of extreme and unbearable injustice, can have little initial probability of success—only hope! This stipulation of discontinuation raises all manner of questions, and thus it is important to have a campaign plan that recognizes the importance of not making things worse and that contains arrangements for de-escalating to nonviolent resistance. A long self-sacrificial struggle that fails, with minimum noncombatant casualties, may be acceptable; but a struggle that brings increased misery to others, without a near certainty of ultimate success, is invalid.[14]

---

14. Adapted from my "Justifiable Resistance," 175–77. I am not separating *jus ad bellum* from *jus in bello* because one feeds into the other.

CHAPTER 8

Just Peacemaking Reduces Terrorism between Palestine and Israel

GLEN H. STASSEN

Pacifism and just-war theory both answer the question: Is war justified? Just Peacemaking Theory does not answer *that* question. So pacifists and just-war theorists, who disagree on the answer to the question, can agree on Just Peacemaking Theory. This explains how 23 scholars (some were pacifists but most were just-war theorists) could work together for five years and reach a consensus on the new ethic of peace and war: the Just Peacemaking Theory.

Just Peacemaking Theory answers the question that is usually overlooked in our discussions and debates: What peacemaking practices are in accord with Jesus' way, work in the real world, and are obligatory for Christians to advocate and practice in the real world?[1]

Situating Just Peacemaking

Figure 1 below illustrates opposing views regarding war and peacemaking. I place pacifism and just-war theory along the *x* axis, corresponding to their respective answers to the question: Is this war justified? Farther to the right on the *x* axis is "right of state": many people simply hand the responsibility to the government to decide whether to make war and do not question the ethics of a war until after they see how it proceeds. This makes the government the lord of our ethics, thus sidestepping Christ's lordship. It is a form of idolatry. It is also a form of authoritarianism, identifying God's will with the will of the

---

1. Just peacemaking theory is explained in Glen Stassen, ed., *Just Peacemaking: Ten Practices for Abolishing War* (Cleveland: Pilgrim, 1998 and 2004). The theory is drawing increasing attention because it offers an ethic that not only seeks to restrain war but presents a paradigm for discussing the practices that prevent war. The ten constructive alternatives or practices in Just Peacemaking Theory are demonstrated by political research to prevent war. An ethical theory ties the ten practices together. This book and articles discuss how the theory applies to terrorism, to the Kosovo War, to humanitarian intervention, to conflicts in Africa, and so on. At the time of writing this essay, I count about 45 articles and book chapters that have been published about just peacemaking theory. More information is available at http://www.fuller.edu/sot/faculty/stassen.

powers and authorities. The New Testament treats the powers and authorities very differently: we are called to follow Jesus and to be independent from the authorities who do violence. For example, they seek wealth and power and neglect the widows and the poor. Both just-war theorists and pacifists are in this sense allies against the right of state, arguing that we are responsible for making judgments about right and wrong and that we need an ethic to guide us.

In fig. 1, I place Just Peacemaking along the *y* axis, illustrating answers to the questions: What peacemaking practices should we attempt? Should we be pushing the government to take peacemaking initiatives? Should we be criticizing the government if it does not? These are two different questions and should not be confused with each other. A person committed to nonviolence and active in taking peacemaking initiatives, such as Martin Luther King Jr., would be placed in the *A* quadrant of the diagram. A person who supports a just war but who actively pursues peacemaking alternatives, such as Kofi Annan, former Secretary General of the United Nations, or former presidents Dwight Eisenhower and Jimmy Carter, belongs in the *B* quadrant. A pacifist who would never support a war but who does nothing to support peacemaking alternatives belongs in the *C* quadrant. A just-war theorist who does nothing to work for peace belongs in the *D* quadrant of the diagram.

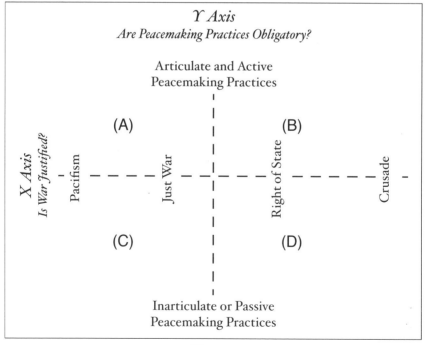

Figure 1.

Each of the 10 Just Peacemaking practices that I will identify below is an actual practice that is working to prevent wars in the real world. For example, when former president Jimmy Carter went to North Korea and persuaded the government to halt its nuclear reactors and to allow inspection and monitoring by the International Atomic Energy Agency in exchange for supplies of oil to make electricity without nuclear reactors, he prevented serious conflict and a nuclear buildup; the Bush administration has finally returned to this solution. This was the practice of conflict resolution. Conflict resolution is a practice in the real world that prevents wars. None of the Just Peacemaking practices is merely an ideal; each is actually happening, and each has been shown by political science research to decrease the number of wars.

Just Peacemaking Theory does not marginalize Jesus' way by relegating it to an ideal realm away from real-world necessity. It does not marginalize and compartmentalize Jesus in the way that some traditions of ethics that are influenced by Platonic idealism do. In contrast to the German Christians who limited Jesus to the inner life and gave their loyalty in the real world to the authoritarian Adolf Hitler, the Barmen Confession in 1934 (written by Karl Barth and signed by leaders of the Confessing church who resisted Hitler) proclaimed that Jesus Christ is the one Lord; there is no other lord or other sphere in which we should serve another lord. Just Peacemaking Theory is congruent with the Barmen tradition: Jesus is Lord over our actions. We are called to support peacemaking practices that fit Jesus' way.

I reject Reinhold Niebuhr's 19th-century, individualistic Jesus who is separated from the real world and marginalized into an ideal realm outside real history. But I think we must learn from Niebuhr's profound understanding of sin. Niebuhr, who was my teacher, explained that sin is in all of us, that no one is righteous, and that we make dangerous errors when we consider our cause to be righteous and the enemy to be unrighteous, refusing to heed what is true in the positions of people with whom we disagree. This is a great danger in the United States, especially after September 11, 2001. We are foolish to close our ears and eyes to differing perspectives. We must learn from Niebuhr about the huge temptations of power and empire and about injustice and how it arises from unchecked and concentrated power. But we must correct his 19th-century, individualistic view of Jesus and his segregating of God's delivering action from the realm of history.[2]

Stanley Hauerwas criticizes Niebuhr for developing an ethic of realism that is split off from the church and marginalizes Jesus. But ironically, Hauerwas's 20th-century ecclesiastical Jesus, similar to Niebuhr's Jesus, is isolated from the real world and so is marginalized. Hauerwas accepts Niebuhr's dualism of

---

2. See his brother's criticism in H. Richard Niebuhr, *Theology, History, and Culture* (ed. Stacy Johnson; New Haven: Yale University Press, 1996).

two kingdoms. Hauerwas, at odds with Niebuhr, limits Jesus' way to the church and thus accepts Niebuhr's isolating of Jesus from the real world outside the church. I maintain that we have much to learn from Hauerwas about our own nationalism and Constantinianism, about practices of the church, about our need for a new Reformation, about nonviolence and following Jesus, about the "peaceable Kingdom,"[3] about the meaning of suffering, about criticism of secular rationalism and the Enlightenment "thinning" of Christian ethics, about our postmodern context, and much more. Niebuhr was my teacher, and I consider Hauerwas my friend; we both have great loyalty to John Howard Yoder, our mutual friend. But I am concerned about the tendency to isolate Jesus from the world outside the church. In the Barmen tradition and Yoder's tradition, Jesus is Lord over all our actions, and there is no realm in which Jesus is not Lord.

Jesus' political context was characterized by the drive to make war on the Roman occupation, just as the Palestinians are making war on Israeli occupation today. He not only taught an ethic for his disciples; he confronted the powers and authorities in Jerusalem as well as the Pharisees for their acts of injustice. Jesus set his teachings in the context of the prophet Isaiah and of Israel. Both deal with the real world. We need a thick Jesus, not a thin and vague Jesus—a Jesus who confronted the real powers and authorities in his day, who prophesied five times in the Gospels that if they did not do the things that make for peace, the temple would be destroyed. This prophecy came true; the temple was destroyed when the Jews rebelled against the Roman Empire, and the Romans destroyed not only the temple but Jerusalem, and they exiled the Jews for 19 centuries.

Peacemaking at Work in the Real World

I will demonstrate how Just Peacemaking Theory is grounded in Jesus' way and also how it works in the real world. Elmer Martens proposes in his essay that we imagine what peace looks like and how it happens.[4] This is what I must help us to see: What do Just Peacemaking practices look like? This question is a fruitful hermeneutical key for unlocking biblical teachings. It causes us to notice meanings that we overlook if we only ask the Bible whether war is allowed.

Cain and Conflict Resolution. The first murder is narrated in Genesis 4. God asks Cain, who is angry with his brother, Abel, "Why are you angry? . . . If you do well, will you not be accepted?" (Gen 4:6). Jesus' teaching about murder (Matt 5:21) refers to a man giving his gift at the altar even though he is

---

3. Stanley Hauerwas, *The Peaceable Kingdom* (Notre Dame, IN: University of Notre Dame Press, 1983).

4. See Elmer A. Martens, "Toward Shalom: Absorbing the Violence," in this volume, pp. 33–57.

angry with his own brother, an echo of Cain and Abel regarding the real danger of murder and killing. Jesus also tells us what it means to do well: go to your brother and make peace. This is the Just Peacemaking practice of conflict resolution. If Cain had gone to his brother to confess his envy and to make peace, he probably would not have killed Abel, and so he would not have been forced to leave home to wander in the land of Nod.

Jacob and Independent Initiative.   On his way home, Jacob fears for his life because of the anger of his brother, Esau (Genesis 32–33). He engages in the Just Peacemaking practice of independent initiatives. He prays, and it occurs to him to send gifts ahead for his brother: sheep, goats, camels, and donkeys. He tells his servants to say, "They are a present sent to my lord Esau" (Gen 32:18). The strategy of independent initiatives worked. Esau accepted Jacob in peace.

Joseph and Forgiveness.   Joseph prays, feeds his brothers (who tried to do away with him), forgives them, and makes peace with the whole family (Genesis 42–50). This is an example of the peacemaking practice of repentance, forgiveness, and acknowledging one's own responsibility in the conflict.

Moses and Righting Injustice.   Jacob's descendants in Egypt need the justice of self-government rather than the tyranny of the authoritarian Pharaoh. They need the justice of their own economy as a covenant people rather than slavery and economic deprivation. Moses is called by God to bring deliverance from the injustice of real slavery and to lead the Hebrews to become a people who really do practice justice in relation to slaves, the poor, widows, orphans, and outcasts.

The Prophets of Israel.   Again and again, prophets call their audiences (and us) actively to attempt to make peace. If we want to avoid the destruction of war and exile, they say, we must repent and practice justice (Amos 5:6, 24). We must cease trusting in idols, warhorses, and war chariots instead of God (Isa 31:1–3, 6). We must repent and return to living a way that is appropriate to individuals who trust in the Lord (Isa 26:4). These are the practices of Just Peacemaking and of reducing trust in offensive weapons and war-making. The threat was judgment by destructive war or exile. It actually happened in the time of Isaiah, as archaeology corroborates.

My point is twofold: When we explore the Scriptures to answer not only the narrow question whether war is justified but also the wider question of specific peacemaking practices, we begin to see a richer and more helpful narrative with regard to ethics. Furthermore, these practices are not mere ideals; they involve real oppression and injustice, real anger and murder, and real modes of deliverance from these vicious cycles of bondage. We see much more clearly what it meant when Jesus confronted the hatred in Israel that would eventually boil up into revolt against Rome, lead to the Roman destruction of the temple and Jerusalem, and end in the exile of the Jews.

Jesus' Way in the Real World:
Peacemaking Practices

The misreading of Jesus' Sermon on the Mount (Matthew 5–7) as idealistic and dualistic must be corrected. This I have tried to do by showing that the way of Jesus is the way of deliverance in the real world—the real world of Jesus' time and our time.[5] In this essay, I can only address the connection between the Sermon on the Mount and Just Peacemaking Theory very briefly.

Matt 5:21–25. Being angry, go make peace with your brother (or sister). The practice of talking with someone for the purpose of resolving conflict has become, in our time, the practice of conflict resolution. This is one key practice of Just Peacemaking.

Matt 5:38–42. Take transforming initiatives to confront injustice nonviolently and make peace. Walter Wink has explained, as have I, that the four transforming initiatives Jesus teaches in the Sermon on the Mount are not merely passive compliance with an oppressor but a transforming initiative that seeks to create a relationship of peace with justice. In Jesus' culture and in the context of the 14 transforming initiatives that constitute the Sermon on the Mount, turning the *other* cheek does not mean complying with the insult but taking the initiative of turning the cheek of dignity; giving the cloak does not mean complying with the oppression but exposing the oppressor's greed; going the second mile does not mean complying with the forced first mile but nonviolently confronting the Roman soldier's oppression; giving to the beggar means responding to the beggar's nonviolent confrontation. All four of the preceding actions are not mere compliance but nonviolent confrontations— initiatives that seek to transform a relationship of injustice and oppression into a relationship of justice and peace. In Just Peacemaking Theory, this is the practice of nonviolent direct action and also the practice of taking independent initiatives.

Matt 7:1–5. Do not judge, but take the log out of your eye. In Just Peacemaking Theory, this action represents acknowledging responsibility for violence and injustice and seeking repentance and forgiveness.

Matt 6:19–33. Do not hoard, but invest your money in God's reign and God's justice. Jesus confronts the injustice of the Jerusalem authorities 37 times in the Gospels. In Just Peacemaking Theory, this is the practice of delivering justice: fostering just and sustainable economic development and advancing human rights, religious liberty, and democracy.

---

5. Glen H. Stassen and David P. Gushee, *Kingdom Ethics: Following Jesus in Contemporary Context* (Downers Grove, IL: InterVarsity, 2003). See also my *Just Peacemaking: Transforming Initiatives for Justice and Peace* (Louisville: Westminster John Knox, 1992); idem, "The Fourteen Triads of the Sermon on the Mount," *JBL* 122 (2003) 267–308; and my *Living the Sermon on the Mount* (New York: Jossey-Bass, 2006).

Matt 5:43–48. "Love your enemies . . . as your Father in heaven."   Here Jesus' teaching is about who is included in our community of neighbors (Lev 19:17–18). He is saying that even our enemies are to be included in the community of neighbors. God is complete and embraces all—including enemies—in the community of rain and sunshine. Children of God the Father are complete and embrace all, including enemies, in the community of regular dialogue and table fellowship. In Just Peacemaking Theory, this entails including diverse nations in the community. Many people who have been committed to preventing another major war or a nuclear war have been working for decades, since World War II, to build community networks that include other nations: international visits and exchanges, international organizations and working relationships that are mushrooming each year, international trade, e-mail, world missions, immigration and emigration, and international student programs. Political-science data demonstrate that the more a nation is involved in these cooperative networks, the less likely it is to be involved in war. The same is true of the United Nations: the more that U.N. organizations are involved in a country, the less likely the country is to make war. These cooperative relationships are analogous to Jesus' teaching about including enemies in the community of neighbors.

Matt 26:52:   *Put up your sword;*
                            those who take up
                               the sword
                                by the sword
                            will die.

This chiastic saying tells Jesus' followers to avoid reliance on swords and, by extension, other weapons of violence. Various ethicists interpret this admonition in different ways, illustrated by the essays in this volume, but Jesus' words correlate directly with this Just Peacemaking practice: reduce offensive weapons and weapons trade.

Finally, Jesus' method was to call out a group of disciples and to form groups of followers in different towns and areas. This inspires the Just Peacemaking practice of joining grassroots peacemaking groups and church and denominational peacemaking groups.

Thus, the 10 Just Peacemaking practices in the new ethic of peace and war are: (1) support nonviolent direct action; (2) take independent initiatives to reduce threat; (3) use cooperative conflict resolution; (4) acknowledge responsibility for conflict and injustice and seek repentance and forgiveness; (5) advance democracy, human rights, and religious liberty; (6) foster just and sustainable economic development; (7) work with emerging cooperative forces in the international system; (8) strengthen the United Nations' and international efforts for cooperation and human rights; (9) reduce offensive weapons and weapons trade; and (10) encourage grassroots peacemaking groups and voluntary associations.

These 10 items are not merely ideals; they are actual practices that are currently happening in many nations. Political-science research is proving that they do, in fact, work. The evidence demonstrates that each practice prevents wars. They all make war less likely. In effect, they abolish wars in many specific cases. And, by contrast, where nations and citizens' groups do not support these practices, wars are significantly more likely to happen.

Realistically, some wars will still develop, so we still need pacifism and just-war theory; but more urgently, we need an ethic to guide us in eliminating the reasons for terrorist anger and recruitment. Just Peacemaking Theory is this ethic.

Peacemaking Theory and the Prevention of Terrorism

I turn now to analyzing two historic examples that show how Just Peacemaking Theory can guide peoples to a more effective set of policies and so prevent terrorism.

Russia and Antiterrorism

Russia has wrestled with terrorism by ethnic-minority Muslim Chechens in southern Russian who are seeking independence. Russia chose a scorched-earth military approach. The result was enormous devastation and no end to terrorism. On September 4, 2004, Chechen terrorists bombed two Russian passenger planes and took a middle school captive in North Ossetia, resulting in over 400 deaths in the school. Prime Minister Putin's policy of reliance on powerful military attacks is being widely criticized in Russia and around the world: it is not only failing; it has led to a dramatic escalation in violence by increasingly angry and bitter terrorists. Putin himself was said to be rethinking his policy; certainly, millions of angry citizens are rethinking it. Fareed Zakaria wrote in December 2003 that in the four previous months,

> seven Chechen suicide bombers, all but one of them women, have detonated explosives that have taken 165 lives, including their own.... In the early 1990s, there were no Chechen suicide bombers, despite a growing, violent movement against Russian rule.... Reporters who covered the Chechen war in the early 1990s mostly agree that there were very few "international Islamists"—Saudis, Afghans, Yemenis—present. They grew in numbers ... as a direct result of the "brutal, botched and unnecessary" Russian military intervention of 1994–96.[6]

---

6. Fareed Zakaria, "Suicide Bombers Can Be Stopped," MSNBC news, December 2003; available online at http://www.msnbc.com/news/953555.asp (accessed December 2003).

Turkey and Antiterrorism

Turkey likewise has wrestled with terrorism enacted by ethnic-minority Muslim Kurds in southern Turkey who are seeking independence. The Kurdish rebellion and terrorism led by the PKK (*Partiya Karkeren Kurdistan*) have killed more than 30,000 persons since their organization in 1984. The Turkish army had been attacking them with widespread force, but in the mid-1990s, the army developed a more-disciplined approach to avoid attacking civilians and introduced health and education for the Kurdish area.[7] One Just Peacemaking practice is *sustainable economic development*, and its key is community development—development of the civic society of local communities. Kurdish areas had been declining economically and were neglected by the central government. However, by shifting its attention to sustainable economic development, the government "initiated huge investments in the southeast, exemplified by the $32 billion Southeastern Anatolia Project, to improve the long-languishing region's economic prospects. Indeed, between 1983 and 1992 the southeast received twice as much investment per capita as any other region in Turkey."[8] Considerable economic development has taken place. Recognition was given to Kurdish language and community customs. The government invested extensively in improving education, including education for girls and women. Instead of trying to break down Kurdish tribal structures, which they previously attempted, the government gave the Kurdish people recognition and sought to enlist them in the struggle for economic development, community development, and political representation.[9]

Another Just Peacemaking practice used in this situation was the *advancement of human rights, democracy, and religious liberty*. Kurds have actually gained more representation in the Turkish parliament than their proportion of the population warrants. This has been in part a response to pressure from the European Union (EU) and Turkey's drive to be accepted as a member of the EU. The Kurds have considered the move toward joining the EU as promising them improved democratization as well as economic development.[10] "Civil associations in Turkey are growing in strength and exerting increasingly effective pressure on the government. . . . The election of Ahmet Necdet Sezer, a prominent democrat from the judicial establishment, to the country's presidency could also have a positive effect."[11]

The pressure from and the allure of the European Union suggests the importance of *working with emerging cooperative forces in the international system*—

---

7. Svante E. Cornell, "The Kurdish Question in Turkish Politics," *Orbis* 45 (Winter 2001) 42.
8. Michael Radu, "The Rise and Fall of the PKK," *Orbis* 45 (Winter 2001) 58.
9. Cornell, "The Kurdish Question," 37.
10. Ibid., 40.
11. Ibid., 45.

another practice of Just Peacemaking. The international community was also important in arresting Abdullah Ocalan, the leader of the terrorist organization. He had been living in Syria, safe from Turkey's military, but Syria expelled him as part of its effort to improve relations with Turkey and join international pressure against terrorism. Ocalan sought refuge in Italy and other countries, but instead Italy arrested him. Turkey then negotiated with Ocalan and achieved his cooperation in ending the terrorism in exchange for immunity from the death penalty. This is the Just Peacemaking practice of *cooperative conflict resolution.* "In 1996 the journalist Franz Schurmann called the PKK 'the biggest guerrilla insurgency in the world,'" but by May 2000, the PKK had basically ended its activities.[12] With the Iraq war, some terrorism has resurfaced.

The painful and tragic irony was that terrorism later resurfaced in Turkey. However, it was not a case of Kurdish terrorism against the Turks but apparently al-Qaeda terrorism against Israel and the British-American "coalition of the willing." As President George W. Bush and Prime Minister Tony Blair were meeting in London on November 20, 2003, terrorists attacked the London-based HSBC bank headquarters and the British consulate in Istanbul. They killed 26 people, including British Consul Roger Short. Five days previously, two Jewish synagogues in Istanbul were bombed: 23 people were killed, and more than 300 were wounded. There had also been several small attacks on U.K. and U.S. diplomatic premises on April 3, April 8, May 31, and June 11.[13]

These attacks are a tragic symbol of the hostility in Turkey that has shifted from Kurdish anger against the government to terrorist anger against Israel and against the alliance between the United States and Britain. The end of Kurdish terrorism against Turkey and the rise of al-Qaeda-like terrorism against England, the United States, and Israel may suggest what works and what does not work in combating terrorism.

Biological Weapons

Many fear that terrorists may attack the United States with biological weapons. Were terrorists to introduce a fatal virus (which would not be detected by the X-ray machines) into an airplane flying from London or Paris to New York, passengers could transmit the infection to their respective cities for a week before their symptoms appeared, and the disease could spread further as doctors took another week to diagnose it.

Fortunately, a treaty called the Biological Weapons Convention that outlaws these weapons has been signed by almost every nation. Though its verifi-

---

12. Radu, "The Rise and Fall of the PKK," 47.

13. Peter Woodman, "Stay Away from Istanbul, Britons Told," *Press Association Limited*, November 20, 2003.

cation procedures are not yet in place, the negotiations to develop them that began in 1995 have produced widespread international agreement. Two Just Peacemaking practices—*work with emerging cooperative forces in the international system* and *strengthen the United Nations and international efforts for cooperation and human rights*—urge support and implementation of treaties of this sort. The practice of *reducing offensive weapons and weapons trade* also applies to biological weapons.

Verification of the Biological Weapons Convention would include annual declarations by nations in which they describe their programs and any of their factories that could be used to produce biological weapons, random visits to declared facilities, and short-notice inspections of suspected facilities. Clearly, this would be useful in preventing many likely sources of bioweapons for terrorists. "The United States has a profound interest in preventing other countries from testing nuclear arms and stopping rogue regimes and terrorists from acquiring biological weapons." The Comprehensive Test Ban Treaty and Biological Weapons Convention "would advance these important goals. If the United States rejects the restraints these agreements impose or declines to negotiate improvements, how can it ask others to embrace them?"[14] Yet, "in the summer of 2001, the United States shocked its peers when it rejected" the agreement establishing verification procedures for biological weapons, an action that reflects the George W. Bush administration's unilateralist course in international policy.

The details of the U.S. actions are as follows: By mid-2001, a consensus text was emerging, and on July 23, 2001, the 24th negotiating session convened. Delegates expected that their efforts would soon result in a final text. During the first three days, more than 50 nations spoke in favor of promptly completing the negotiations. Then, U.S. Ambassador Donald Mahley brought the entire process to an end: "The United States has concluded that the current approach to a protocol to the Biological Weapons Convention . . . is not, in our view, capable of . . . strengthening confidence in compliance with the Biological Weapons Convention. . . . We will therefore be unable to support the current text, even with changes."

Later in 2001, "the United States tried at the last minute to terminate protocol negotiations completely, throwing the meeting into disorder and leaving no option but to suspend the conference until November 2002." The United States earned disappointment, criticism, and anger from the world community for blocking enforceable inspections of sites where terrorists could develop, purchase, or steal biological weapons for their own use.

---

14. Mark Wheelis, Malcolm Dando, and Catherine Auer, "Back to Bioweapons?" *Bulletin of the Atomic Scientists* 59 (January/February 2003) 40–47. The following information and quotations are from this well-informed essay.

When the attack on September 11, 2001, demonstrated the urgent threat of terrorism, the U.S. representative did not try again to block annual study meetings or to block the proposal to reattempt adoption of the treaty in 2006. However, as of the writing of this essay, the protocol for inspections has not yet been adopted.

In the summer of 2004, the international community was developing an international treaty to halt the development of weapons-grade uranium and plutonium. Keeping these nuclear-bomb fissile materials out of the hands of terrorists constitutes a top priority in preventing terrorism. Nevertheless, the policies of the Bush administration have been to place its trust in U.S. military weapons and to avoid restraints by international treaties. Therefore, the U.S. government announced in August of 2004 that it would oppose any inspection programs to verify that nations are complying with the treaty.

My own university studies were in nuclear physics; I did nuclear-physics research for the U.S. Naval Research Laboratory. Other people may disregard the threat of nuclear weapons in the hands of the wrong people, but I cannot. Nor can I place my trust in U.S. nuclear weapons or oppose international treaties that work to end their proliferation. This administration has withdrawn its support of the Comprehensive Test Ban Treaty, the Anti-Ballistic Missile Treaty, the Biological Weapons Convention, and the Fissile Materials Cut-Off Treaty. The U.S. opposition tears apart the fabric of the treaties that hinder the spread of these horrible weapons. In an age of international terrorism, I have a strong commitment to the Just Peacemaking practices of cooperating with international forces and the United Nations to prevent the spread of these dangerous weapons.

Israel and Palestine

The greatest source of anger for Arabs and Muslims in the Middle East is the ongoing and worsening occupation of Palestine by Israel, including the U.S.-supported assassinations of Palestinian terrorist leaders as well as Palestinian citizens in their vicinity. This widespread Arab anger against Israel and the United States aids recruiters of potential terrorists enormously. If Arabs had witnessed the U.S. government working energetically to bring a more just solution to Palestinian problems during the year before the disastrous attack of September 11, 2001, one cannot help but wonder if the attack would have been averted. The U.S. government could have given strong support to implementing the Oslo Accords, to which both Israel and Palestine had agreed but which were canceled by Prime Ministers Netanyahu and Sharon, or the government could have supported continuing the negotiations at Taba that were canceled by Sharon. One wonders if the continuing U.S. refusal to work for justice for Palestinians and peace for Israelis and the continuing U.S. blessing on Sharon's building of the wall, funding of settlement expansion, and assassinations of Palestinian leaders and civilians, will lead to new al-Qaeda attacks against the United States as well as against Israel.

The prophets of the Hebrew Bible announce again and again that, if Israel does not repent and practice justice, it will be driven into exile. The prophet Jeremiah says repeatedly that injustice by Israel will result in great destruction. "This city must be punished; it is filled with oppression. . . . Violence and destruction resound in her. . . . Take warning, O Jerusalem, or I will turn away from you and make your land desolate so no one can live in it" (Jer 6:6–8; see also 2:18, 5:17, 5:20–31, 6:13, 8:10, 17:11, 21:12, 22:13–17). The result of injustice and idolatry will be exile from the land. Similar warnings abound in other prophets as well as in Deuteronomy. Jesus likewise wept over Jerusalem because the Jerusalemites did not know the practices that would bring them peace, and he prophesied that Jerusalem would be destroyed (Luke 19:41–44). This prophecy was fulfilled in A.D. 70.

It is not Christian to block a process that can provide peace for Israel. It is not Christian to teach that Israel will possess the land regardless of whether it offers justice to the poor, the widows, and the orphans of Palestine and engages in the practices that bring peace. It is not Christian to place trust for security in military weapons and expansion of land (Jer 2:18, 5:17; Isa 31:1). True and effective support for Israel is to join the prophets' call for repentance, justice, and peacemaking. This is what will provide more security for the people of Israel and Palestine. Jesus calls us to be peacemakers. We must pray earnestly that this hope will come to pass. Jeremiah exhorts,

> Reform your ways and your actions, and I will let you live in this place. . . . If you really change your ways and your actions and deal with each other justly, if you do not oppress the alien, the fatherless or the widow and do not shed innocent blood in this place, and if you do not follow other gods to your own harm, then I will let you live in this place, in the land I gave your forefathers for ever and ever. (Jer 7:3–7)

The prophet reaffirmed this hope often (Jer 7:23, 9:23–24, 22:3–4, 23:5–8, 29:4–14, 30:1–31:40). The hope is real. God has not changed. Let us obey the LORD.

My subtheme is that the call for Just Peacemaking practices and Jesus' teaching of peacemaking practices are not merely about ideals; they are about the real world. Hence, I point out the obvious: the prophets' warnings and Jesus' warnings were about real destruction in real history. Today, Israel, which is only the size of New Jersey, is surrounded by Arab nations. If Israel does not offer justice to the Palestinians, it faces the serious threat of its own destruction (perhaps by weapons of mass destruction) and of exile yet again. Some object to this notion on the basis that God has made a covenant with Israel, and God's covenants are eternal. I hope I have demonstrated above that, if this is true, the prophets were wrong. They knew full well of God's covenants with Israel and warned repeatedly that, if Israel did not practice justice and if Israel did not stop placing its trust in military weapons instead of God, it would experience the destruction of war and be sent into exile. Their warnings were based precisely on the covenants and the consequences of disobeying the covenants, which demanded justice.

Unfortunately, Christian Zionist organizations and the religious right are opposed to the prophets' call for peacemaking by practicing justice. One Christian Zionist Web site states:

> The victory in Iraq will likely usher in a period of unprecedented American dominance in world affairs. . . . The Arabs will be livid with rage, [and the rest of the world will be severely critical of the U.S.]. . . . The easiest way for Bush to patch up America's relations with the world, and bring down the price of oil, will be to impose a peace settlement on Israel and the Palestinians, bringing about an end to the century-old Middle East conflict. . . . It is therefore essential [to rally supporters] and prevent such a scenario from unfolding. . . . [Christian Zionists] have the ability to bring together millions of American Christians on Israel's behalf. These people form the backbone of Bush's support in the Republican Party, and they must be mobilized at once to work against the creation of an independent Palestinian state.[15]

The Strategic Logic of Suicide Terrorism and Initiatives to Save Lives

The way that Just Peacemaking can enable us to see connections we otherwise miss is nicely illustrated by Robert Pape's study "The Strategic Logic of Suicide Terrorism." Pape argues that suicide terrorist leaders are not merely fanatical; they have a rational strategy to achieve specific goals, and they often succeed. Suicide terrorism almost always has the twin objectives of withdrawal of an occupying force from a national homeland and achievement of self-rule. Suicide terrorism is unlikely to cause the target nation to abandon goals central to their wealth or security. But "suicide terrorism often does get limited results, such as a withdrawal from unimportant territory," or "a temporary and partial withdrawal from a more important area."[16] Accordingly, he reports the facts of several time sequences in relations between Palestine and Israel, noting that times of terrorism were followed by limited Israeli withdrawals.

Viewing events from the perspective of the Just Peacemaking practice of independent initiatives, we notice another dimension of the same facts. In

---

15. Michael Freund, "Striding toward Palestine—Bush Makes It Personal. Beware, Pax Americana Ahead," *Jerusalem Post*, March 5, 2003; also available at http://web.israelinsider.com/views/2047.htm.

16. Robert Pape, "The Strategic Logic of Suicide Terrorism," *American Political Science Review* 97 (2003) 355.

previous decades, Israel outlawed negotiating with leaders of the Palestine Liberation Organization (PLO). But in the early 1990s, Israel and its neighboring Arab countries engaged in small independent initiatives with each other, opening telephone communications between their people and opening new trade relations. A small amount of trust began to build—enough to allow secret negotiations to begin in Oslo between leaders of Palestine and Israel. Thus, independent initiatives were followed by serious negotiations to give major areas of occupied homeland back to the Palestinians. The outcome in September 1993 was the Oslo Accords, in which Palestine promised to recognize Israel's right to exist in peace, and Israel promised to return first an *A* section, then a *B* section, and then a *C* section of the West Bank and Gaza to Palestinian self-rule by specified deadlines. These were not strictly *independent* initiatives because they were not independent of prior negotiated agreements. Perhaps we could call them "on-time initiatives," because the Oslo Accords did set specific deadlines for the return of each section of occupied Palestine to self-rule. The Oslo Accords laid out a series of visible and verifiable initiatives for one side to accomplish by specific dates, while the other side was expected to reciprocate with initiatives of peacemaking. The strategy of independent initiatives emphasizes that the initiatives must absolutely be taken by the announced deadline, regardless of provocations. The point of the strategy is to decrease distrust and threat by taking visible initiatives, thus opening opportunities for solutions, improvements, or peacemaking. If the initiatives miss the deadlines, the distrust will be confirmed.

Pape reports:

> In April 1994, Hamas [began] a series of suicide bombings in [retaliation] for the Hebron Massacre [in which an Israeli settler killed 29 Palestinians]. After two attacks, Israel decided to accelerate its withdrawal from Gaza, which was required under the Oslo Agreement but which had been delayed. Hamas then suspended attacks for five months. From October 1994 to August 1995, Hamas (and Islamic Jihad) carried out a total of seven suicide attacks against Israel. In September 1995, Israel agreed to withdraw from certain West Bank towns that December, which it earlier had claimed could not be done before April 1996 at the soonest. Hamas then suspended attacks until its retaliation campaign during the last week of February and first week of March 1996. . . .
>
> When Israel agreed to withdraw more promptly than expected, Hamas decided to forgo the remaining three planned attacks.[17]

Initiatives Must Be on Time

Pape considers suicide attacks to be efficacious in persuading Israel to withdraw. Just Peacemaking understands another alternative: the efficacy of

---

17. Ibid., 352–53.

Israel's withdrawal in persuading Hamas to end the attacks. And it realizes one thing more: Israel failed to meet the agreed deadline for the withdrawals, thus missing a crucial rule in the strategy of independent initiatives designed to disconfirm distrust.

Pape reports:

> [In 1995] Hamas leaders deliberately withheld attacking during the spring and early summer in order to give PLO negotiations with Israel an opportunity to finalize a withdrawal. However, when in early July, Hamas leaders came to believe that Israel was backsliding and delaying withdrawal, Hamas launched a series of suicide attacks. Israel accelerated the pace of its withdrawal, after which Hamas ended the campaign.[18]

Moreover, Pape continues:

> Israel agreed on March 29, 1995 to begin withdrawals by July 1. Later, however, the Israelis announced that withdrawals could not begin before April 1996 because bypass roads needed for the security of Israeli settlements were not ready. Hamas and Islamic Jihad then mounted new suicide attacks on July 24 and August 21, 1995, killing 11 Israeli civilians. In September, Israel agreed to withdraw from the West Bank towns in December (Oslo II) even though the roads were not finished. The suicide attacks then stopped and the withdrawal was actually carried out in a few weeks starting on December 12, 1995.[19]

In four different presentations that he has entitled "The Facts," Pape recounts the following sequence of events each time: (1) Israel delayed one of its withdrawals agreed to in the Oslo Accords; (2) Hamas and Islamic Jihad engaged in a campaign of suicide terrorism to compel Israel to carry out the promised withdrawal; (3) Israel finally carried out the promised withdrawal; and (4) the leaders of the suicide terrorists halted the attacks for months, until Israel was late again in a promised withdrawal.[20] The theorists of independent initiatives note this twofold lesson: (1) never miss the announced deadline for taking the promised initiative; and (2) the initiative strategy does work efficaciously to halt the attacks.

The independent-initiatives strategists have come to one other conclusion: when the initiatives miss the deadlines, the other side then takes coercive action, and the initiatives are finally taken late—at this point, the other side may believe that the initiatives came because of their coercive action, not because of the trustworthiness of the party taking the initiative. The other side views its coercion as having been rewarded. Consequently, they take coercive action again the next time there is a delay. Pape demonstrates that

---

18. Ibid., 348.
19. Ibid., 354.
20. Ibid., 348, 352–54.

Hamas and many Palestinians concluded that suicide terrorism effected the withdrawals. He suggests that this is probably the wrong conclusion. Israel withdrew because the Oslo Accords obligated them to withdraw. But the fact that Israel repeatedly missed deadlines convinced Hamas otherwise:

> Although the Oslo Accords formally committed to withdrawing the IDF from Gaza and the West Bank, Israel routinely missed key deadlines, often by many months, and the terrorists came to believe that Israel would not have withdrawn when it did, and perhaps not at all, had it not been for the coercive leverage of suicide attack.[21] . . . The bottom line is that the ferocious escalation of the pace of suicide terrorism that we have witnessed in the past several years cannot be considered irrational or even surprising. Rather, it is simply the result of the lesson that terrorists have quite reasonably learned from their experience of the previous two decades: Suicide terrorism pays.[22]

Because Terrorism is Purpose Driven, Preventive Initiatives Make a Difference

The point of Pape's study is to demonstrate that the leaders of suicide terrorists are motivated by a rational purpose. He does so convincingly with reference to 16 suicide terrorist campaigns from 1980 to 2001, including Sri Lanka and the Tamil Tigers, Turkey and the Kurds, Russia and Chechnya, and the United States and the Arabian Peninsula, as well as numerous campaigns between Israel and the Palestinians. It has been demonstrated that the leaders of suicide terrorists are rational strategists whose objective is the withdrawal of occupying troops from their national homeland. One would expect that this observation would lead to the conclusion that the efficacious way to stop their terrorism is to enable them to achieve their objective by peaceful means. For example, implement the Oslo Accords, continue the Wye negotiations at Taba rather than canceling them, accept the offer of peace from the 12 surrounding Arab nations with a two-state solution, implement the Roadmap for Peace, and implement the Geneva Accords. If the terrorist leaders are rational strategists with the rational objective of self-determination in their homeland, a two-state solution would give them the self-determination they rationally desire.

Pape briefly discusses what he calls the strategy of concessions, arguing that they can be effective in reducing popular support for and recruitment of terrorists, "improving the standing of more moderate nationalist elites."[23] However, "concessions" differ from the strategy of on-time initiatives in key ways. First, "concessions," as Pape uses the term, are responses to coercion by

---

21. Ibid., 353.
22. Ibid., 355.
23. Ibid., 356.

terrorists—giving in or conceding to their demands. *Initiatives* are creative actions to decrease distrust and are designed to meet the needs of the people but not necessarily of the terrorists. Second, "concessions," as Pape describes them, follow not meeting or delaying deadlines for initiatives and the subsequent use of terrorism. The strategy of on-time *initiatives* carries out an explicit series of steps strictly on time, never delaying. Third, concessions are responses to terrorism; initiatives are not responses to terrorism but obedience to one's own (previously announced) schedule. Fourth, concessions often carry a condition: for example, "We will give this land back only if you disarm your terrorists." This removes the opportunity from the conceding side to set the timetable and empowers the terrorists to set the timetable. Initiatives carry no condition, but they invite positive reciprocating action that will be rewarded by further initiatives. Thus, the incentive is for reciprocating action, not for renegade terrorists to jam the process by committing a violent act. The initiative is carried out regardless of the actions of any would-be jamming renegade; because the initiative brings beneficial results, there is less incentive for a renegade to attempt to jam it. Fifth, concessions are often granted grudgingly, in fear that terrorism is being rewarded, and so are often accompanied by assassinations or additional punishment of the terrorists. Thus, an opportunity to create trust and invite reciprocation is lost. Initiatives should be done graciously and, if possible, a statement of hope for reciprocation and the possibility of additional future initiatives should be included.

Pape states that six of eleven Palestinian terrorist campaigns did appear to lead to modest concessions, although in only three of the cases were the concessions clearly the result of the terrorism. I contend that only two of the Palestinian terrorist campaigns led to a real gain. Two of the six alleged successes were Israeli withdrawals from parts of occupied territory, which, as Pape concedes, Israel subsequently reoccupied in retaliation against further terrorism. One success was the release of Sheikh Ahmed Yassin from prison, "which was actually done not in response to terrorism but in order to obtain the release of Israeli agents [who] were captured, and also was the product of American and Jordanian pressure." In the meantime, Israel has increased settlements in the occupied territories severalfold and has assassinated Sheikh Yassin. Thus, only two of the eleven campaigns achieved lasting results.

More clearly, the results of the terrorist campaigns have been to undermine Israeli voter support for parties that were willing to offer negotiated solutions and to strengthen support for Sharon and hawkish parties whose policies have been truly disastrous for Palestinians. Terrorism has indeed *worked*; it has worked to drive Israel to the right, to excuse massive assassination, invasion, and occupation actions by Israel, and to justify the building of the wall (in the process of which additional Palestinian territory has been annexed and Palestinians have been cut off from essential travel and former employment). The First Intifada, which was primarily nonviolent direct action, achieved much better results: the Oslo Accords and subsequent negotiations toward a two-state solution. This history appears to me to be a clear demonstration of the superiority of the Just Peacemaking practice of nonviolent direct action over terrorism.

Testing the Theories

One test of the two theories—reluctant concessions versus independent initiatives—is to determine whether Israel has ever withdrawn from an occupied territory on time and whether this led to more or less suicide terrorism. Several incidents provide adequate data.

Withdrawal from the Sinai Desert

Israel had occupied the Sinai Desert as a result of the 1967 war. Egypt insisted that the Sinai be returned to Egyptian control. Israel insisted that it was needed as a buffer zone to protect against Egypt's mobilizing its tanks and weapons along Israel's border. President Carter, Anwar Sadat, and the United Nations employed the Just Peacemaking practice of cooperative conflict resolution. They proposed that the desert be returned to Egypt in exchange for Egypt's promise not to move its tanks and weapons across the desert to Israel's borders. The U.N. would monitor the desert electronically and physically so that the world would know whether Egypt kept its promise. This brilliant conflict-resolution solution was accepted by Israel and Egypt. Israel did withdraw from the desert by the deadline. The U.N. did monitor the desert and still does. Egypt upheld the agreement and to this day does not engage in terrorism against Israel. The result is only a cold peace, but this is surely better than a hot war.

Oslo Agreement, 1993

When the two sides signed the Oslo agreement in 1993, recognizing Israel and its need for security and setting dates for return of Palestinian land to Palestinian rule, there was reason to expect that Israel would return the land as promised. Palestinian support for the agreement was initially 67 percent in the key poll, and this rose to 80 percent as the first parts of land were returned. Support for violence against Israel plummeted to 20 percent, and actual violence was very low. Prime Minister Netanyahu took office in 1996 and postponed the return of land indefinitely. Expectations of a permanent peace settlement in polls of Palestinians dropped from 44 percent to 30 percent in Netanyahu's first year, to 24 percent under Prime Minister Ehud Barak (with settlements expanding more rapidly than previously), and to 11 percent under Ariel Sharon, with his cancellation of the negotiations at Taba following Barak's offer of a two-state solution. Support for violence against Israel increased inversely, both in the polls and in actuality.[24] "Polls by the Jerusalem Media and Communication Centre indicate that increased coercive measures by Israeli forces during the Second Intifada (fall 2000–present) are positively correlated with Palestinian popular support for attacks. Support for suicide attacks, in turn, directly correlates with" increased support for the radical Islamic groups, decreased support for the Palestinian Authority, and decreased Palestinian readiness to support the peace process toward a negotiated solution.[25]

The Lebanon Border Incident

For ten years, Israel's army, led by Ariel Sharon, occupied southern Lebanon in order to prevent Hezbollah from shelling northern Israel. Hezbollah responded with continuing violence, and Israeli soldiers were being killed. Israeli Prime Minister Ehud Barak saw that Israeli occupation of southern Lebanon was indefensible both morally and militarily and announced that Israel would withdraw by July. He met the deadline, the troops withdrew, Lebanon celebrated, and southern Lebanon was not used for violent attacks against Israel, until recently, when Israel made large-scale attacks against Gaza and re-occupied Gaza in 2007. Polls in Israel showed strong support for the action, and the world applauded. Again, this series of events is susceptible to two interpretations, both of which seem true. It solved the problem of southern Lebanon and Hezbollah shelling. The on-time independent initiative did work. But Hezbollah and Hamas interpreted it as a victory that was due to their violent attacks against the Israeli soldiers. It did end Hezbollah violence intended to reclaim their land in Lebanon, but it did not end Hamas violence in protest against the Israeli occupation of Gaza and the West Bank. This double interpretation raises the question, if Israel withdraws from its occupation of Gaza, will this basically end violence from Gaza? Prediction based on the Lebanon example leads to the conclusion "mostly so." But will it end violence from the West Bank in protest against the occupation of the West Bank? Most likely, it will not. And then the final question is, if Israel withdraws from occupying the West Bank to the borders required by the Geneva Accords, will this end violence by Hamas and Islamic Jihad? Embittered leaders of Hamas claim that they will not stop until they have driven Israel completely out. But the poll data predict that a huge majority of Palestinians will support peace when they see Israel giving back most of their land in accordance with the Oslo Accords. The PLO and the 12 surrounding Arab countries promise to accept Israel within its borders. Just Peacemaking strategists say that indepen-

---

24. Khalil Shikaki, "Palestine Divided," *Foreign Affairs* (January/February 2002) 90ff.

25. Scott Atran, "The Strategic Threat from Suicide Terror" (December 2003) 9. Online: http://www.aei-brookings.org/publications/abstract.php?pid=410.

dent initiatives do work. The withdrawals thus far demonstrate this, and for Israel's security as well as Palestinian security and justice, independent initiatives must be taken.

Based on these test cases, the "disreward" theorists draw the conclusion that land in exchange for peace did not work. Hamas learned from Lebanon that violence works; Egypt offered only a cold peace and not a friendly peace; Palestine halted terrorism for only a three-month test period and did not disarm its terrorist organizations. Strategists of independent initiatives learned that, because these initiatives were taken by the deadlines, Hezbollah halted shelling and attacks against Israel and Israeli forces until Israel engaged in massive attacks against Gaza in 2007; Egypt halted violence against Israel permanently; and suicide attacks against Israel halted for a three-month test period (with one maverick exception). The Egyptian test case is significant: the withdrawal was carried out, not in response to terrorism, but in response to conflict-resolution negotiations, and was carried out on time. The result has been a permanent halt in violence from this source.

The Bush administration announced from the beginning that it was disengaging from conflict resolution in the Middle East. This resulted in a weak Palestine with a powerful Sharon-led Israeli government, a lack of expectation of withdrawal, and a huge increase in terrorism.

> By any measure 2002 was an astonishing year for Israel in terms of suicide bombings. An average of five attacks a month were made, nearly double the number during the first fifteen months of the second intifada—and that number was itself more than ten times the monthly average since 1993. Indeed, according to a database maintained by the National Security Studies Center, at Haifa University, there were nearly as many suicide attacks in Israel [in 2002] (fifty-nine) as there had been in the previous eight years combined (sixty-two).[26]

Just Peacemaking urges the administration to reengage in practicing conflict resolution. In fact, Tony Blair persuaded President Bush to become engaged in the "Roadmap for Peace." The Roadmap is, or was, the Just Peacemaking practice of *independent initiatives*. Palestine chose a prime minister who could act somewhat independently from Arafat, as Israel had demanded. The new prime minister persuaded the leading terrorist organizations to suspend terrorist acts for a three-month trial period. Israel freed most of Gaza from military occupation, freed a few prisoners, and loosened curfews and checkpoints in a few places. These are independent initiatives. However, Israel did not remove any significant settlements from the West Bank, and it continued armed attacks in Palestinian territory to assassinate Palestinian leaders whom it identified as terrorists. Palestine did not disarm terrorist organizations. The

---

26. Bruce Hoffman, "The Logic of Suicide Terrorism," *Atlantic Monthly* 291 (2003) 44.

United States did not push forcefully for implementation of further initiatives, and President Bush gave his blessing to the assassination of Abu Ali Mustafa, the beloved head of the Democratic Front for the Liberation of Palestine, in the summer of 2001, after which came the suicide bombing of September 11, 2001.

The Limits of Unilateral Power and the Need for a Cooperative Foreign Policy in Pursuit of Justice

There is a limit to how much the United States can do or will do, and there is a limit to what U.S. military power can accomplish without major help from Europe and other nations. Reinhold Niebuhr pointed this out persuasively when the Eisenhower administration was debating whether to enter the Vietnam War in the 1950s, as the French were being defeated at Dienbienphu.[27] He argued, as Isaiah also argued, that there is always the temptation to put idolatrous trust in what one's own military can do.

Surely this applies to the struggle against terrorism. The international terrorist networks operate in 60 or more nations. A "go-it-alone" policy of relying on U.S. military strength cannot stamp out terrorism in 60 nations. Donald Rumsfeld himself has ruminated that, in many nations, the terrorists are recruiting more new members because of increased anger than the number of terrorists that the United States military is destroying.

It could not be clearer that defeating terrorism requires international cooperation. In order to get the cooperation of other nations, the United States must cooperate with other nations. Working with emerging cooperative forces in the international system is a key Just Peacemaking practice. Failing to work cooperatively to strengthen international networks and instead using the enormously powerful U.S. military to set the example of unilateral initiation of war, combined with withdrawing from or blocking seven international treaties designed to stop the spread of weapons of mass destruction, is already causing increased international anger against the United States. It portends more terrorism in the U.S.'s future. Just Peacemaking offers a wiser and more effective way to dry up the sources of terrorism.

---

27. Reinhold Niebuhr, "The Limits of Military Power," *New Leader* (May 30, 1955) 16ff.

Index of Authors

Index of Scripture

Old Testament